Secret London

Secret London

ANDREW DUNCAN

NEW
HOLLAND

This edition first published in the UK in 2000 by
New Holland Publishers (UK) Ltd
London • Cape Town • Sydney • Auckland

Garfield House
86–88 Edgware Road
London W2 2EA
United Kingdom
www.newhollandpublishers.com

80 McKenzie Street
Cape Town 8001
South Africa

14 Aquatic Drive
Frenchs Forest, NSW 2086
Australia

218 Lake Road
Northcote
Auckland
New Zealand

13 15 17 19 20 18 16 14

First published in 1995

ISBN 1 85974 675 6

Publishing Manager: Jo Hemmings
Indexer: Paul Barnett
Maps: Claire Littlejohn

Printed and bound in Singapore by Kyodo Printing Co (Singapore) Pte Ltd

Photographic Acknowledgements
All photographs by the author, with the exception of the following:
Bank of England: Plate 30; Berry Bros. & Rudd Ltd: Plate 24; Cabinet War Rooms: Plate 7;
Cecil Denny Highton (architects)/Adam Woolfit: Plate 22; Coutts & Co: Plate 33; Lloyd's of
London: Plate 29; Public Information Office, House of Commons: Plate 20; The Stafford
Hotel: Plate 27; Thames Water plc: Plate 6; Whitechapel Bell Foundry: Plate 34

Front cover: Apothecaries' Hall by Andrew Lawson

NOTE: Place and other names in the text printed in **bold type** have an entry in the
Opening Times, Addresses and Further Information section at the end of the book.

CONTENTS

Maps   6

Introduction   7

Key to maps contained in the book   8

1 Hidden Landscape   10

   The Campden Hill spur walk   13

   The Islington spur walk   19

   The Westbourne river walk   23

   The Tyburn river walk   29

   The Fleet river walk   37

2 The Subterranean City   44

3 Private Landowners   55

4 Taken for Granted   73

5 Westminster   87

6 Whitehall   101

7 St James's   112

   Exploring the hidden courts and passages of St James's 118

8 The City   127

   The City – East of St Paul's walk   136

   The City – West of St Paul's walk   143

9 Special Collection   150

Acknowledgements   161

Opening Times, Addresses and Further Information   162

Bibliography   168

Index   169

MAPS

Key to maps contained in the book pp. 8–9
London's landed estates (Chapter 3) pp. 56–7
Westminster area (Chapter 5) p. 90
Whitehall area (Chapter 6) p. 102
The Clubs of St James's (Chapter 7) p. 113
The City (Chapter 8) pp. 130–1
Each walk has its own individual route map

Key to Maps
····→····   Route of walk
Underground station
Railway station
Public toilets
Viewpoint
All maps are drawn on a north–south axis unless otherwise indicated.

INTRODUCTION

Any city of six and a half million people is bound to be a very public place. But London also has its private side, that part which is deliberately kept covered up against prying eyes, or which is simply invisible because it is behind the scenes in some way. It's this private, this secret, side of London which is explored in this book.

In a place as big, as old and as multi-faceted as London there are naturally many things that can be described as secret in one way or another. On the one hand there are things that are purposefully concealed, such as the locations of our secret service headquarters or the identities of publicity-shy aristocratic landowners. On the other hand there are things that are secret simply because the vast majority of people do not know about them. Here one might mention the natural landscape buried beneath London's streets and the true stories behind Dick Whittington and Marble Arch.

In uncovering these and other facets of secret London, my aim has been to penetrate as far as possible to the very heart of the city. One way I have tried to do this is by creating 20 miles of walks, revealing, among other things, the winding courses of three long-buried rivers. My other method has been to seek out new and unusual places to visit. Altogether, the book contains details of about 30 such places, including a roof garden in Kensington and a bell foundry in the East End.

In security-conscious Whitehall and Westminster I inevitably had less luck than elsewhere in pushing back the frontiers of public accessibility. However, I have at least been able to include in the book first-hand descriptions of some of the more historic government offices. I describe what goes on backstage in the Houses of Parliament and reveal how many people live there.

The one part of secret London I have not been able to explore is the extensive network of tunnels, sewers and abandoned tube stations that honeycombs the cold London clay beneath the city's streets. However, by combining other researchers' findings with my own observations, I have been able to draw what I hope is a fairly complete outline of the subterranean city.

Any further light that readers can shed on this shadowy area and on any of the other aspects of secret London investigated in this book would be very welcome. Please e-mail your comments to me at andrew@andrewduncan.co.uk. For details of my other books visit my website at www.andrewduncan.co.uk.

Andrew Duncan

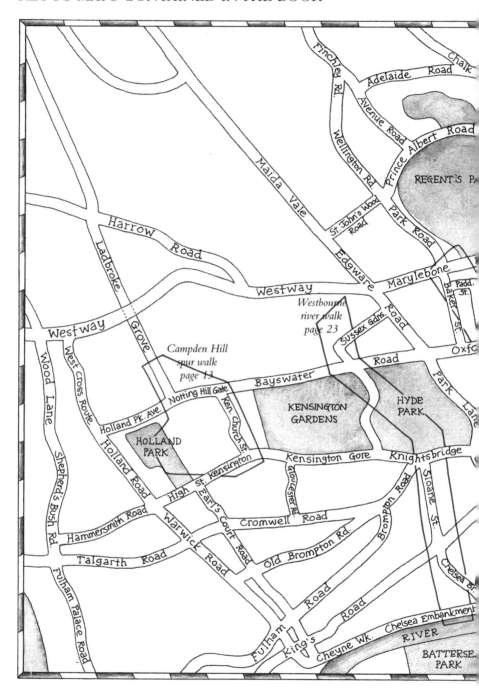

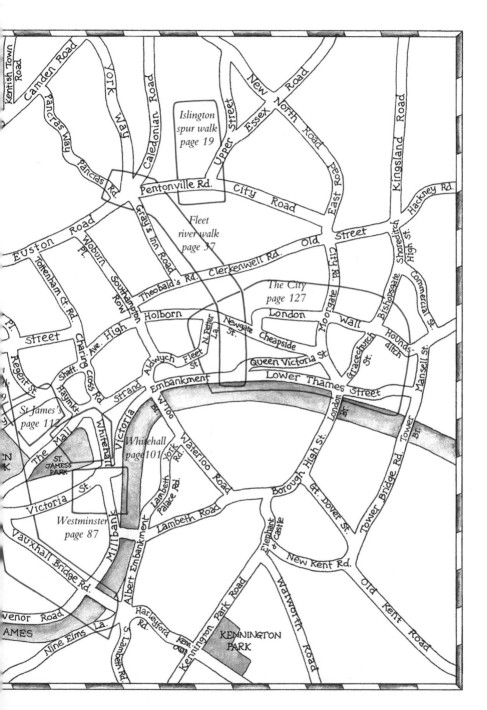

Chapter 1

HIDDEN LANDSCAPE

Beneath the streets of London lies a hidden landscape. Over the centuries it has been built on, covered up and generally obscured, but it is still very much in existence. Few Londoners are probably aware of it, even though it dictates things that affect their everyday lives, such as the layout of roads and streets, the position of important buildings and the routes of railways and canals, as well as less tangible things like boundaries and place names.

There's something about living in a city which seems to blind people to obvious geographical features that stand out in the countryside. Perhaps we just don't think about hills and valleys and streams when all we can see are endless vistas of bricks and mortar and tarmac. Travel is another factor: it is only when you provide your own motive power that you really become aware of ups and downs. That's why cyclists are usually the only ones who know where the ground rises and where it falls. But even they might find it difficult to say how the apparently unrelated humps and troughs on their regular routes fit into London's overall physical geography.

THE THAMES VALLEY

London's main geographical feature is of course the river valley in which it sits. The Thames valley is about 10 miles (16 kilometres) wide and 400 feet (120 metres) deep. One of the best places to see this is from Parliament Hill (319 feet; 97 metres) on Hampstead Heath.

It takes 20 minutes to walk there from Hampstead Underground station (Northern Line) and the route is as follows. Turn left out of Hampstead station and take the first left into Flask Walk. Follow the road (at first pedestrian-only) down and to the right as far as the crossroads. Burgh House, Hampstead's community centre and local history museum, is on the left. Turn right into Willow Road and follow it down the hill to the junction with Downshire Hill. Here turn left, cross the main road and enter Hampstead Heath. Walk along the tarmac path with one of the Hampstead ponds – a source of the River Fleet (see page 37) – on your right. When you come to a track crossing left and right, go left and follow this main track round to the right between two more ponds. On the far side, follow the path up the hill, bending slightly right then left. When you come to a fork, go right (where it says NO CYCLING). Soon you come out of the trees and, a minute later, reach the top of the hill.

View from Parliament Hill

Parliament Hill is not the highest spot in London, but it is higher than most and it commands extensive views east, south and south-west right across the valley, with the main landmarks to the south picked out on a panorama board. From this vantage point you can see that the city has slowly filled the bottom of the valley and then crept up and over the sides. You can also clearly see some of the features mentioned later. The first are the two valleys, one either side of the hill, from which flow the two streams that later come together to form the Fleet river. The second, to the left, is the long spur that starts up at Highgate and gently descends towards the City. A prominent landmark near the end of this spur is the former Caledonian market clocktower, which is visible when you step back and left from the panorama board about 10 paces.

At the bottom of the valley, the Thames meanders through its flood plain. Generally the plain is about 2 or 3 miles (3–5 kilometres) wide, and less than 25 feet (7.5 metres) above sea level. To get an idea of its extent, take a map of London and draw a line south of the river from Greenwich to Putney. All the land between that line and the river is low flood plain. On the north bank, draw a line from Trafalgar Square to Hammersmith. Apart from a raised spit under Chelsea, all the land between that line and the river, including Westminster and Whitehall, is also flood plain.

Before it was drained, embanked and built on, the whole plain, especially on the south side, was subject to flooding. Indeed, in London's Roman era, Southwark and Lambeth, then tidal marsh (a modern street near Waterloo Station is even called Lower Marsh), were inundated with every high tide. Because south-east England is gradually sinking into the sea, the lowest parts of central London would still be subject to flooding were it not for the **Thames Barrier**.

THE TERRACES

Rising above the flood plain are two terraces, one at about 50 feet (15 metres) and the other at about 100 feet (30 metres). The terraces were caused by fluctuations in the volume of water flowing in the Thames. These fluctuations were in turn caused by variations in the speed at which local glaciers were melting. Millions of years ago the Thames flowed much further north than it does now. Then about 500,000 years ago the advancing glaciers of the Ice Age blocked the old river's drainage system, forcing it to seek a route further south. Starting 400 feet (120 metres) above where it is now, that is on a level with places like Hampstead and Highgate – which, though high ground now, were low ground then – it gradually wore its way down to its present level. For two eons during this gradual process, it flowed at relatively stable levels, hence the terraces. These are most evident on the north side of the river where the flood plain rises gradually to the Northern Heights around Hampstead (440 feet; 134 metres) and Highgate (420 feet; 128 metres). On the south side, the plain rises more abruptly to places like Richmond, Wimbledon, Clapham Common, Forest Hill and Greenwich (with the first and last places – Richmond and Greenwich – being the closest hills to the river on the south side and thus the best places to go for river views).

The 50-foot terrace
In the West End and the City, the southern edge of the 50-foot terrace follows a line roughly along Piccadilly, the Strand, Fleet Street, Cannon Street and Eastcheap. From Piccadilly, walking west to east, you can see the ground sloping steeply away to the right down Constitution Hill, Green Park and St James's (St James's Street and Duke Street St James's show it clearly). From the Strand, the slope is even more pronounced, but then one would expect that because the river, bending right at Charing Cross, has eaten into the hillside here, creating a sharp escarpment. The best places from which to view it are Waterloo Bridge and Adelphi Terrace. Further east, two good places to see the drop are Essex Street at the eastern end of the Strand and Dorset Rise at the eastern end of Fleet Street. Essex Street is built out on a sort of mound so that you have to go down a flight of steps at the end to descend to river level. The natural incline here is shown by adjacent Milford Lane. Dorset Rise climbs up from Tudor Street to Salisbury Square (see page 149). Dorset Buildings, leading off on the City side, ends in a vertical drop into the Fleet valley.

In the City, the brink of the terrace continues along St Paul's Churchyard, Cannon Street and Eastcheap. Take any right turn off these streets and you will find yourself plunging down to the river. Not surprisingly many of these side streets have the word 'hill' in their names: St Andrew's Hill, Addle Hill, White Lion Hill, Bennet's Hill, Lambeth Hill, Old Fish Street Hill, Huggin Hill, Garlick Hill, College Hill, Dowgate Hill, Laurence Pountney Hill, Fish Street Hill, St Mary-at-Hill and St Dunstan's Hill. The best place to view the slope is the top of the wide steps at Peters Hill leading down from **St Paul's Cathedral**.

The 100-foot terrace

The 100-foot terrace is a bit more difficult to explore than the lower terrace because it covers a much bigger area and is cut through by deeper and wider valleys. However, you can see it in the Islington area from the Primrose Hill viewpoint, as described below (see pages 17–18). And you walk on it when you do the Campden Hill and Islington spur walks, described below and on pages 19–22, respectively.

THE SPURS

The valleys just mentioned are the valleys of rivers running down from the Northern Heights to the Thames. There are seven rivers altogether. From west to east they are Stamford Brook, Counter's Creek, the Westbourne, the Tyburn, the Fleet, the Walbrook and the Lea. Four major spurs of high ground ending in more or less pronounced escarpments separate these rivers from each other and form prominent features of London's landscape.

The most westerly ends in two hills – Notting Hill (98 feet; 30 metres) and its higher neighbour Campden Hill (124 feet; 38 metres) – which are the main features of our first spur walk.

The Campden Hill spur walk

Notting Hill and Campden Hill are two of London's most sought-after residential areas, in particular Notting Hill, where the designers of the Victorian Ladbroke estate included large communal gardens in their development. With all the trees in these gardens, and in Holland Park on Campden Hill, the views on the walk are somewhat restricted. However, the hilliness of the terrain and the variety of the architecture more than compensate.

Start:	Notting Hill Gate Underground (District, Circle and Central Lines)
Finish:	Kensington Underground (District and Circle Lines)
Length:	2½ miles (4 km)
Time:	1½ hours
Food:	The Windsor Castle pub, which serves better than average food and has a large walled beer garden, is at the half-way stage; towards the end of the walk there is a good café in Holland Park; otherwise there are plenty of places to eat and drink in Notting Hill Gate at the start of the walk, and in Kensington High Street at the end.

Sights: The Ladbroke estate, Holland Park and its **Ice House gallery**, the **Commonwealth Institute**, Kensington High Street for shopping. Note: The views on this walk are in the western half of the compass so it is best done in the morning with the sun behind you.

Come out of Notting Hill Gate Underground at the Notting Hill Gate north side/Portobello Road exit and walk straight on west across Pembridge Road and under the block of flats. Already you can see the ground dropping away to the west down Holland Park Avenue. At the end of the terrace of shops, just by the phone booth and traffic lights, turn right into an unnamed passage and continue straight on through the traffic barrier into Victoria Gardens. At the end turn left into Ladbroke Road.

Again, as the ground begins to drop away, turn right into Ladbroke Terrace and walk towards the private gardens in Ladbroke Square, the second largest in London and centrepiece of the Ladbroke estate. Turn left into the square. Once again, the ground ahead begins to fall away and in the far distance, framed by the trees, you can see the tops of blocks of flats nearly 2 miles (3 kilometres) away in Shepherd's Bush.

Notting Hill

The first road you come to is Ladbroke Grove. Turn right here and walk up the hill to the summit, marked by St John's Church with its landmark spire. This is

Notting Hill. If you go a little way beyond the church to the brink of the hill on the north side, you can see down into Notting Dale with the Westway elevated motorway crossing Ladbroke Grove by the Underground station. This is where the annual Notting Hill carnival takes place in August. Beyond lies North Kensington and Kensal Town, and, though you can't see it, the famous cemetery of Kensal Green, modelled on Père Lachaise in Paris.

Before the Ladbroke estate and the surrounding district were built up, from the 1840s onwards, Notting Hill was the central feature of a dramatically landscaped racecourse called the Hippodrome. Spectators watched from the summit where you are now, while the horses galloped round the circular course laid out around the base of the hill. For a while the course was a great success, but its long-term future was undermined by the exceptionally heavy going in Notting Dale, which was a menace to the horses. The Hippodrome closed in 1841, having been open for only four years. Crossing the Grove, if you have not already done so, and returning to the church, turn right into Lansdowne

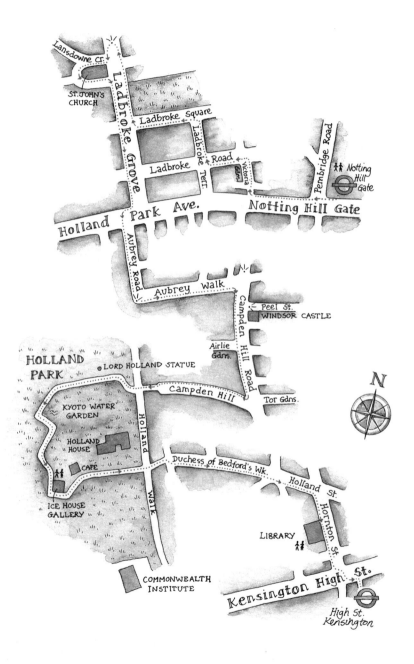

Crescent. Now, as you follow the road round to the other end of the church, you see how the ground falls as steeply away to the west as it did to the north. The low ground at the bottom was drained by the stream called Counter's Creek before it was covered over and turned into a storm sewer.

Campden Hill

Once you have regained Ladbroke Grove, turn right and go back down the hill, keeping going until you reach Holland Park Avenue, the main road at the end. Cross and turn right and then immediately left up the very steep Aubrey Road. Having descended Notting Hill, you are now climbing to the higher summit of Campden Hill. At the top of Aubrey Road, look back and you will see the tower and spire of St John's Church on the far side of what seems to be a valley filled with a dense mass of trees.

The big house just here is Aubrey House, named after Aubrey de Vere, one of Kensington's medieval lords of the manor. In the 18th century when it had its own farm, Aubrey House was the home of the eccentric Lady Mary Coke, and there are many references to it in her diaries. All the farm and most of the extensive grounds have now been built on, but there is still a huge secret walled garden, completely invisible except from the south side of the house. Follow Aubrey Road round to

the left where it becomes Aubrey Walk. To the right the courts of the tennis club cover reservoirs built here about 1810 by the West Middlesex Water Company. Looking left down Campden Hill Gardens, the top of a block of flats in Kensal Town called Trellick Tower comes into view. When you get to Campden Hill Road, the main road running over the hill, turn right and walk past the Windsor Castle pub, opened in 1837 when you could indeed see Windsor Castle from Campden Hill. As you look down Peel Street, next to the pub, the BT Tower 3 miles (5 kilometres) away in the West End punctures the horizon.

Holland Park

Beyond the Windsor Castle, you begin to descend the south side of Campden Hill. Carry on past Airlie Gardens and take the next right into Campden Hill. At the road end, continue on along the path that cuts through Holland Park School. Cross Holland Walk, go into Holland Park and turn right up the tarmac path.

Follow this path round to the left and go past the statue of the third Lord Holland, to whose family this park once belonged. Now the ground falls steeply away again as you approach both the end of the Camden Hill spur and the western edge of Campden Hill and the 100-foot terrace. Although the thick foliage of the trees obscures the view at this point, the vista opens up a little at the first crossroads you come to. Here turn left and walk past the Kyoto water garden, following the path round to the left where it is joined by another one coming up the hill. Then take the first right. This takes you on to the terrace in the formal garden area of the park. Walk along to the corner past the restaurant and art gallery. Although the trees are still quite thick, there are occasional glimpses of the long views west over the flat ground formerly drained by Counter's Creek and Stamford Brook. Turn left round the corner and walk through the colonnade out on to the broad walk that takes you in front of the remains of Holland House, a 17th-century mansion almost completely destroyed by bombs in the Second World War. (The grounds became a public park a few years later.) Now you are on the south side of the hill and the ground slopes gently away towards the green copper roof of the **Commonwealth Institute** and Kensington High Street beyond. Go straight on out of the park, over Holland Walk and through the bollards into Duchess of Bedford's Walk. Skirting the hill in a slightly downhill direction, cross Campden Hill Road into Holland Street, heading for St Mary Abbots Church ahead. At Hornton Street turn right and walk down the hill past Kensington town hall and library to Kensington High Street and the end of the walk. The Underground station is on the other side of the High Street.

CAMPDEN HILL'S EAST SIDE AND THE OTHER SPURS

To the north and west, as this walk has just shown, the Campden Hill spur comes to a relatively precipitous conclusion, but in the east, in other words towards central London, it slopes very gently down to the valley of the Westbourne, dammed in the 18th century to form the Long Water and the Serpentine lake dividing Kensington Gardens and Hyde Park.

The spur on the other side of the Westbourne runs away from the Hampstead region of the Northern Heights along Fitzjohn's Avenue and Finchley Road, and then stops short on the north bank of the Serpentine. Its descent from there, through Belgravia to Pimlico, is much more gentle. Cycle from Marble Arch to Victoria and it's downhill all the way.

The next spur is a dramatic one featuring Primrose Hill, an excellent viewpoint close to central London and therefore to some extent a better one than Parliament Hill despite the fact that it is 100 feet (30 metres) lower. It takes about 10 minutes to walk to Primrose Hill from Chalk Farm Underground station. Come out of the station on Adelaide Road and cross to Bridge Approach. This leads straight into Regent's Park Road. Follow this road round to the park and turn right into Primrose Hill Road. Go immediately left through the gate and climb straight up to the top of the hill.

Beginning at Hampstead, the Primrose Hill spur runs down to a pronounced saddle where Elsworthy Rise crosses King Henry's Road. The spur is at its narrowest here so several major railway lines – including those from St Pancras and Euston stations – take the opportunity to tunnel through at this point, as a quick glance at a London map will show.

From the saddle (165 feet; 50 metres) the ground rises steeply to Primrose Hill (220 feet; 67 metres) where a panorama board identifies the major landmarks in the City and the West End. In addition, to the left you can clearly see across the valley of the Fleet river to the next spur, with the old Caledonian market clock-tower a prominent landmark. To the west, the rather narrower valley contains the Tyburn. Beyond are the chimneys of Battersea Power Station and the distinctive silhouette of Erno Goldfinger's Trellick Tower. South beyond the West End you can make out the streets on the far side of the river, the Crystal Palace TV mast and, on the horizon, the Surrey hills.

At the foot of the hill, the Regent's Canal cuts across the spur in a slight depression. Between Regent's Park and the river, the ground slopes gently down across Oxford Street to Piccadilly, from where, as we have seen, the descent to the flood plain (i.e. St James's Park and **Buckingham Palace**) is quite steep.

The Islington spur

The fourth and most easterly spur – the Islington spur – is aligned in a more south-easterly direction than its neighbours. Running away from Highgate down Dartmouth Park Road, it forms a saddle in the vicinity of Tufnell Park Underground station. Here the railway line tunnels through in the Cathcart Hill/Spencer Rise area. The spur then rises again – its crest followed by Brecknock Road – to Caledonian Park (158 feet; 48 metres). Here the old clocktower of the Caledonian market (1855–1939) forms a landmark visible for miles around. Headwaters of the rivers on either side of the spur once again cut back here, creating another narrow saddle or col, and this time it is the east-coast main line from King's Cross that seizes the tunnelling opportunity. By contrast, the Caledonian Road bravely climbs over the top.

The spur turns east here for about half a mile (1 kilometre) and then, in the Barnsbury Street area of Islington, resumes its southerly drift for over a mile (1.6 kilometres), dropping less than 20 feet (6 metres) over the whole of this distance. The drop to the lower terrace begins at Claremont Square on Pentonville Road. This is where we take the second of our spur walks.

The Islington spur walk

This circular walk through some of the most elegant but least-known streets and squares in London explores both a prominent snout on the spur and the edge of the 100-foot terrace. It includes a spectacular view of the BT Tower and, at its furthest point, an excellent pub called the Albion.

Start/Finish: Angel Underground (Northern Line)
Length: 2 miles (3 km)
Time: 1½ hours
Food: The Albion pub as above; otherwise all manner of places around Angel Underground station at the start/finish point.
Sights: Camden Passage antiques market (Wednesdays and Saturdays) is literally within a stone's throw of Angel Underground station.
Note: The views are mainly to the west so the walk is best done in the morning with the sun behind you.

Turn left out of Angel Underground station and walk down to the crossroads. Cross to the right and stand on the corner in front of the Cooperative Bank. You are not quite on the snout of the spur here (the ground rises up to it on the right), but looking left you can see the fall-away to the east, and ahead down St John Street you can see the ground level beginning to descend to the 50-foot terrace level of the City. On a bicycle you can freewheel from here virtually all the way to Smithfield

Market, a distance of almost a mile (1.6 kilometres).

Cross over Pentonville Road and walk down the right-hand side of St John Street. At Chadwell Street turn right. In Myddelton Square, go left round St Mark's Church and continue on into River Street. All the time the ground is sloping steadily downhill to the left.

Spectacular view
From River Street cross Amwell Street into Lloyd Baker Street. When you get

to Lloyd Square turn right and then left along the north side of the square. Now you have come round to the west side of the spur and the ground falls sharply away to the Fleet valley, providing a spectacular view of the BT Tower over a mile (1.6 kilometres) away. Walk down the north side of this pretty and little-known square (developed by the Lloyd Baker family in the 1820s and in their possession until as recently as 1975), and, just as you are about to go out of the square, turn right up some steps into Cumberland Gardens. (This, incidentally, must surely be one of the most desirable places in London to live: peaceful location, good views, elegant architecture and all within walking distance of the City.) At the end of the road turn right up Great Percy Street and then left into Amwell Street and walk up to the junction with Pentonville Road. At this point you are on the snout of the spur and on the edge of the 100-foot terrace. To the left down the hill the spire and roofs of St Pancras Station are the main feature. To the right the embankment in the middle of the square contains a reservoir with a history stretching back well over 300 years. The original one was constructed in the early 1600s to hold water brought from Amwell in Hertfordshire (hence Amwell Street), 20 miles (32 kilometres) away, by means of a special canal constructed by the New River Company (hence River Street). City merchant Sir Hugh Myddelton

(hence Myddelton Square) was the head of the company. From the reservoir the water flowed down the hill in pipes to the City. The New River still supplies water to London, but its terminal reservoir is now at Stoke Newington, 3 miles (5 kilometres) north of here.

The last viewpoint

Now cross Pentonville Road into Penton Street and keep walking when Penton Street becomes Barnsbury Road. At this point you are directly above the tunnel which takes the Regent's Canal straight through the Islington spur. You are also walking across the 100-foot terrace and following the eastern edge of the spur. This becomes more clear when, having crossed Copenhagen Street, you arrive at Barnard Park and look out west over the Fleet valley, much broader here than it was back at Lloyd Square.

This is the last viewpoint on the walk. Next is the Albion pub and then the return to Angel Underground. Carry on to the end of Barnsbury Road and then go right and left by a little garden into Thornhill Road. The Albion is on the right. To return to the Angel, carry on along Thornhill Road to Barnsbury Street. Here turn right and then right again into Lonsdale Square, built about 1840 on land belonging to the Drapers' Company (one of the City livery companies – see page 142) in a Gothic style. Go

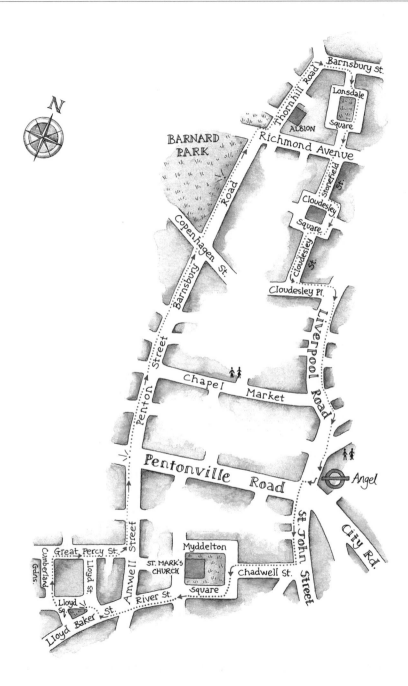

right or left through the square and
cross Richmond Avenue into
Stonefield Street. This leads to
Cloudesley Square, of a more conven-
tional design. Again go right or left

through the square and into
Cloudesley Street. Then turn left into
Cloudesley Place and right into
Liverpool Road. Soon you are back at
Angel Underground station.

END OF THE ISLINGTON SPUR

The Islington spur ends in two little 60-foot (18-metre) high hills in the City,
Ludgate Hill and Cornhill, divided by a depression. These are the most historic
parts of London, for its Roman founders planted their most important buildings
on the summits: the amphitheatre and fort on Ludgate Hill (today the site of **St
Paul's Cathedral**) and the forum and basilica on Cornhill (today the site of
Leadenhall Market). In the olden days, people thought Ludgate Hill was the higher of the two, hence the 300-year-old inscription on a stone on the left-hand side
of the entrance to Panyer Alley Steps next to St Paul's Underground station: 'When
ye have sought the City round, yet still this is the highest ground. August 27th,
1688.' In actual fact, Cornhill is about 1 foot (30 centimetres) higher.

The Walbrook river valley
The depression dividing the two hills – obvious, for example, in the way Cannon
Street dips between Budge Row and Walbrook – is all that remains of the valley
of the Walbrook river. Originally this was quite steep-sided, but as early as the 15th
century it was flattened out when the river was covered over. Accumulations since
then have further smoothed it over.

Today the Walbrook, known to sewer engineers as the London Bridge Sewer,
runs 30–35 feet (9–10 metres) below ground level and meets the Thames about
120 feet (35 metres) west of Cannon Street Station. Its route is marked by All
Hallows London Wall Church (the river entered the City through a culvert in the
wall just to the west of the church), St Margaret Lothbury Church (built on vaults
over the river), the exposed foundations of the Roman Temple of Mithras in
Queen Victoria Street (the temple stood on the river's western bank), the aforementioned dip in Cannon Street (although the lowest point in this dip seems to
be at Walbrook, the river's course is actually about 150 feet (45 metres) west) and
a monument in Cloak Lane marking the site of the church of St John the Baptist
upon Walbrook (the river flowed past the west wall of the church, which was
destroyed in the Great Fire). If you look at a map of the City's wards, you will find

that the western boundaries of Walbrook and Dowgate wards correspond exactly to the river's course.

THE LOST RIVERS OF LONDON

With the exception of the Lea, all the other central London tributaries of the Thames on the north side of the river have gone the same way as the Walbrook; in other words they have been covered over or piped in and turned into storm sewers whose main function is to carry away rainwater from roadside gutters. Despite the fact that they have been buried, however, many clues to their existence remain visible on the surface.

We will now set out on foot to discover some of them. The three routes chosen follow the lower, most interesting reaches of central London's most significant 'lost' rivers: the Westbourne, the Tyburn and the Fleet. In general, these walks reveal a secret London of winding lanes, narrow back streets and picturesque mews to which few people go except those who happen to live or work there.

The Westbourne river walk

The Westbourne (meaning West Stream) begins as several streamlets flowing down the hill to the west of Hampstead. One of these streamlets can apparently be seen beneath a manhole at the west end of Alexandra Road in NW8. The major streamlets flow together to form the main river in the region of Kilburn High Road station. In the 18th century a spring on the bank of the river here (commemorated today in Springfield Lane and Spring Walk) was developed into a popular spa called Kilburn Wells. A stone plaque at first-floor level at the corner of Kilburn High Road and Belsize Road marks the spa's site. From Belsize Road the river flows through Maida Vale and Carlton Vale and then having picked up a tributary from Kensal Rise turns east along Shirland Road. At the end of Shirland Road it veers south under the Regent's Canal and the humpy Westbourne Green. From here it flows down Gloucester Mews West and Upbrook Mews to Brook Mews North just outside Hyde Park where we pick it up. First, however, we have to make our way to Brook Mews from Paddington Underground station.

Start: Paddington Underground station (District, Circle, Hammersmith & City and Bakerloo Lines)

Finish: Sloane Square Underground station (District and Circle Lines)

Length:	3 miles (5 km)
Time:	2½ hours
Food:	Around the half-way stage you have a choice of either the Dell café/restaurant in Hyde Park next to the Serpentine or, just a little bit further on, one of the cosy pubs in picturesque Kinnerton Street. Otherwise, Paddington Underground near the beginning of the walk and Sloane Square Underground towards the end are both surrounded by all kinds of eating places, cheap and expensive.
Sights:	Hyde Park, the Serpentine, Knightsbridge, Belgravia, Sloane Square, **Chelsea Hospital**.
Note:	If possible, plan to finish the walk at low or lowish tide on the Thames, otherwise it may not be possible to see the Westbourne's outfall. To find out when low tide is, either consult the current edition of *Whitaker's Almanack* in your local library or ring the Port of London harbourmaster on 020 7265 2656.

Come out of Paddington Underground station opposite the Hilton London Paddington Hotel and turn left. Cross Spring Street and carry on down the hill, passing the entrance to Conduit Mews on the left. Spring Street and Conduit Mews (and nearby Conduit Place, which you don't see) commemorate a local spring which was used to supply the City of London with water from 1471 until 1812. This was the main spring in the area, and its name, Bayard's Watering, became, in a slightly altered fashion, that of this whole district: Bayswater.

Brooks and mews

Cross Westbourne Terrace and go past the entrance (on the left) to Smallbrook Mews, probably taking its name from a little tributary of the Westbourne. Cross Gloucester Terrace. When you get to the next mews entrances – Upbrook Mews on the right and Brook Mews North on the left – you are on the actual course of the Westbourne, which flows from right to left. Turn left into Brook Mews North and walk down to the far end. If the gate on the left is open, go through it, turn right and make your way to the far right-hand corner of the garden. Here turn left into Elms Mews. If the gate is closed, follow the road round to the right, turn left into Craven Terrace, and then, when Craven Terrace bends right, branch left down some steps (i.e. down the river bank) into Elms Mews. Elms Mews brings you out on to the Bayswater Road at a definite low point. When this was still open country there was a bridge here, with a coaching inn called the Swan next to it. The bridge has gone, but look to your right and you will see that the Swan, opened in 1775, is still very much in existence.

Hyde Park

Turn left on Bayswater Road, cross at the lights to the other side and go through Marlborough Gate into Hyde Park. Ahead of you now is a long stretch of water: first, four fountains and then the Long Water, the latter created in the 1730s by the simple expedient of damming up the Westbourne. In the foreground is the ornate fountain pump house, and, just in front of that, the Westbourne's original outfall into the Long Water with the tops of its three brick-lined arches poking up through the grass. Today the Westbourne flows not into the Long Water (which is filled by rainwater run-off from the surrounding slopes) but into the Ranelagh Sewer, a Victorian conduit constructed beneath the lake's left bank.

Go to the left of the pump house and walk along beside the fountains and then the lake. As you do so, you are contouring round the end of the spur running down from the Northern Heights described earlier. After a while you come to a fork. Keep right here to stay close to the water and walk underneath the bridge. On the other side (where the lake is known as the Serpentine) you can see to the right the tower of Knightsbridge cavalry barracks. Later another tower comes into view in the far distance: the Victoria Tower of the Palace of Westminster.

The Dell

Carry on to the end of the lake and the dam. Just beyond the Dell café turn right down the slope into the Dell. On the way you pass, on the right, an inscription commemorating another ancient water supply, this time not for the City but for Westminster. This one was started before the Norman Conquest (1066) and was not cut off until 1861, so it lasted for 800 years; not a bad record. The Dell is a pretty little water garden formed beneath the Serpentine's dam. The overflow from the lake here is not the Westbourne, but it does flow into the buried Westbourne (i.e. the Ranelagh Sewer) if the Serpentine is full. If the Serpentine is not getting enough run-off from its catchment area, the overflow is recycled back into the lake.

Carry straight on from the Dell, crossing first a tarmac cycle track, then the Rotten Row riding track and then South Carriage Drive. Beneath this road is a huge brick-lined cavern where the Westbourne is joined by the overflow from the Serpentine and by a little tributary called the Tyburn Brook (not to be confused with the Tyburn)

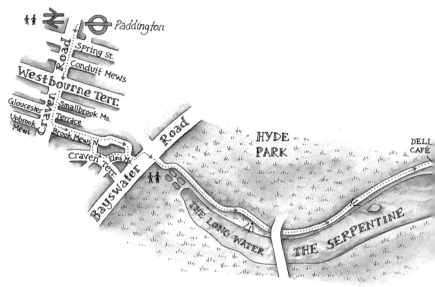

which runs down from the Marble Arch area.

Knightsbridge

Having crossed South Carriage Drive, go through Albert Gate to come into Knightsbridge. As the second part of the name suggests, there was indeed a bridge here once carrying the main road – since ancient times an important highway to the west – over the Westbourne. Where 'knight' comes from, however, is not as obvious as it seems; it is probably a corruption of a quite different word such as Neyt, the name of the adjoining manor.

From this point – the junction of Albert Gate and Knightsbridge – the Westbourne continues its southerly course across the Thames flood plain.

Being so flat, the plain reveals few signs of the river's course, but there are one or two clues, for example in the layout of certain streets, which help to keep us on the right track. To find the first of these clues, we have to make a short detour to the east of the river.

The east bank

Cross Knightsbridge at the lights and turn left. Take the first right into Wilton Place and then go right again into Kinnerton Street and turn left. Off to the right there are lots of little dead-end mews running off the street at right angles. Altogether there are eight of these little enclaves, all belonging to the Duke of Westminster's Grosvenor estate (notice the estate signs and the wheatsheaf plaque fixed to the fronts of some of the houses – more details on page 65). Today they provide bijou residences for the wealthy, but originally they were yards and workshops used by the tradesmen serving the grand houses on the Duke's newly-built Belgravia estate. The river ran along the far end of them (no doubt making a convenient lavatory and rubbish tip), which is why they are all blocked off.

At the end of Kinnerton Street, turn right into Motcomb Street. The impressive façade of the Pantechnicon (a supposedly fire-proof warehouse burnt down in 1874) stands on the right just about directly over the river's course. Carry on to the end of the street. The

river crosses from left to right in the vicinity of Zafferano's restaurant at No. 15 to your right. Now turn left into Lowndes Street. When you get to the traffic lights in Chesham Place, turn right into Pont Street, so named because of another bridge over the Westbourne here. The French word was probably chosen in order to make the new development (dating from the 1830s) sound more chic and attractive.

Pont Street to Sloane Square

The bridge, marked on maps up to the 1820s at least, seems to have been where Cadogan Lane now is, so turn left into the lane when you come to it and walk on right down to the end where it becomes D'Oyley Street. Follow D'Oyley Street round into Sloane Terrace and take the first left into Sedding Street. A zebra crossing at the end brings you into Sloane Square.

Sloane Square Underground station ahead provides a good opportunity to get a new fix on the exact course of the Westbourne, for the river is carried over the tracks in a huge iron pipe clearly visible from the platforms. You can try persuading the staff to let you down free to have a quick look, but they will probably make you buy a ticket first. From the station, the river carries on down Holbein Place, first left out of the station. At the end of Holbein Place it splits up into several different channels to form a kind of delta. The main one

carries straight on under Chelsea Barracks and cuts across Chelsea Bridge Road and the grounds of Chelsea Hospital before flowing out into the Thames through an arched tunnel in the embankment wall.

The Chelsea Hospital channel

The barracks are inaccessible for obvious reasons so we cannot follow this route directly, but we can go through the grounds of Chelsea Hospital (the home for old soldiers, founded in 1682) and pick up the river again just before its confluence with the Thames. From Holbein Place, turn right into Pimlico Road. Cross Chelsea Bridge Road at the lights and walk along Royal Hospital Road to the Hospital entrance on the left. Turn in here and walk down the road and through the big gates leading to the tree-lined avenue. The river cuts across Ranelagh Gardens – from which the Ranelagh Sewer gets its name – on the left, crosses the avenue and meets the Thames almost directly ahead. Go down the little slope in the avenue and turn right by the tennis courts. Then go left down the central path leading past the 1849 Chilianwallah memorial towards the gutted but still majestic Battersea Power Station on the far side of the river. (Chilianwallah, incidentally, was the British Army's costliest battle in the conquest of India.)

Go through the gates at the far end and cross Chelsea Embankment using the traffic island on the left. Where the pavement meets the wall you will see the date 1858 carved into one of the granite blocks. What this refers to is not known (it can't be the building of the embankment because that was 15 years later) but it serves as a useful pointer to the mouth of the Westbourne, for if you look over the wall you will see it directly below. For the intrepid who want to get a closer look, there are some stairs about 100 yards to the right. Otherwise you can get a good view from Battersea Park opposite.

Other channels

When you come back from the park, cross the bridge on the downstream (i.e. power station) side. From here you will see two more tunnel entrances and the entrance to a large dock in between the road bridge and the railway bridge.

These are the ends of the delta channels mentioned earlier.

The dock is all that remains of an extensive canal and reservoir system begun by the Chelsea Waterworks Company in 1725 to supply drinking water to Mayfair. A century later it was extended by the Grosvenor family, hence its present name, the Grosvenor Canal. Until the mid 1990s Westminster City Council used it for barging away rubbish to tips in the Thames estuary. Now it is being regenerated with houses, shops and offices surrounding a marina. For a closer view of the dock, stand on Grosvenor Road where it crosses the dock entrance and look over the railings.

To return to Sloane Square Underground station and the end of the walk, follow Chelsea Bridge Road and its continuation, Lower Sloane Street, straight up to Sloane Square.

The Tyburn river walk

The Tyburn (meaning Boundary Stream) rises on Haverstock Hill near Hampstead in the vicinity of Shepherd's Walk and its junction with Fitzjohn's Avenue. Flowing down through Swiss Cottage, it is then said to cross the Regent's Canal and enter Regent's Park by means of an aqueduct incorporated into pedestrian-only Charlbert Bridge. The park manager, however, says this is not the case. He also says that the Tyburn does not supply Regent's Park lake although other authorities claim that it does. Whatever the truth on these points, the Tyburn certainly begins its journey through the West End in the Baker Street area, where we pick it up.

Start: Baker Street Underground (Jubilee, Metropolitan, Bakerloo, Hammersmith & City and Circle Lines)

Finish:	Pimlico or Vauxhall Bridge Underground (both Victoria Line)
Length:	3½ miles (5.5 km)
Time:	2½ hours
Food:	There are plenty of pubs, restaurants, wine bars and sandwich bars along the whole length of this walk, except for the last half mile (kilometre). Shepherd Market in Mayfair, one of London's most attractive little enclaves, is perhaps the best refreshment stop: it's about half way and it has a good selection of all types of eating and drinking places.
Sights:	Oxford Street, Mayfair, Green Park, **Buckingham Palace** and the **Queen's Gallery**.
Note:	If possible plan to finish the walk at low or lowish tide on the Thames, otherwise it may not be possible to see the Tyburn's outfall. To find out when low tide is, either consult the current edition of *Whitaker's Almanack* in your local library or ring the Port of London harbourmaster on 020 7265 2656.

Come out of Baker Street Underground station on the south side of Marylebone Road and walk down the left-hand side of Baker Street, heading in the same direction as the traffic. At the second left, Paddington Street, turn left. The river actually continues south for a little way almost as far as Blandford Street before it also turns left, but because of the unhelpful street layout we have to make our turn here. If you look down Kenrick Place on the right you can see the low point where the river runs across just before Blandford Street.

Carry on along Paddington Street until you reach Paddington Street Gardens. Turn right into the gardens and make your way diagonally across to the far left-hand corner. Go through the gates out of the park into Moxon Street and turn right into Aybrook Street (the river was sometimes known as the Aye Brook as well as the Tyburn). At the bottom of the street, where we pick up the river again, turn left into Blandford Street.

Marylebone

When you get to Marylebone High Street, cross over to the Angel in the Fields pub and continue on along Marylebone Lane. The High Street was the centre of the old village of Marylebone, its name derived, via St Mary-le-bourne, from Tyburn. The lane was the road connecting the village with London. At this point the lane stuck to the riverside, hence its distinctly winding course. Elsewhere in this part of London the streets are laid out on a more or less regular grid.

Stay with Marylebone Lane until you come to a fork with a shop called The Button Queen at its dividing point. Here the lane goes off to the left away from the river; we go right into pedestrian-only Jason Court. At the main road (Wigmore Street) turn right and then, crossing over at the lights, turn left into James Street, a popular place to eat out in summer. Walk on down this street to its junction with Oxford Street. Here, look left and right and you will see that you are definitely in the river valley. In 1941 the river was seen flowing through the bottom of a bomb crater here.

Mayfair

Carry on now into Gilbert Street and so into the exclusive residential district of Mayfair. Somewhere here the river bends east again, but the street levels have been so much altered that it is impossible to pinpoint the exact course. However, the steep drop into St Anselm's Place is at least a clue. Turn left here, right at the end into Davies Street and then immediately left into Davies Mews. At the end of the mews, turn right into South Molton Lane, cross Brook Street (note the watery name) and enter narrow Avery Row, built in the 1720s over the newly culverted Tyburn by bricklayer Henry Avery. The low point in the middle is the real ground level and the west side of the valley can be seen stretching up Brook's Mews to your right. Behind and in front of you, Brook Street and Grosvenor Street respectively have been raised up on artificial embankments. It's these embankments, or causeways, which create the constant ups and downs as we walk along what should be a flat river bed.

Now climb up to Grosvenor Street, cross over and go through the opening into Bourdon Street. Again, there is a pronounced descent to the valley bottom. Ideally we want to go straight on here but buildings block our path so we have to make a short detour. Turn right up the hill (keeping left when the road forks) and then left near the top into pedestrian-only Jones Street. This brings you out into Berkeley Square. From the corner on the left you can see the bottom of the valley at the far end of the square and the bank on the far side rising up to Piccadilly. We shall come to this point shortly, but first we must return as nearly as we can to the point where we left the river in Bourdon Street. We do this by turning left into Bruton Place and going down to the bottom past the Guinea pub. Here follow the road round to the right, cross Bruton Street and then continue along Bruton Lane, keeping the Coach and Horses pub on the left.

Near the end of Bruton Lane, a gated private road follows the course of the

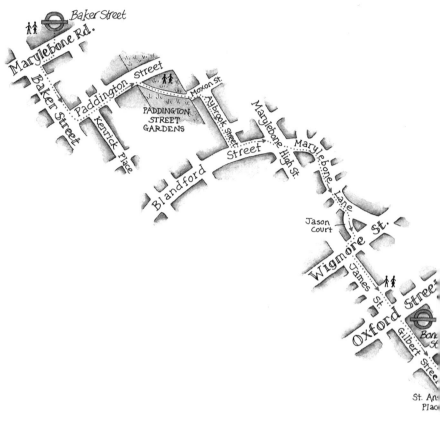

river. Bear right here and then turn left into Berkeley Street. Hay Hill and the rising ground up to Piccadilly bar the river's southerly progress towards the Thames and force it to pursue a more westerly course. We follow it by crossing Berkeley Street into pedestrian-only Lansdowne Row. This little street of small shops and sandwich bars was created by paving over the river when it formed a boundary between the grounds of two former aristocratic town houses: Devonshire House and Lansdowne House.

Shepherd Market

From Lansdowne Row, continue on into Curzon Street. Just beyond the Third Church of Christ Scientist on the right, turn left through the opening at No. 47 leading into Shepherd Market. Go down to the bottom by the King's Arms and turn right. The original market from which this little enclave of narrow streets, pubs and restaurants takes its name must have grown up on the banks of the river, for after flowing west to avoid Hay Hill the Tyburn continues its southerly course here, possibly through Carrington Street (second on your left), Yarmouth Place and the bottom of Brick Street. Carrington Street (significantly) is a dead end, so we must detour round it to get to Yarmouth Place and Brick Street.

Carry on a little way and turn left into Hertford Street. Follow the road round to the right and take the first left into Down Street. (Ahead on the right is the entrance to the disused

Down Street Underground station – see page 47.) Turn left again into Brick Street. Yarmouth Place is at the bottom of the hill on the left. Follow Brick Street which used to be called Engine Street ('engine' referring to a mill or other machine powered by the river) round to the right and you come out on Piccadilly. That you are back on the actual course of the river is confirmed by the way the ground rises to both your left and your right.

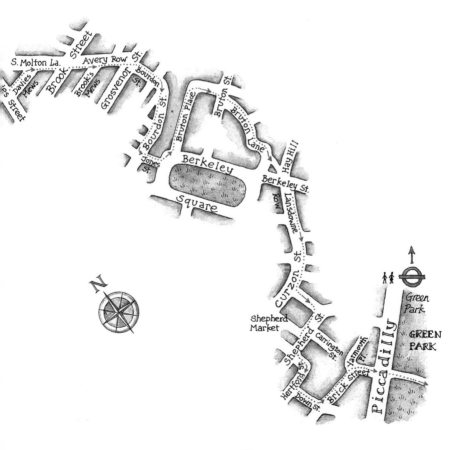

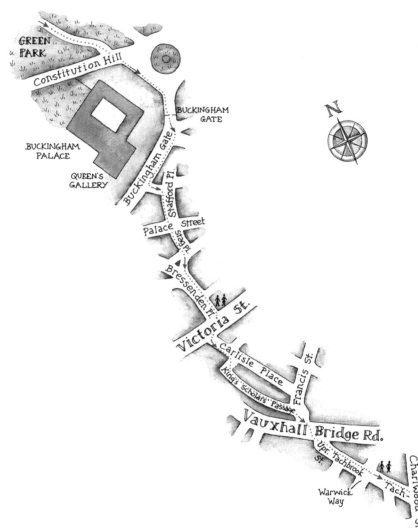

Green Park

Cross Piccadilly and go through the gate into Green Park. You can now see the gently sloping valley, shorn of buildings, curving gently to the right and then, near the bottom, nudged by Constitution Hill protruding from the right, equally gently to the left. Here, in very ancient times, the open Tyburn disappeared into the marshy ground of the Thames flood plain, as described above. Later it was used to fill the lake in St James's Park (a function fulfilled today by artesian wells). Now, safely contained in its brick-lined tunnel, it continues on its way beneath

Buckingham Palace to its meeting point with the Thames, about 1⅓ miles (2 kilometres) away.

To the Thames

It has to be admitted that the walk from here to the Thames, which takes about 50 minutes and is along flat ground, is not quite as interesting or varied as the stretch from Marylebone to Green Park, but it is well worth doing none the less. The reward at the end is to see where the Tyburn flows out into the Thames.

To begin, cross Constitution Hill at the lights, pass in front of Buckingham Palace, and keep following the railings round to the right. After passing

through Buckingham Gate, cross the main road (also called Buckingham Gate) and turn right. Turn left at No. 4 Buckingham Gate (opposite the entrance to the Queen's Gallery) and walk through the pedestrian-only opening into Stafford Place. Turn right here, cross Palace Street and continue on into Stag Place. At the far end, go through the colourful sculpture and then straight on into Bressenden Place. At the lights, cross straight over Victoria Street to Carlisle Place and take the first right into King's Scholars' Passage. (If the gates are closed, carry on along Carlisle Place and turn right on Francis Street.) The passage is a rather smelly service road between the

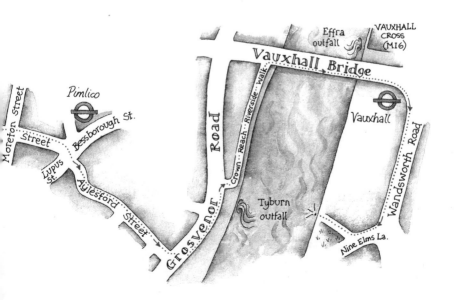

backs of tall buildings. Its curious name comes from King's Scholars' Pond, into which the Tyburn flowed somewhere near here when the area was still open countryside. The King's Scholars themselves were schoolboys at nearby Westminster School (see page 98). When the Tyburn was covered over, this section was christened the King's Scholars' Pond Sewer.

At the end of the passage, cross busy Vauxhall Bridge Road diagonally into Upper Tachbrook Street. You could be forgiven for thinking that Tachbrook is in some way a reference to the Tyburn. In fact it is a place in Warwickshire which in the 18th century was owned by a man who also owned land here. (The man, incidentally, was royal gardener Henry Wise.)

Carry on along Tachbrook Street, crossing Warwick Way, Charlwood Street and Moreton Street on the way. At the end, the river carries straight on across the main road (Lupus/Bessborough Street) but we have to deviate slightly and bear right along Aylesford Street. At the end of the street, cross Grosvenor Road and turn left back towards the river's course, passing the derelict Thames-side Chester Wharf.

The Tyburn outflow

When you reach Tyburn House and Rio Cottage, you are back with the river once more. This, moreover, is the precise point where it finally flows into the Thames. Beneath the houses there is a semi-circular opening in the river wall about 10 feet (3 metres) high and 15 feet (4.5 metres) across. Set back about 20 feet (6 metres) inside it is a heavy iron sluice gate installed, as the plaque on Rio Cottage says, in 1832. If you go round the corner into Crown Reach Riverside Walk and look over the parapet, you can see the river's outflow channel.

To get a close-up view of the actual brick-lined tunnel and sluice gate, you have to climb down the ladder on to the mud flats (not advisable unless you are strong and well shod). A safer alternative is to go to the public garden on the opposite bank. To reach it, walk along the riverside to Vauxhall Bridge. Cross the bridge, turn right into Wandsworth Road and right again into Nine Elms Lane, and keep going until you come to the garden. As an added incentive to make this extra effort at the end of a long walk, if you cross the bridge on the left-hand side you will also see, at the point where the bridge meets the bank, the sluice gate of the Effra, one of the main 'lost' rivers on the south side of the Thames. Above it towers the monstrous new headquarters of MI6 (for more on this and other Secret Service HQs, see page 110).

Locations of both Pimlico and Vauxhall Underground stations, at either of which the walk can end, are shown on the map.

The Fleet river walk

The highly conspicuous sources of the Fleet (Anglo-Saxon for tidal inlet) are the large bathing ponds on the Hampstead and Highgate sides of Hampstead Heath, and the lake in the grounds of Kenwood. The Hampstead source flows down Fleet Road and is joined by the Highgate source just before passing under Kentish Town Road in the vicinity of its junction with Hawley Road. Having flowed under the Regent's Canal in the Lyme Street area, it links up with St Pancras Way at the latter's junction with Pratt Street. St Pancras Way is an old road and the Fleet once flowed beside it just as the Tyburn flowed beside Marylebone Lane. Passing Old St Pancras Church, the river then flows between St Pancras Station and King's Cross Station, where we join it.

Start:	King's Cross Station (Circle, Victoria, Northern, Piccadilly, Hammersmith & City and Metropolitan Lines and trains)
Finish:	Blackfriars Station (District and Circle Lines and trains)
Length:	2 miles (3.2 km)
Time:	1½ hours
Food:	There are pubs, sandwich bars and restaurants all along the route, but Clerkenwell Green is undoubtedly the best place to stop. It's got a good selection of places to eat and drink in, is exactly half way, has a villagey atmosphere and has seats if you want to sit outside.
Sights:	**Mount Pleasant Sorting Office**, the **Clerks' Well**, Clerkenwell Green, Smithfield Market, **St Paul's Cathedral**, Fleet Street, Bridewell.
Note:	If possible plan to finish the walk at low or lowish tide on the Thames, otherwise it may not be possible to see the Fleet's outfall. To find out when low tide is, either consult the current edition of *Whitaker's Almanack* in your local library or ring the Port of London harbourmaster on 020 7265 2656.

On the forecourt of King's Cross Station facing away from the entrance, turn left. Cross York Way into Pentonville Road and walk along to the traffic lights. Ahead, Pentonville Road climbs the steep hill forming both the west side of the Barnsbury spur, running down from the Northern Heights, and the east side of the Fleet valley.

Cross right into King's Cross Bridge, a short road covering the railway and

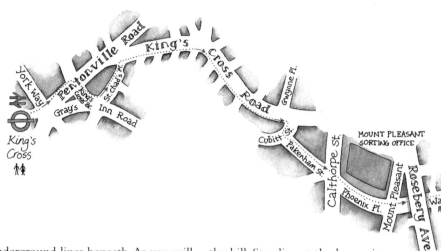

Underground lines beneath. As you will see at various points along the course of the walk, both these lines run through a deep cutting – sometimes open, sometimes covered – as far as Farringdon Station, where they divide. The railway line, continuing on through City Thameslink Station and crossing the river at Blackfriars, is one of only two lines in central London to run right through the city. Significantly, both use river valleys to do so. This one, the Thameslink Line, obviously uses the valley of the Fleet. The other one, the West London Line passing the Olympia and Earl's Court exhibition centres, follows the course of Counter's Creek.

St Chad's spa

From King's Cross Bridge, take the first left into St Chad's Place and walk down the hill. Standing at the low point, you can see over the wall into King's Cross Thameslink Station in the cutting below. The building of the Underground line through this district in the 1860s destroyed the last remaining part of St Chad's Gardens, a pleasure ground surrounding a once popular medicinal well which in the 18th century attracted up to a thousand people a week to drink its waters. Later in the walk we come to the site of another Fleet-side spa which was an even bigger draw than that.

St Chad's Place now narrows into a passage, and, bending left, brings you out on King's Cross Road. Turn right and follow the road as it bends round to the right. On the left the roads all climb up the east side of the Fleet valley and several (Weston Rise, for example) feature the tell-tale word 'Rise' in their names. Beyond the former magistrates' court and police station, the road changes direction and swings round to the left, keeping close to the river's meandering course.

Bagnigge Wells

Just beyond the garage on the right there is a terrace of houses, all with balconies at first-floor level. Here stood Bagnigge Wells, the other

famous spa mentioned earlier and one of the best-attended of all the spas surrounding London during the spa-crazy 18th century. The Fleet itself flowed through the spa gardens and there were seats on the bank 'for such as chuse to smoke or drink cyder, ale etc. which are not permitted in other parts of the garden'. Today the only relic of the spa (besides the name of nearby Wells Square) is the inscribed stone set into the front wall of the first house in the terrace, thought to mark the north-western boundary of the gardens. The stone is dated 1680, which is particularly interesting because this is about the time when Bagnigge House was used as a summer retreat by Charles II's mistress, Nell Gwynne. Nell's association with the area is commemorated in Gwynne Place on the opposite side of the road. The 'Pinder a Wakefeilde' mentioned on the plaque refers to a famous old pub called the Pindar of Wakefield on nearby Gray's Inn Road. It survived until just a few years ago when it was taken over and renamed The Water Rats. The original Pindar opened in 1517.

Mount Pleasant

Beyond the terrace turn right into Cubitt Street and then first left into Pakenham Street. The river swings right here towards Pakenham Street to avoid a knob of high ground ahead called Mount Pleasant. As you rise up towards the junction with Calthorpe Street, the knob comes into view with a huge **Royal Mail sorting office** on top. Go straight on into Phoenix Place and down the hill, probably an artificial one intended to graduate the incline of Calthorpe Street up the west side of the Fleet valley. When you get to the road called Mount Pleasant, the true valley bottom reappears to the right. Carry straight on here into Warner Street and go under the bridge carrying Rosebery Avenue across the valley. The river now cuts into the bank on the right, up which climb several streets with 'hill' in their names, for example Eyre Street Hill and Back Hill. The top of the hill was once a large garden attached to the Bishop of Ely's London house, hence other local horticulturally flavoured street names such as Vine Hill and Herbal Hill.

Clerkenwell

At the end of Warner Street, turn left into Ray Street, its sides framing the spire of Clerkenwell parish church ahead. Cross Farringdon Road and follow Ray Street Bridge round to the right towards the City Pride pub. Clerkenwell's name comes from the **Clerks' Well**, a spring of pure water on the east bank of the Fleet which in the Middle Ages was associated with the Company of Parish Clerks in the City. Having been lost for centuries, the old well was rediscovered in 1924

Plate 1: *The entrance to the Grosvenor Canal in Pimlico (see the Westbourne river walk, page 29).*

Plate 2: *Holborn viaduct was built to span the Fleet river valley and improve communications between the City and West End (see the Fleet river walk, page 41).*

Plate 3: *Tyburn House and the Tyburn river outfall into the Thames (see the Tyburn river walk, page 36).*

Plate 4: *A view of the BT Tower across the Fleet river valley (see the Islington spur walk, page 19).*

Plate 5: Entrance to the Goodge Street deep level tube shelter, one of several such structures constructed beneath existing tube stations during the Second World War. This particular one housed General Eisenhower's D-Day communications centre (see page 46).

Plate 6: Access shaft to Thames Water's London Tunnel Ring Main (see page 51). This vast new engineering feat deep below ground is planned to supply fully half of London's water needs.

Plate 7: The Central Map Room in Winston Churchill's Second World War Cabinet War Rooms, excavated beneath Whitehall in the 1930s (see page 44).

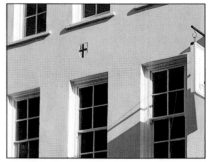

Plate 8: Kinnerton Street on the Grosvenor estate in Belgravia (see pages 27 and 66). The Grosvenor estate is one of the few privately owned estates in London which advertizes its presence in various signs and plaques.

Plate 9: The City's coat of arms on a shop front in South Molton Street, Mayfair (see page 58). The property was acquired by the City Corporation in 1628 in return for making substantial loans to King Charles I.

Plate 10: The Statue of Eros in Piccadilly Circus (see page 74). Is the downwards pointing arrow a pun on the name of Lord Shaftesbury, in whose memory the statue was sculpted by Sir Arthur Gilbert in 1893?

and is now visible through a window in No. 16 Farringdon Lane (Well Court) just beyond the City Pride. The display beside the well includes an exhibition with writing big enough to read from outside and, on the left wall, an enlarged reproduction of a 16th-century map which clearly shows Clerkenwell and the broad River Fleet flowing down beside it towards the Thames. From the well, carry on along Farringdon Lane and past the entrance to Clerkenwell Green. Cross Clerkenwell Road and continue into Turnmill Street, so named because of three water mills worked here by the Fleet in the Middle Ages. At the end of the street, turn right by Farringdon Station into Cowcross Street, cross Farringdon Road into Greville Street and turn left into Saffron Hill. This is a reminder that the Bishops of Ely grew a rich crop of saffron crocuses in their hilltop garden here, saffron being widely used in the Middle Ages to mask the taste of rancid meat. Saffron Hill slopes quite steeply down to what is probably something like real street level. At the end you have to climb up some steps to regain the artificially elevated street. The difference between the two must be all of 20 feet (6 metres). From the top of the steps turn left. Ahead on the other side of the valley is Smithfield Market. When this ancient market dealt in live meat, it was the cause of many of the Fleet's

problems, for the river was used to wash away the blood and entrails of butchered animals. The resulting pollution can all too easily be imagined.

Holborn Viaduct

At the crossroads, turn right into Farringdon Street and walk down to Holborn Viaduct. Stairs at three of the viaduct's four corners make it easy to climb up on to it to view the valley to both north and south. To the north, Farringdon Road was constructed over the Fleet in the 1840s, erasing some of London's most infamous slums at the same time. To the south, the river had been covered over as early as the 1730s and the Fleet Market – two rows of one-storey shops connected by a covered walkway – built on top. By the early 19th century, however, the market had become so badly dilapidated and such a nuisance that it was cleared away and replaced by Farringdon Street.

Holborn Viaduct itself was built in 1869. Connecting Holborn with Newgate Street, the new bridge put an end to the difficult and sometimes dangerous ascents and descents of the steep sides of the Fleet valley, making it much easier for horse-drawn traffic to pass to and fro between the City and the West End.

Continuing on from Holborn Viaduct along Farringdon Street, the names of several streets on the left provide more clues to the presence of the 'lost' river. Turnagain Lane was a cul-de-sac ending at the riverside: when you reached it you had to 'turn again' and go back the way you came. When Londoners cooked their food and heated their homes with open fires, much of their coal came by sea from the Newcastle area. Newcastle Close, therefore, may allude to the coal brought up the Fleet by barge, though this is not certain. Old Fleet Lane is obvious. Old Seacoal Lane is definitely a reference to coal traffic on the Fleet. The river was navigable as far as Old Seacoal Lane until 1765, when New Bridge Street, the next and final section of the walk, was built over it.

New Bridge Street and Bridewell

New Bridge Street begins at Ludgate Circus, the meeting point of two ancient thoroughfares: Fleet Street and Ludgate Hill. Here the river slices its way through the 50-foot terrace described earlier. As you make your way down the street, you can see how the ground continues to rise steeply on either side until quite near the Thames.

For 300 years the wide mouth of the Fleet was dominated by a royal palace-turned-prison called Bridewell (another watery name). Although the main part of the Tudor building was pulled down in the 1860s, a reminder of it exists in the name of Bridewell Place on the right. Also, a little further on, the prison's 1805 gatehouse, complete with black

spiked gate, still stands. A little further on still is a street with the resonant name of 'Watergate'. This marks the position of the prison's river entrance. It is some distance from the modern Thames ahead, showing how much land has been reclaimed over the past couple of centuries or so, particularly at this point.

The Fleet outflow

Near the entrance to Watergate you will see an entrance to the Blackfriars subway. Go down here for the final stage of the walk: the search for the point at which the Fleet finally flows out into the Thames after its 4½-mile (7-kilometre) journey from Hampstead Heath. At the foot of the stairs go left and then right, making for exit 5 on the subway map. When you come out into the open air again, don't go up the steps on to the bridge, but turn right down to Paul's Walk. At the foot of the steps, lean out over the water and crane your head to the left: if it's low tide you should be rewarded with your Holy Grail, a clear, if oblique, view of the arched entrance to the Fleet tunnel.

Unfortunately, this is the only view you will get. With the Tyburn and the Westbourne it is possible to go to the other side of the Thames and look back to see the river mouth front-on. But here the bridge support is in the way and it is so close to the bank that it is impossible to get even an oblique view by walking up- or downstream.

The walk ends at Blackfriars Station, accessible through the subway.

Corresponding with the seven Thames tributaries on the north side of the river are seven more on the south side.

SOUTH OF THE THAMES

Starting in the west, these are (with places of confluence with the Thames): Beverley Brook (Putney), the Wandle (Wandsworth), Falcon Brook (Battersea), the Effra (Vauxhall), the Neckinger (Bermondsey), the Earl's Sluice (Rotherhithe) and the Ravensbourne (Deptford). However, the terrain on the south side is not so interesting as on the north side (either to describe or to explore) and the south-side rivers are more suburban than the north-side ones. Also, the south-side rivers are less 'secret'. No fewer than three of the seven – Beverley Brook, the Wandle and the Ravensbourne – flow on the surface; a fourth, the Effra, appears in the grounds of a publicly owned country house called Belair in Gallery Road, Dulwich. The mouth of a fifth – the Neckinger – can be seen at St Saviour's Dock next to the Design Museum on Butler's Wharf.

Chapter 2

THE SUBTERRANEAN CITY

There is a lot more to London than meets the eye. The hidden parts are not just behind walls; they are also beneath the surface. People have been tunnelling through the London clay for well over a century and a half now and the result is an extraordinary honeycomb of structures extending up to 200 feet (60 metres) deep below the city streets. Generally, the only signs on the surface are grilles, vents and manhole covers. Of course, much of this subterranean world is familiar to millions of people through the Underground system and the various road and foot tunnels under the Thames. But equally much is not, as we shall see.

UNDERGROUND CITADELS

Probably the most interesting individual complex is the government's system of offices and tunnels under Whitehall. At its heart is a huge subterranean office block beneath the Treasury at the junction of Horse Guards Road, Storey's Gate and Great George Street. Secretly converted within the existing building by filling in the ground floor above with 17 feet (5 metres) of concrete to form a protective shield, it was built in the 1930s and used during the Second World War by Prime Minister Winston Churchill and his War Cabinet. Today most of its 200-odd rooms continue to function as office space, although the most historic parts – the rooms used by Churchill and the Cabinet – have been opened to the public as the **Cabinet War Rooms** museum. If you should visit this evocative relic of Britain's darkest hour, remember that what you see is only a relatively small part of a much bigger complex extending over 6 acres (2.5 hectares) around you. The army engineer responsible for building the War Rooms (Brigadier James Orr) died only in 1993. He received an OBE for his work, but the whole project was so secret that he was never given a citation.

Extending north and south from the War Rooms are two tunnels. The southerly one goes as far as former government offices in Marsham Street. Built during the last war to connect the War Rooms with the government's Rotunda citadel constructed within the old Horseferry Road gasometers, the tunnel (rumoured to emerge in the basement of Westminster Hospital) is now believed to be disused. The partly ivy-clad Rotunda has been incorporated at ground level within the Marsham Street offices and is best viewed from the rear in Monck Street. The northern tunnel, which is the oldest part of the government system, connects the War Rooms via the 'Q' Whitehall exchange with the government telephone exchange in Craig's Court and Northumberland Avenue, near Charing Cross Station.

It is believed (the government system is very secret) that several branch tunnels lead off this telephone-exchange tunnel. One goes east to the pre-Second World War army citadel under the Ministry of Defence. (At the end of 1993 news broke that this citadel had just been converted into a brand new state-of-the-art headquarters to replace the old Cabinet War Rooms.) Another branch tunnel goes west to the Admiralty citadel, the above-ground section of which forms the ivy-covered concrete blockhouse at the junction of Horse Guards Road and the Mall. A third tunnel burrows its way in the Pall Mall direction and apparently has an exit at the Duke of York's Steps, where there is a door with a doorbell next to it. Behind this door is a vestibule from which another door leads possibly into the tunnel. You can see this vestibule by peering through a louvred window in the men's lavatory in the Institute of Contemporary Arts, entered from the Mall. There is also thought to be another tunnel connecting the Duke of York's Steps with Buckingham Palace, although its existence has never been confirmed. It's supposed to have been constructed before or during the Second World War so that, in the event of an invasion, the Royal Family could make a quick getaway via Charing Cross tube station and Paddington mainline station to Bristol and so to Canada.

Before and during the war further 'citadels' were built outside the Whitehall district: for the Admiralty at Cricklewood; for the Air Ministry at Harrow; for the Cabinet Office under the Post Office Research Station at Dollis Hill; for MI5 under their building in Curzon Street, Mayfair; for the London civil defence organization next to the old Geological Museum (now part of the Natural History Museum) in South Kensington's Exhibition Road; and for the Post Office (now British Telecom, BT) next to the Faraday House telephone exchange in the City. All these citadels still exist, and the Admiralty one in Cricklewood was brought back into action in 1982 for the Falklands War.

Post Office cable tunnels

The government system links via the 'Q' Whitehall exchange tunnel with a 12-mile (19-kilometre) network of Post Office cable tunnels. Two tunnels fan out from Colombo House near Waterloo Station. One goes north-west to Trafalgar Square post office. The other goes north-east to the Faraday House telephone exchange in the City, between Blackfriars Bridge and London Bridge. The rest of the network is on the north bank and extends as far as Shepherd's Bush in the west and Shoreditch in the east. Two-thirds of the network was built in the late 1940s and early 1950s in response to the Cold War atomic-bomb threat. The tunnels constructed at this time are over 16 feet (5 metres) in diameter and contain a 2-foot (60-centimetre) gauge railway for laying heavy cables. The later tunnels (the most recent of which, linking Paddington with Shepherd's Bush, was finished as late as 1976) are rather smaller. Access is through post offices, and ordinary manhole covers like the one at the junction of Bethnal Green Road and Sclater Street in the East End. It used to be so easy to get into the tunnels that the *New Statesman* magazine was able to hold its Christmas party in one in 1980!

The Post Office cable tunnels, now the responsibility of BT, connect with the Kingsway telephone exchange 100 feet (30 metres) down on either side of High Holborn under Chancery Lane Underground station. Also built in the early 1950s in response to the atomic-bomb threat, its existence was almost completely unsuspected outside official circles until the late 1960s, despite its being directly beneath one of London's busiest streets. The exchange, which fills a number of interconnecting tunnels extending south down Furnival Street, is said to be so large that it takes as much as an hour and a half to walk round it. BT's large office at the eastern end of Holborn no doubt connects with it.

Deep-level shelters

Two of the tunnels in the Kingsway telephone exchange were originally built in 1942 to form the Chancery Lane deep-level shelter. This was one of eight such shelters, all beneath existing Underground stations and seven of them on the Northern Line. Each consisted of two parallel tunnels 1,200 feet (365 metres) long and divided into two floors. Four of the shelters (Belsize Park, Camden Town, Clapham North and Clapham South) were fitted with bunks for 8,000 people and used as public air-raid shelters. The other four were retained for government use. Chancery Lane and Clapham Common provided emergency citadels for use during V1 and V2 rocket attacks. Stockwell housed American troops and Goodge Street, linked to the Cabinet War Rooms by pneumatic despatch tube, became a subterranean D-Day communications centre for General Eisenhower, the Allied supreme commander.

Today the shelters still exist. Chancery Lane is part of the Kingsway exchange. The remaining seven are all on the Northern Line and are identifiable on the surface by their distinctive blockhouse-type entrances. Three (Belsize Park, Camden Town and Goodge Street) are used by a firm called Security Archives for storing commercial data. The remaining four (Stockwell, Clapham North, Clapham Common and Clapham South) are vacant. The leases for the shelters contain a clause which allows the government to re-occupy them should the need ever arise, which we hope it does not.

UNDERGROUND RAILWAYS

During the 130 years of the existence of the Underground railway in London, some 40 stations above and below ground have become, for a variety of reasons, surplus to requirements. Fourteen below-ground stations still exist. The closest to central London is Down Street, just off Piccadilly near Hyde Park Corner. Opened on the Piccadilly Line in 1907, it was closed in 1932 because it was so close to both Hyde Park Corner and Green Park. During the Second World War it came into its own again when the government took it over as an emergency HQ, equipping it with a telephone exchange, meeting rooms and living quarters. It was used mainly by the Railway Executive Committee, the organization responsible for co-ordinating the still-private railways during the war years. But Churchill and his War Cabinet also used the centre occasionally during the Blitz, though their main base was of course the Cabinet War Rooms. Churchill's bath, near the stairs at the far end of the platform, is still in place, as is the old telephone exchange.

Today, the station forms part of the Underground's ventilation system. At street level, the red-tiled façade is a typical example of Underground-station architecture in the early years of this century. Below ground, the only indication of the station's existence is a glimpse of a platform between Green Park and Hyde Park Corner.

King William Street

One of the most historic of the old stations is King William Street in the City. Opened in 1890, it was the northern terminus of the world's first electric tube railway, the City and South London Railway, which connected the City with Stockwell via a mile-long (1.6-kilometre) tunnel under the Thames. When this pioneering line was extended northwards to Moorgate in 1900, the engineers could not fit King William Street and its tunnel into the new system and they had unfortunately to be abandoned. The station entrance was removed in 1933 but the platforms survived and were used during the war as an air-raid shelter. There are still old wartime posters on the walls.

'Passing Brompton Road'

Another ex-station with wartime relics is Brompton Road, opened in 1906 on the Piccadilly Line. Some trains were already passing straight through it by 1910 because two other Piccadilly Line stations (Knightsbridge and South Kensington) were so close. The guard's cry 'passing Brompton Road' became so well known (a bit like 'mind the gap' today) that it was adopted as the title of a popular West End play about commuting and the rat race. During the Second World War the station, which had closed in 1934, became the operations room of the Anti-Aircraft Command (not, as some books have it, an air-raid shelter). Below ground, the platforms have been walled off so you cannot see them from passing trains. One has a screen at one end on which films were shown during the war. At street level one of the original maroon-tiled entrances survives on the east side of Cottage Place, near the junction with Brompton Road.

Wood Lane

Wood Lane in Shepherd's Bush opened as a surface station on the overground section of the Metropolitan Line to serve the White City Franco-British exhibition of 1908. In 1920 two Underground platforms were added when the Central Line was extended from Shepherd's Bush to Ealing. But the station proved difficult for Central Line trains to use, so in 1947 a new Central Line station a little further up Wood Lane was built. This is the existing White City Underground station. Wood Lane reverted to Metropolitan Line-only use and eventually closed in 1959. From Wood Lane itself you can see the station building with its name in relief above the entrance. The upper platforms are hidden behind high walls. Below ground, travelling east on the Central Line from White City to Shepherd's Bush, you pass one of the lower station platforms adorned with enamel nameplates and tattered posters half a century old.

North End

North End on the Northern Line was never actually opened as a station. Indeed, it was never even finished. After completing the platforms and short sections of the stairway, the Hampstead Tube Company abandoned the project in 1906 when Hampstead Heath was scheduled as a public open space and further suburban development in the immediate vicinity (the station's prospective market) scrapped. Had the station been completed, its entrance would have been at the junction of Hampstead Way and North End Road. Underground engineers tend to refer to it colloquially as Bull and Bush after the nearby pub of music-hall fame.

With its extreme depth – at 200 feet (60 metres) it's London's deepest Underground station – North End was given a new lease of life during the Cold War of the 1950s when London Transport converted it into a control centre for activating the London Underground's floodgates in the event of a nuclear attack. That danger is long since perceived to have disappeared. Today, the station is abandoned and the platforms are gone, but the site is visible from passing trains.

Disused tunnels

Besides disused Underground stations, London Underground also has several disused Underground tunnels. At New Cross there is a 472-foot (144-metre) tunnel built in 1971–2 for an uncompleted Jubilee Line extension to Thamesmead. Between St Pancras Station and a railway subterranean goods depot at Smithfield, there is a Metropolitan Line link abandoned after the war. And under the Thames there are three disused tunnels, all formerly part of the Northern Line. Two in the region of London Bridge form the abandoned double tunnel which used to carry the City and South London Railway from Borough Station to King William Street in the City. The third, between Hungerford and Blackfriars Bridge, formed the Northern Line's now-abandoned Charing Cross loop. This was bombed during the war and is now flooded.

Mail Rail

London Underground is not the only organization to run Underground railways in London. Besides the Post Office's cable tunnel railway already mentioned, the Post Office also has its own tube railway which it uses for transporting sacks of mail between sorting offices and railway stations. **Mail Rail**, as it is called, can be seen in operation during the tour of Mount Pleasant Sorting Office in Clerkenwell.

Mail Rail runs from Paddington in the west to East London Sorting Office in Whitechapel, stopping *en route* at Liverpool Street railway station and several sorting offices, including Mount Pleasant. It is electrically operated, driverless and about the size of those miniature steam engines you can ride on at fun fairs and amusement parks. When it opened in 1927 it immediately took a quarter of London's mail vans off the roads, thus helping to reduce the traffic congestion which had prompted its construction in the first place. The 9-foot (3-metre) tunnels are 70 feet (21 metres) below ground and it takes less than half an hour for one of the 34 trains on the circuit to travel all the way across London, including stops. In a van it would probably take three or four times that.

TUNNELS UNDER THE THAMES

It has been calculated that there are well over 20 tunnels under the Thames, making it the most undermined capital river in the world. Besides the three disused tube tunnels and two Post Office cable tunnels already mentioned, there are nine tube tunnels, eight service tunnels, three road tunnels and two foot tunnels. The public tube, road and foot tunnels are, by definition, relatively well known; the service tunnels, being closed to the public, are not.

Passing beneath the Thames between Barnes and Hammersmith in the west and Woolwich Reach in the east, these service tunnels mostly carry water mains and electricity cables. The most interesting historically is the Tower Subway running from Tower Hill next to the Tower of London to Vine Lane, Tooley Street, on the opposite bank. Opened in 1870, it was originally used by people crossing the Thames, first by 12-passenger cable car and then on foot. Following the opening of Tower Bridge in 1896, it was closed to the public and has not been opened again since.

Until the 1970s it was used by the London Hydraulic Power Company (see below) as a conduit for its mains. Today, owned by Cable and Wireless Communications and the only privately owned tunnel under the Thames, it carries phone lines, cable TV and water mains. The tunnel is about 7 feet (2 metres) in diameter.

UTILITY SUBWAYS

The public utilities have always been Underground animals both because the earth cradles and protects their precious pipes and ducts and because there is nowhere for these conduits on the surface. For the most part the networks are buried in specially dug channels and trenches, but there are beneath London's streets several purpose-built service subways which enable maintenance and repair to be carried out without ripping up roads and pavements.

Altogether, there are nearly 12 miles (19 kilometres) of service subways in London, mainly underneath the West End, the City and Docklands. The principal system radiates out from Piccadilly Circus to Trafalgar Square, Shaftesbury Avenue, Regent Street, Charing Cross Road and Holborn. There is another in the vicinity of Holborn Viaduct and a third in the northern approaches to London Bridge around Arthur Street. There is also a little-known one under the Kensington Court estate in west London. The longest is probably the one in the Embankment. It runs all the way from the Houses of Parliament to Blackfriars Bridge before turning inland to the Bank of England. The door at the base of the Boudicca statue on Westminster Bridge is the Westminster entrance.

Most of these subways, mainly designed to accommodate proliferating gas and water mains, were built as part of Victorian street-improvement schemes. The oldest, under Garrick Street in Covent Garden, was built in 1861. A modern one is the circular tunnel built under Oxford Street in 1968 to contain services diverted by the modernization of Oxford Circus Underground. There are no signs on the surface that this tunnel exists, but the routes of the older subways are generally marked on pavements by the long, wide rectangular grids through which the heavy cast-iron pipes were inserted. Some of these pipes, still in excellent order, are 3 feet (1 metre) in diameter. One of the newest service subways in London is the complex of tunnels under Ludgate Hill near St Paul's, built in 1992 as a result of the lowering of the Snow Hill railway tunnel.

The London Hydraulic Power Company (LHPC)

The LHPC was founded in 1871 and for a hundred years supplied hydraulic power for heavy lifting machinery, including lifts and cranes, and safety curtains in West End theatres. In its heyday in the 1920s its network of mains carrying water at a pressure of 600 lb/square inch (42 kg/cm²) spanned London from Limehouse in the east to Earl's Court in the west. The wonder is that it survived so long when electricity had more than come into its own as a source of power.

When the LHPC eventually ceased its century of operations in the 1970s, it bequeathed to the late 20th century a subterranean legacy of nearly 200 miles (320 kilometres) of 19th-century, 12-inch (30-centimetre) cast-iron pipes. A consortium including Rothschilds bought the network and has since occupied itself finding new uses for the pipes. As mentioned above in the description of the Tower Subway, Cable and Wireless Communications have taken over part of the system for their phone lines.

Giant waterworks

Virtually the entire water network in London is Underground and therefore invisible. Could it but be brought to the surface and revealed in all its glory, it would be seen to be a marvel of engineering: beautiful brick-lined Underground lakes with vaulted roofs (as at Putney Heath) and now, the latest feat of Thames Water, the London Tunnel Ring Main, a 50-mile (80-kilometre) bore 130 feet (40 metres) down and big enough to drive a car through. In fact in 1993 something approaching this actually happened when ten cyclists rode along a 1.5-mile (2.5-kilometre) section of the tunnel as part of a charity bike race.

Completed in 1996, the ring main encircles London and supplies about half its water. Huge pump-out shafts big enough to put a bus in and extending right down to the main, bring up the water and channel it into local distribution systems. The closest one to central London is under the traffic island at the bottom of Park Lane, though you wouldn't know it from the surface.

Electrical network

As with water, much of London's electricity network is hidden from view, especially the small sub-stations, of which there are 12,000, mostly invisible, strung out across the capital. These stations take power at 11,000 or 6,600 volts from larger converter stations and transform it down to 405 or 240 volts for distribution to individual customers.

One of the newest sub-stations is bang underneath Leicester Square. Three storeys deep, it contains three large transformers and is entered via a large automatic trapdoor concealed in the pavement in the south-west corner of the square. The theatre ticket office in the square is also the ventilation extract shaft. A new mile-long (1.6-kilometre) tunnel, crossing four tube lines and passing 65 feet (20 metres) below Grosvenor Square, connects it with the ground-level Duke Street substation in Mayfair. In 1993–4 London Electricity built a new 6-mile (10-kilometre) tunnel between Pimlico and Wimbledon via Wandsworth to strengthen power supplies in south-west London.

The sewers

Last but not least in the reckoning of London's utilities with substantial Underground structures is the capital's sewer system. Essentially this is another Victorian creation, and a particularly impressive and effective one at that. Its main feature is a series of large brick-lined tunnels running west to east on both sides of the Thames and parallel to it. These large tunnels, constructed with all the attention to design and detail so characteristic of the Victorian Age, intercept smaller sewers flowing north and south down towards the river and carry the effluent away to treatment works in east London (the northern one is at Beckton and the southern at Plumstead).

This very simple system, still performing well 130 years after its completion, was the brainchild of Sir Joseph Bazalgette, engineer to the Metropolitan Board of Works. The intercepts start out about 4 feet (1.2 metres) high and then gradually grow in size as they take in more tributary sewers. By the time they get to east London they are about 11 feet (3.5 metres) high. It is of course possible to walk around in the main intercepts, and people do (those whose job it is to keep the muck flowing and the structures themselves in good repair) but unfortunately they are never open to the public. Unlike the Paris sewers, which can be visited, London's do not have raised walkways. Anyone venturing into them has to put on a pair of waders and take the plunge and, as you might imagine, this is a dangerous business.

Although the sewers themselves are not open, you can at least visit two of the sewer system's magnificent, cathedral-like pumping stations: **Abbey Mills** on the north side of the river and **Crossness** on the south. They have both been converted to electricity now, but Crossness still has its giant steam engines *in situ* and Abbey Mills is worth seeing for its superb iron work.

SOME ONE-OFFS AND FAR-OUTS

The features of subterranean London described so far have generally been networks of tunnels and other types of buildings in the centre of the city. The ones that follow now are either one-offs or some distance from the city centre.

The Camden Town Catacombs, an extensive series of Underground passageways and vaults lit via tell-tale cast-iron grilles in the road surface above, honeycomb the ground beneath the old canal–railway interchange at Camden Lock. They run from Camden Lock market and the old Gilbey's gin warehouse next door, pass under the Primrose Hill goods yard and connect with a vast subterranean chamber which used to house the stationary steam winding engine that hauled trains up the incline into Euston mainline railway station. The catacombs were originally used for stabling ponies employed in shunting goods wagons in the yards above. Although disused, they are still railway property.

Underneath a former school behind Clerkenwell parish church on the northern fringes of the City is an amazing network of subterranean prison cells. They originally formed part of the Clerkenwell House of Detention, an overflow to the Bridewell women's prison a mile (1.6 kilometres) or so away beside the Thames. The first Clerkenwell was built in 1616 and the cells may well date back to that time, but it is more likely that they are a relic of a later rebuilding. They are now part of the **House of Detention** museum.

Away out in east London there are two unknown tunnel systems. In Greenwich Park there is a series of what appear to be medieval brick-lined conduits west of the Observatory under the slope of the hill. No one knows exactly why they were built or when or, indeed, what for. The most common explanation is that they supplied water to the old royal palace of Placentia (no longer surviving), but that does not account for their large size: in parts they are like passageways and high enough for a person to walk through.

The Woolwich Arsenal system, extending from Thamesmead to Shooters Hill, dates from the 18th century and was once part of the enormous Royal Artillery/Royal Arsenal complex at Woolwich. Today it is used by the British Library as a bookstore.

Never outdone in anything, Harrods, the great emporium, of course has its own tunnel system. The main thoroughfare under the Brompton Road links the store with its warehouse (scheduled for conversion into a hotel) in Trevor Place. A network of smaller tunnels and cellars leading off it provide deep-freeze stores, wine cellars and last, but not least, a lock-up for shoplifters. Harrods is definitely not the place for claustrophobic kleptomaniacs.

In addition to four tube lines, the Thameslink tunnel, the Fleet Sewer, several gas mains and the London Tunnel Ring Main, the congested ground beneath King's Cross Station also envelops a pair of abandoned railway tunnels known as the 'York Road' and 'Hotel' curves. Linked to the mainline station by a ramped opening that gradually rises from a siding on the York Way side, these tunnels will probably be incorporated into the planned sub-ground enlargement of the mainline station and the construction of the new Channel Tunnel terminal, also Underground.

Kingsway tram tunnel and more air-raid shelters

The Kingsway tram tunnel runs from Waterloo Bridge to Theobald's Road, via Aldwych and Kingsway. It was originally used by trams, but in the 1960s the southern section was converted into a traffic underpass as far as Holborn. The short section from Holborn to Theobald's Road, including the subterranean Theobald's Road tram station, was then used by the Greater London Council as its flood-control centre. The GLC has now gone and, with the building of the Thames Barrier, so has the imminent danger of flooding. The centre is now believed to have been abandoned.

To protect civilians caught outside by air raids in the Second World War, covered trench systems were built in many London squares and parks, including Hyde Park, Green Park, St James's Park, Queen Square, Woburn Square, Leicester Square, Russell Square, Bloomsbury Square and Lincoln's Inn Fields. The one in Lincoln's Inn Fields was nearly 1,500 feet (450 metres) long, 7 feet (2 metres) deep and roofed with concrete and 2 feet (60 centimetres) of earth. The Lincoln's Inn shelter and most of the others are believed still to exist, although the entrances have been blocked off. In Leicester Square the shelter was destroyed when the new electricity sub-station was built. The former entrance has survived half-way down the steps to the men's lavatory in the north-east corner of the square, but it now appears to have been blocked off.

Chapter 3

PRIVATE LANDOWNERS

One of the best-kept secrets in London is the fact that large chunks of the capital belong to historic estates which have been owned by the same institutions and families for hundreds of years – and, in the case of the Crown, for nearly a thousand years. It is impossible to say precisely how much land is owned in this way. Landowners as a rule do not publicize the extent, or even the existence, of their estates and there is nowhere you can go (such as a comprehensive public land registry, indexed by owner) to find out. However, at the very least, the total (excluding parkland) must be something like 4,500 acres (1,800 hectares); in other words, getting on for seven times the size of the City.

Quite what all this must be worth to the fortunate owners in question is impossible to compute. As an indication, the value of the Queen's central London property (in the City, West End, Regent's Park and Kensington, excluding parkland) is currently put at over £1 billion ($1.5 billion).

Traditional landowners own most of their property freehold and make their money from letting it to leaseholders for a fixed term of years. Leaseholders may in turn sublet to an occupier, or even to another leaseholder. Sometimes there are whole chains of leaseholders between freeholders and occupiers, an arrangement which makes it even more difficult to establish who owns what. To take one conspicuous but relatively simple example: the Queen is the freeholder of Spencer House in St James's; Earl Spencer, brother of the late Princess of Wales, is the head leaseholder; and Lord Rothschild's St James's Place Capital plc is the sub-leaseholder and occupier.

THE CITY

The City Corporation owns nearly a third of the City's 677 acres (274 hectares) in its twin guises of private landowner and government-appointed local authority. In its local-authority role, it owns a 115-acre (46-hectare) 'Planning Estate' mainly acquired after the Second World War to expedite the rebuilding of blitzed areas like the Barbican.

In its private capacity, the Corporation owns two historic estates whose origins go way back to the beginnings of the modern City in the early Middle Ages.

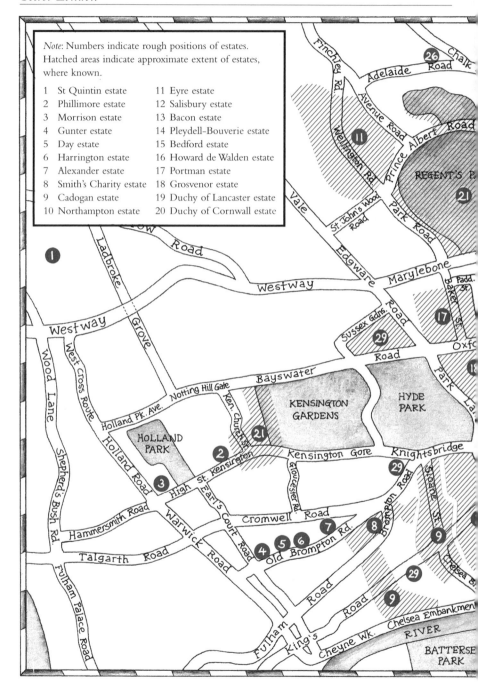

Note: Numbers indicate rough positions of estates.
Hatched areas indicate approximate extent of estates,
where known.

1   St Quintin estate   11 Eyre estate
2   Phillimore estate   12 Salisbury estate
3   Morrison estate   13 Bacon estate
4   Gunter estate   14 Pleydell-Bouverie estate
5   Day estate   15 Bedford estate
6   Harrington estate   16 Howard de Walden estate
7   Alexander estate   17 Portman estate
8   Smith's Charity estate   18 Grosvenor estate
9   Cadogan estate   19 Duchy of Lancaster estate
10 Northampton estate   20 Duchy of Cornwall estate

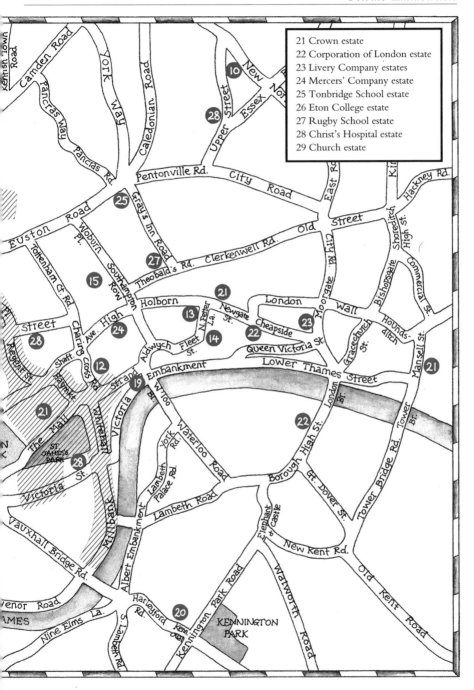

21 Crown estate
22 Corporation of London estate
23 Livery Company estates
24 Mercers' Company estate
25 Tonbridge School estate
26 Eton College estate
27 Rugby School estate
28 Christ's Hospital estate
29 Church estate

The larger of the two is the so-called 'City's Cash' estate. The Cash estate derives originally from the City's ancient right to acquire any 'wastes and open spaces' in the City. Today it owns land both in and outside the City. The core holding is the 35-acre (14-hectare) estate actually in the Square Mile. This includes the Old Bailey, parts of New Broad Street, Whitefriars and Fenchurch Street and the City's two surviving markets, Smithfield and Leadenhall. Outside the City, the Cash estate also owns two relocated City markets – the Spitalfields fruit and vegetable market, now in Leyton and the Billingsgate fish market, now in Docklands. It also owns a 27-acre (11-hectare) Mayfair estate called Conduit Mead.

Conduit Mead

Conduit Mead has an interesting history. In the 17th century it was a Tyburn-side field which the City leased from the Crown so that it could draw water from a spring in the field. Then in 1628 King Charles I, gearing up for his 11-year rule without Parliament and therefore taxes, needed to obtain money from the City. The Corporation duly obliged with the cash and received the freehold of Conduit Mead in return. From the 18th century the estate was developed with houses. Today it is bisected by New Bond Street and takes in all or part of Brook Street, Maddox Street, Grafton Street, Conduit Street and South Molton Street. Since these streets are now among the most fashionable and expensive in London, the estate should by rights be netting the City an extremely healthy annual income. Unfortunately, this is not quite the case. The original leases, granted in 1754, had to be 'perpetually renewable' in order to attract tenants. This means that, despite the huge increase in the value of the property that has taken place since then, all holders of the leases have been able to renew them endlessly at the original 18th-century rent. So today it is the leaseholders not the City who are making all the money. And they will continue to do so for centuries to come. The 1925 Property Act did reduce 'perpetually' to 2,000 years maximum, but that still leaves another 1,800 years to go before the City can get its hands on Conduit Mead again and bump up the rent to more realistic levels. Meanwhile the City's presence in Mayfair can be seen most clearly in South Molton Street where its red-and-white coat of arms has been fixed to the fronts of Nos 13, 44 and 65 (the latter painted over) and where the blue plaque to the poet William Blake at No. 17 is of the distinctive square City type rather than the usual circular sort.

In total, the Cash estate brings into the City a reasonably respectable £70 million ($105 million) a year. A large slice of this money goes straight out again to maintain the largest part (in area) of the Cash estate, namely the 9,000 acres (3,650 hectares) of forests, common and open spaces in and around London, acquired since 1878 specifically for the recreation of cooped-up city dwellers. The largest is the 6,000-acre (2,400-hectare) Epping Forest, north-east of London. Also in the portfolio are West Ham Park, Highgate Wood and Queen's Park further in. The newest addition is Hampstead Heath, taken over from the defunct Greater London Council in 1989. All these properties are non-income-generating and are hugely expensive to keep up: the 800-acre (320-hectare) Hampstead Heath, for example, costs anything up to £4 million ($6 million) a year to look after.

Bridge House Estates

The City Corporation's other historic landholding goes by the name of the Bridge House Estates. This estate consists of land given or bequeathed in the Middle Ages and later for the maintenance of old London Bridge, completed in 1201. The last bequest was in 1675. Most of the land is south of the river in areas like Borough High Street and Hay's Wharf which were opened up by the construction of London Bridge and later bridges across the Thames.

The income from the estates was, and still is, used for building and maintaining the bridges across the Thames owned by the City. There are four of these – London Bridge, Blackfriars Bridge, Southwark Bridge and Tower Bridge – but the estate has actually paid for six: the medieval London Bridge's two replacements, 1831 and 1972; the new Blackfriars Bridge, 1869 (the 1769 original was paid for mainly with money from another source); the two Southwark Bridges, 1819 and 1921; and Tower Bridge, completed in 1894. Today there is over £300 million ($450 million) in the Bridge House kitty and it is growing at the rate of £20 million ($30 million) a year. City officials are naturally wondering what to do with the embarrassing surplus: a new bridge to ease the pressure on Tower Bridge is one option under consideration.

THE LIVERY COMPANIES

The old-established livery companies (see pages 129–35) are another major traditional landowner in London, particularly in the City. Nobody knows exactly what or how much they own, but a mid-1980s' estimate put their property in the Square Mile alone at 15 per cent of the total City area, in other words about 100 acres (40 hectares).

Most livery-company property consists of their livery halls and surrounding land. Between them, the Carpenters and the Drapers own all Throgmorton Avenue, where both have their halls. Just to the west the Drapers own a great swathe stretching back from Throgmorton Street to London Wall which was once their garden (hence the street Drapers Gardens running through the middle), and another block in St Swithin's Lane where their first hall stood. To the east, the Leathersellers own every freehold around their hall in St Helen's Place, and more either side in Bishopsgate and St Mary Axe. To the west, the Grocers own nearly all the west side of Prince's Street around Grocers' Hall Gardens, opposite the Bank of England, plus more land in Cornhill and Old Jewry. To the south, the Merchant Taylors at 30 Threadneedle Street have since the 14th century owned virtually everything on their island site bounded by Finch Lane, Cornhill and Bishopsgate.

Of course, the livery companies also own plenty of property in London outside the City. The Mercers, for example, rumoured to be the biggest landowners of all the livery companies, have an estate in Covent Garden around Mercer Street. And the Goldsmiths have 200 acres (80 hectares) of Ealing, left to them by a member called John Perryn in 1657. Much of the estate consists of playing fields. There is also an impressive range of almshouses built in 1811.

Public school landowners

Several livery companies have close connections with old-established public schools, and in one case at least the school has an old London estate which is still managed for it by its sponsoring livery company. In 1553 Sir Andrew Judd, Muscovy merchant and member of the Skinners' Company, founded a school in his home town of Tonbridge in Kent and endowed it with an estate in St Pancras. That estate is now around Tonbridge Street, Cartwright Gardens and the top end of Judd Street, near St Pancras Station, and it is still looked after by the Skinners' Company. Hence the Skinners Arms pub at 114 Judd Street.

Besides Tonbridge, several other old public schools have estates in London. Eton College in Windsor owns the 60-acre (24-hectare) Chalcot estate north of Primrose Hill. Formerly a farm, it was given to the school by King Henry VI, founder of Eton in 1440. Today it can be identified by street names such as Eton Villas, Provost Road and King Henry's Road. Rugby School in Warwickshire was founded in 1567 with an estate around what is now Rugby Street, close to the famous children's hospital in Great Ormond Street, WC1. The land on which the hospital stands was bought from the school, so reducing the original 8-acre (3-hectare) endowment somewhat. Today the school, having missed the boat on development, is saddled with huge bills for maintaining its inheritance of handsome 18th-century listed houses, so there may not be a Rugby estate in the area for much longer.

The Rugby estate includes the northern section of Lamb's Conduit Street. The southern section, along with Dombey Street, Emerald Street and part of Bedford

Row, belongs to the Harper estate, the endowment of Bedford School founded by William Harper in 1566. This estate was originally 13 acres (5 hectares) in extent, but it has now shrunk to 3 acres (1.2 hectares). Probably the largest old school estate in central London belongs to Christ's Hospital. Besides land in Soho, Islington and Westminster (most of Queen Anne's Gate, where the National Trust is based, Old Queen Street and Carteret Street), it includes the freehold of two West End theatres (the Queen's and the Gielgud in Shaftesbury Avenue) and an industrial estate in the East End. The school, now based in Horsham, West Sussex, was originally founded in the City by King Edward VI in 1553. Today its wealth is such that all but six of its 800-plus pupils are on subsidized fees.

The largest old school estate in Greater London must be that belonging to Dulwich College in south London. The school's founder, actor Edward Alleyn, endowed it with the 1,500-acre (600-hectare) manor of Dulwich in 1619. Today the manor remains virtually intact (although Dulwich Park has been acquired by the local authority), and with its woodlands and large open spaces has all the appearance of a country, rather than an urban, estate. Through the middle runs a College-owned road which is barred half-way by the last toll-gate in London. The revenue is about £17,000 ($25,500) a year. In the centre of Dulwich village is the school's public **picture gallery** with its world-famous collection of Old Masters.

CHURCH ESTATES

You may have noticed that, with the exception of Eton, all these schools were endowed around the same time, that is to say in the 1550s and 1560s. The reason for this is that in the Middle Ages it was the monasteries which ran the schools. When the monasteries were dissolved as part of the Protestant Reformation in the middle of the 1500s, other ways of funding schools had to be found: endowing them with their own estates was the obvious method since that is how monasteries also had been supported.

Although the monasteries lost their estates during the Reformation, the rest of the Church clung on to its extensive landholdings. Today these estates, managed since 1948 by the Church Commissioners, generate income which mainly goes towards paying clergy stipends. Once upon a time the Church of England's estate in London, handed down from Bishop of London to Bishop of London, covered hundreds of acres, but this century it has diminished in size considerably.

The largest single block today is the Hyde Park estate, a 90-acre (40-hectare) tri-angle of up-market houses between Sussex Gardens, Edgware Road and Bayswater

Road. Originally developed from 1827 onwards with increasingly large stuccoed terraces, much of this area has been rebuilt since the 1950s with more manageable town houses. This has enabled it to retain its social cachet and therefore its value to the Church. Elsewhere in London, in places like Brixton, Lambeth, Vauxhall and Stoke Newington, the Church owns the Octavia Hill housing estates. Unlike the Hyde Park estate, which is purely an investment, these fulfil a social purpose by providing homes for people on small incomes who need to live in central London. As well as residential property, the Church also has an extensive commercial property portfolio in London, though to what extent this is the result of the development of historic estates or modern property dealing is not clear. Some of the more conspicuous commercial premises are the Royal Lancaster Hotel at Lancaster Gate (the western corner of the Hyde Park estate), offices at 107–169 Victoria Street and shops in Connaught Street (also on the Hyde Park estate), Knightsbridge (55–91) and King's Road, Chelsea (virtually every one between 195 and 277).

THE CROWN ESTATE

Historically, the Church and the Crown were the two biggest landowners in London. But, whereas the Church has either lost or disposed of most of its property (one recent disposal was its historic estate in Maida Vale, where it is believed Harrow School also has an estate), the Crown has managed to hang on to its possessions so that today it is far and away the largest historic landowner in London.

The official **Crown Estate** consists essentially of 12 million – yes, 12 million – square feet (over 1.1 million square metres) of commercial space, mainly shops and offices, in central London, and over 1,000 acres (400 hectares), mainly residential land and golf clubs, in outer London. Not part of the official Crown Estate but still royal property are the 5,000 acres (2,000 hectares) of parkland in both central and outer London, and the small Duchy of Cornwall and Duchy of Lancaster estates.

Central London
With one significant exception, most of the central London Crown Estate is described either as 'ancient possession', which means it has been owned by the Crown for as long as there have been records (i.e. approaching 1,000 years), or was acquired during the 16th century. As an example of the latter, Regent's Park, originally part of Barking Abbey's manor of Tyburn, was appropriated by the rapacious Henry VIII in 1544 following the closure of the monastery and the seizure of its property.

The 'significant exception' is Regent Street: although a major part of the central London estate today with nearly a quarter of the Crown's commercial space in London, it was not acquired until the early 19th century. Its purchase was made necessary by John Nash's ambitious scheme to link Regent's Park with Carlton House, the Prince Regent's palace overlooking St James's Park.

The core of the Crown Estate in London is a broad and virtually continuous strip of land between Primrose Hill in the north and Millbank/Victoria Street in the south. Broken only by Portland Place, the strip follows Regent Street, Lower Regent Street and Haymarket, Trafalgar Square and Whitehall. Among other things it includes the gleaming stucco terraces of Regent's Park and Carlton House Terrace (where the Crown Estate Commissioners have their office); all the famous shops like Liberty and Mappin & Webb on both sides of Regent Street; Piccadilly Circus and its lights; the clubs, art dealers and Green Park-facing mansions of St James's; cinemas and theatres in Haymarket, including the Theatre Royal; and the two large buildings facing each other across Trafalgar Square, Canada House and South Africa House. There is also a clutch of big West End hotels like the Intercontinental, the Inn on the Park, Le Meridien Piccadilly and the Strand Palace.

In the City, the Crown Estate has over a million square feet (100,000 square metres) of office space, mainly blocks of offices in Holborn Viaduct, Cornhill, East Smithfield (Royal Mint Court) and Leadenhall Street. Away to the west, the Kensington estate is made up of two components: first, the individual mansions in Kensington Palace Gardens and Palace Green, now mostly used as embassies; and, second, half a million-plus square feet (50,000 square metres) of shops and offices in lucrative Kensington High Street, including the former Derry & Toms department store, with its large roof garden (see page 150).

Greater London

In outer London, almost all the 1,000-plus acres (400 hectares) of houses and golf clubs are divided between Eltham and Richmond. Eltham in south-east London, an ancient possession where the remains of the royal palace can still be seen, has 490 acres (200 hectares). The golf clubs are the Royal Blackheath and Eltham Warren. Richmond in south-west London, another ancient possession where again the remains of the royal palace can be seen, has 375 acres (150 hectares), including the Old Deer Park and the Royal Mid-Surrey Golf Club between Kew and Richmond.

In Richmond itself, Richmond Park is, at 2,470 acres (1,000 hectares), by far the largest royal park in London. Then come in descending order of magnitude: Bushy Park and Hampton Court Park, 1,099 acres (445 hectares); Hyde Park and

Kensington Gardens, 615 acres (250 hectares); Regent's Park, 420 acres (170 hectares); Greenwich Park, 200 acres (80 hectares); Primrose Hill Park, 112 acres (45 hectares); St James's Park, 90 acres (36 hectares); and Green Park, 53 acres (21 hectares).

Duchies of Lancaster and Cornwall estates

The Crown Estate is really semi-public property, for all its income (minus management expenses) is surrendered to the Government in return for a royal family operating grant known as the Civil List. The estates of the Duchies of Lancaster and Cornwall, however, are very much personal possessions and the Queen is entitled to keep every penny they earn. Both these estates are mainly agricultural and therefore mainly outside London, but each has its central London nucleus.

The Duchy of Lancaster's London estate consists of 3 or 4 acres (1–1.5 hectares) under and around the Savoy Hotel in WC2 and essentially covers the site of the medieval palace of Savoy, home of royal earls and dukes of Lancaster in the 13th and 14th centuries. The land has always been Crown property except for a brief period in the mid-13th century when it was granted to the Queen's uncle, the Count of Savoy, and then bequeathed by him to the monastery of St Bernard in Savoie in 1268. Queen Eleanor bought it back in 1270 and gave it to her second son, Edmund, Earl of Lancaster. Today, the only surviving part of the palace is the Savoy Chapel in Savoy Street. The estate is managed from the Duchy office in Lancaster Place.

The 45-acre (18-hectare) Duchy of Cornwall estate is south of the river in the Kennington area. Although it has some shops and offices, it mainly consists of 600 flats and houses – mostly let on low rents, often to ex-royal family employees – and the 10-acre (4-hectare) Oval cricket ground, on long lease to Surrey County Cricket Club. Ever since 1337 when Edward III created his eldest son Duke of Cornwall, the income from the estate has been used to support the heir to the throne. Prince Charles is the 25th Duke of Cornwall: he receives three-quarters of the income and gives the rest – maybe as much as £500,000 ($750,000) a year – to the government. The Duchy is managed from an elegant office at 10 Buckingham Gate with a panelled first-floor boardroom known as the Prince's Council Chamber.

NON-ROYAL ESTATES

Below the royal family, at least a dozen non-royal families own more or less substantial historic estates in London. Three of the largest holdings are in the lucrative West End and they have helped put their owners – worth collectively about £4.3 billion ($6.5 billion) according to one recent survey – high in the ranks of the wealthiest men in Britain. Indeed, the owner of the largest of these estates, Gerald Grosvenor, 6th Duke of Westminster, is said to be the richest commoner in the country. It is also said that his estate has an asset value equivalent to that of the eighth largest company in the UK.

The Grosvenor estate

Although an ancient Norman family who came over to England either with William the Conqueror in 1066 or not long after, the Grosvenors were mere country gentlemen in Cheshire until a fortuitous marriage in 1677 brought them 300 acres (120 hectares) of boggy farmland on the western fringe of London. Careful development of that land in the 18th and 19th centuries, besides catapulting the family into the peerage stratosphere, created the districts we know today as Mayfair, Belgravia and Pimlico. From the beginning Mayfair and Belgravia have been two of the smartest addresses in London, but Pimlico, south of Victoria Station, degenerated before and after the Second World War into a seedy area of slums and brothels. Embarrassed by the frequency with which his name was figuring in prosecutions of brothel-keepers, the 2nd Duke sold Pimlico in 1950 and invested the money overseas, primarily in Vancouver.

The Mayfair estate, around 100 acres (40 hectares) with roughly 1,500 properties, stretches from Park Lane across to South Molton Lane and Avery Row (in other words the River Tyburn (see page 31) and from Oxford Street down to South Street and Bruton Place. (The City's Conduit Mead estate is immediately to the east.) In the middle is Grosvenor Square, one of the largest squares in London. The whole of the west side is taken up by the US Embassy; it's the only US embassy in the world where the USA does not own the freehold.

The Grosvenor estate in Belgravia, about 200 acres (80 hectares) with roughly 3,000 properties, takes in all the land between Knightsbridge and Ebury Bridge Road/Buckingham Palace Road, and between Sloane Street/Chelsea Bridge Road and Grosvenor Place, except for a thinnish strip up the side of Sloane Street. This strip is on the other side of the covered-in River Westbourne (see page 26). The centrepiece of Belgravia is Belgrave Square, although Eaton Square (more of an elongated rectangle really) to the south is also a prominent feature.

Both Mayfair and Belgravia were built as residential areas, but today only a third of the former and half the latter are lived in. The majority of the houses have been taken over by firms and embassies seeking central locations and prestigious addresses, so enhancing the value of the estate considerably.

The Grosvenor estate, operating from the **Grosvenor estate office** at 70–72 Grosvenor Street in Mayfair, exercises strict control over the appearance of its properties. Satellite dishes, for example, are not allowed and all stucco exteriors have to be regularly painted in a special kind of magnolia paint. The estate also adopts a far higher public profile than any other private landlord in London. There are places (such as Kinnerton Street in Belgravia) where you can see GROSVENOR ESTATE signs and wheatsheaf plaques fixed to the walls of some of the houses: the wheatsheaf is the main feature of the Grosvenor coat of arms. And there are even walking guides to Mayfair and Belgravia, published by the estate, which accurately delineate the extent of the Grosvenors' London property. Not even the City or the Crown go this far.

Portman estate

Immediately north of the Grosvenors' Mayfair estate is the 110-acre (45-hectare) Portman estate, centred on Portman Square and bounded by Crawford Street, Oxford Street, Edgware Road and Manchester Square. Given to Lord Chief Justice Portman by Henry VIII back in 1533, this is possibly the oldest private estate in London. The owner today is Christopher, 10th Viscount Portman, who lives on a 3,000-acre (1,200-hectare) estate at Clifford in Herefordshire.

Howard de Walden estate

Adjoining the Portman estate on its east side is the Howard de Walden estate. This also covers 110 acres (45 hectares) and occupies all the land between Marylebone Road and Wigmore Street, and from Marylebone High Street to Great Portland Street. In the early 18th century the estate was owned by the Harleys, Earls of Oxford, hence Harley Street. From them it passed to the Dukes of Portland. In 1879 the 5th Duke died unmarried and his sister brought it into the Howard de Walden family. The owners today – along with 3,000 acres (1,200 hectares) in Berkshire – are the four daughters of the 9th and last Baron Howard de Walden, who died in 1999. There are 1,200 houses on the estate and they all have planning permission for use as offices, so very few of them are actually lived in. The estate is run from an office at 50–52 New Cavendish Street. You can find out more about it from the estate's own magazine, *The Marylebone Journal*, available in local libraries.

Bedford estate

Still moving east, the next old family estate to be encountered is the Bedford estate, a much-reduced 20-acre (8-hectare) holding in the British Museum area. One part is in and around Bedford Square, London's finest surviving Georgian square. The other is in the Russell Square area between Montague Street and Bedford Row. Henry Russell, Marquess of Tavistock and heir to the 13th Duke of Bedford, is owner of this estate, plus 13,000 acres (5,300 hectares) of Bedfordshire around Woburn Abbey. He inherited, reluctantly, in 1974 when his father went to live in Monte Carlo as a tax exile. The Russells acquired the property as a result of Lord William Russell's marriage to the Earl of Southampton's daughter in 1669.

Small estates in the Covent Garden/Fleet Street area

South of the Bedford estate are three smaller family estates in the Covent Garden/Fleet Street area, the sizes of which are unknown. The westernmost, incorporating Cecil Court between St Martin's Lane and Charing Cross Road, belongs to the Cecils, Marquesses of Salisbury, a family that first rose to prominence under Elizabeth I in the late 1500s. William Cecil and his son Robert, the first Earl of Salisbury, were both chief ministers to the queen. Lord Salisbury acquired the estate in 1609 and 1610. Development began at once: first the west side of St Martin's Lane, then Leicester Square, then the ground in between. Today the property is much reduced in size. The present owner is Robert Cecil, the 6th Marquess. Born in 1916, he lives at Hatfield House, a massive Elizabethan mansion just off the A1 north of London. His heir, Viscount Cranborne, lives at Cranborne on the family's 13,000-acre (5,300-hectare) Dorset estate. In early 1994 an amusing incident occurred when, during an altercation in a restaurant on Cecil Lane, an irate waiter said to Lord Valentine Cecil: 'Do you think you own this place?' In response, Lord Valentine is reported to have merely smiled – and nodded.

Going east, the next estate is the tiny Colville estate in the heart of legal London. Bounded by Southampton Buildings and Rolls Passage on the east side of Chancery Lane, it was acquired 400 years ago by Sir Nicholas Bacon, a prominent lawyer and Lord Keeper of the Great Seal under Elizabeth I. One of Bacon's sons was Sir Francis Bacon, philosopher and Lord Chancellor. Another was created premier baronet of England in 1611. It is the baronet's descendant, Sir Nicholas, the 14th baronet and another lawyer like his ancestors, who owns the estate today. Besides the Colville estate, Sir Nicholas also owns 14,000 acres (5,660 hectares) of Norfolk at Raveningham, where he lives, and a further 9,000 acres (3,600 hectares) in Lincolnshire.

Across Fleet Street from the Colville estate, the Pleydell-Bouveries, Earls of Radnor, have a small estate in and around Bouverie Street in the heart of the old Fleet Street newspaper quarter. The estate once owned the Harmsworth House and Northcliffe House West newspaper offices. The Bouverie family came from the Château des Bouveries near Lille in Flanders in the 16th century and established themselves in London as merchants trading with Turkey. A baronetcy came in 1714 and then the earldom of Radnor in 1765. It was about this time that they are believed to have bought the London estate. Today, Jacob, the 8th Earl, lives on the 10,000-acre (4,000-hectare) Longford Castle estate near Salisbury surrounded by a fabulous picture collection. It is his son and heir, Viscount Folkestone, who actually owns the London estate (and a large chunk of the south-coast port of Folkestone as well).

North London family estates

On the northern fringes of London there are two old family estates, one in Islington and one in St John's Wood. The Canonbury estate in Islington, now centred on Canonbury Square, originally belonged to the Priory of St Bartholomew in Smithfield. After the closure of the priory, it was bought by John Spencer, later Lord Mayor of London. His daughter and heiress Elizabeth married the Earl of Northampton. Four hundred years later, the owner is Spencer Compton, the five-times-married 7th Marquess of Northampton. Lord Northampton lives at Compton Wynyates, the picture-book Tudor manor house in Warwickshire. He has another fine house and estate at Castle Ashby in Northamptonshire. It is unknown how large the Islington estate is.

On the far side of the Fleet valley from Islington, the Eyre family, based on the Sadborow estate in Chard, Somerset, owns a substantial estate of about 130 acres (55 hectares) in the expensive residential district of St John's Wood, north of Regent's Park. It stretches from Lord's up to Belsize Road and across from Abbey Road to Avenue Road. City wine merchant Henry Eyre, brother of the Lord Chief Justice, bought the estate for £20,000 from Lord Chesterfield of *Letters* fame in 1732. At that time it covered nearly 500 acres (200 hectares) of farmland. His descendants started developing it about 1815, prompted by John Nash's work in nearby Regent's Park.

Two houses in Norfolk Road (Nos 15 and 16) dating from this period are the oldest surviving semi-detached houses in London. Lord's cricket ground was laid out by Thomas Lord on 8 acres (3 hectares) of land leased from the estate in 1814. The MCC eventually acquired the freehold in 1866. On the opposite side of the estate, the Board of Ordnance leased some land in 1820 and built a new barracks on it, together with a fine riding school and officers' mess. Today the modernized barracks, incorporating the Georgian riding school and mess, are home to the King's Troop, Royal Horse Artillery, which fires official salutes in Hyde Park on the Queen's birthday and other occasions.

KENSINGTON AND CHELSEA

In one west London borough – Kensington and Chelsea – at least nine historic estates survive.

Cadogan estate

Kensington and Chelsea stretches all the way up from the River Thames just west of Westminster to the Harrow Road north of Notting Hill. In the southern part 90 acres (37 hectares) of fashionable Chelsea belong to the Cadogan estate, the property of Earl Cadogan, who lives at 7 Smith Street SW3, and his eldest son, Viscount Chelsea. The Cadogans, originally from Wales, also have estates in Oxfordshire and Perthshire. They acquired Chelsea in 1717 when a soldier ancestor, Charles Cadogan, married the daughter of wealthy physician Sir Hans Sloane, benefactor of the British Museum and, more to the point, Lord of the Manor of Chelsea. Eighty per cent residential, the Cadogan estate is today quite fragmented. The main block, including Sloane Street and Cadogan Square, stretches from Knightsbridge down to below Sloane Square. West, there are other blocks both sides of the King's Road as far as Beaufort Street.

Smith's Charity estate

Abutting the Cadogan estate, on the north side of Fulham Road and Walton Street, is the 58-acre (24-hectare) **Smith's Charity estate**, acquired for £2,000 under the will of Alderman Henry Smith, who died in 1628. Smith's aim in financing the posthumous purchase of the land (then market gardens and farmland) was to raise money to ransom English seamen captured and enslaved by Barbary pirates, and to support such of his poor relations as could not earn their own living. By the 18th century the Barbary pirates no longer posed a threat, so from 1772 all the income from the estate was handed out among the neediest of his descendants.

In the 19th century, when the estate was developed into a prime residential area and started producing serious money, the aims of the charity were amended again to allow most of the income to be devoted to proper charitable projects, such as medical research. As late as 1992, however, Smith's 'poor kindred' were still receiving nearly £200,000 a year from the estate. In 1995 Smith's Charity sold out to the medical charity Wellcome Trust for the huge sum of £280 m. The old Smith's Charity estate stretches from Harrods west to Evelyn Gardens. You can get a history and plan of it from the estate office at 48 Pelham Street near South Kensington Underground station.

Alexander estate

In between South Kensington Underground station and the Smith's Charity estate is the Alexander estate. Originally this covered 54 acres (22 hectares). It is believed to be much smaller than this now, but it still includes Alexander Square and Thurloe Square directly opposite the Victoria & Albert Museum.

The tradition is that the estate was given by Oliver Cromwell to his secretary of state John Thurloe, but the truth probably is that a grandson of Thurloe's married the heiress of the property, Anna Maria Harris, in the early 18th century. At the end of the century, the then owner left it to a fortunate godson named John Alexander. A century later, after the Alexander family had developed it, an Alexander girl married a Campbell, one of the sons of the Duke of Argyll, bringing the estate with her. A descendant of that marriage, Ian Fife Campbell Anstruther, owns the estate today. He lives at 13 Thurloe Square.

Harrington estate

Immediately to the west of the Alexander estate, in the Stanhope Gardens/Harrington Gardens area, Charles Stanhope, Viscount Petersham, heir to the 11th Earl of Harrington, owns the 12-acre (5-hectare) residue of the Harrington estate. The Harringtons acquired it in the 18th century when the 3rd Earl married one of the daughters of Sir John Fleming, who died in 1763.

Lord Petersham also has a country estate at Westbury in Wiltshire. His father lives on a 700-acre (280-hectare) stud farm in County Limerick, Eire. The family used to have a castle at Elvaston in Derbyshire. There are both Elvaston and Petersham street names on the part of the estate north of the Cromwell Road which is believed to have been sold.

The Day estate

Bordering the Harrington estate to the south is the Day estate. This spans Old Brompton Road west of its junction with Gloucester Road and includes Hereford Square, Wetherby Place, Rosary Gardens and the northern section of Drayton Gardens, named after the village of Drayton near Norwich where some of the Days lived in the 1830s. Originally 13 acres (over 5 hectares) in extent, the estate is now quite a bit smaller following sales such as the one in 1972 when 28 properties were disposed of. The land came into the Day family after Benjamin Day, a mercer in Covent Garden, married the daughter of a neighbour named Walter Dodemead, who had himself acquired it when he foreclosed on a mortgage in 1735. Simon Day is the owner of the estate today.

The Gunter estate

West of the Day estate is the Gunter estate in Earl's Court and West Brompton. Originally this covered over 100 acres (40 hectares), but much was sold in 1917. The founder of the Gunter family fortunes was Robert Gunter, proprietor of Gunter's Tea Shop in Berkeley Square, one of the great institutions of Regency London. George III bought his buns there and the aristocracy of Mayfair lounged about outside on hot days cooling themselves with Gunter's renowned ices and sorbets. As well as creating a successful catering business which is still going under the name of Payne & Gunter, Gunter also bought land in Kensington, between Barkstone Gardens and Wetherby Gardens in the north and Gunter Grove and Edith Grove in the south. The profits from the development of this land, starting with the Boltons in the 1850s, enabled the Gunters to acquire a large estate near Wetherby, North Yorkshire. They lived there until Sir Ronald, the third and last baronet, died in 1980. His daughters and grandchildren have no doubt inherited the property.

Holland House estate

Across Kensington High Street from the Gunter estate, Charlotte Townshend, daughter of Lord Galway, owns what is left of the Holland House estate. Originally this comprised 200 acres (80 hectares), but sales over the years have reduced it, particularly the disposal in 1951 of 52 acres (21 hectares) of gardens and parkland surrounding the bombed-out remains of Holland House. These remains, incorporating a youth hostel, can still be seen in the middle of Holland Park, which is now a public open space (see page 16).

Mrs Townshend also owns a 3,000-acre (1,200-hectare) estate in Nottinghamshire and a 15,000-acre (6,000-hectare) estate around Melbury House near Dorchester, Dorset, where she lives. She inherited Melbury and the Holland estate from the Earls of Ilchester, who in turn acquired it from their cousins the Hollands in the 19th century. The first Lord Holland, father of rake and politician Charles James Fox, originally bought the estate in 1768.

Phillimore estate

To the east of Holland Park is an estate belonging to Lord Phillimore. His ancestors acquired it through the marriage of Joseph Phillimore, a Gloucestershire clothier's son, to Ann D'Oyley, daughter of a wealthy City merchant, in 1704. Originally 64 acres (26 hectares) but now much reduced, the estate covers the southern slope of Campden Hill and is made up of brilliant white stucco terraces in streets like Phillimore Walk and Phillimore Place. In 1874 artist and *Punch* cartoonist Edward

Linley Sambourne leased one of these houses – then virtually new – and lived in it for the rest of his life. His family kept it unchanged after his death and it is now a fascinating Victorian time-capsule **museum**. Lord Phillimore, who is the 5th Baron, lives at Binfield Heath, near Henley, in Oxfordshire.

St Quintin estate

In the remote northern part of the borough, up near the canal and the railway lines, the Legard family of Scampston Hall near Malton in North Yorkshire own the very small remains of the 200-acre (80-hectare) St Quintin estate in the vicinity of St Quintin Avenue. The St Quintin family, Yorkshire squires since the Middle Ages, acquired the estate in the form of a farm called Notting Barns in 1767. The farm was developed in the 19th century. Many of the freeholds were sold off in the 20th century. Lady Legard of Scampston Hall is the daughter of the last of the St Quintins.

THE END OF THE ESTATES?

It seems fitting to end with an estate like the Legards' which has all but disappeared, because all the old freehold estates in London (with the exception of the Queen's) are threatened with extinction. The menace comes from a piece of legislation called the Leasehold Reform, Housing and Urban Development Act 1993. It sounds innocuous enough, but its consequences are potentially revolutionary. Under this act, all leaseholders in flats and houses have the right to buy their freeholds, subject to certain conditions. It remains to be seen how many of them will be either able or willing to exercise their new right but, if significant numbers of them do, the old estates will inevitably be broken up and they will become yet another chapter in the long history of London.

There are those, such as the Leasehold Enfranchisement Association, who think this may not be such a bad thing. Perhaps it is not, for the freeholders have benefited greatly from the increase in the value of their land over the centuries without actually putting anything into its development. In virtually every case, all the capital for building was provided by the actual house builders, many of whom went bust as a result. Maybe it is time, therefore, for the freeholders' free ride to come to an end.

Chapter 4

TAKEN FOR GRANTED

Many features of London have become so familiar to us that we take them completely for granted. Sometimes they are conspicuous things, landmarks even, like Cleopatra's Needle or the BT Tower. Sometimes they are less obvious things like drinking fountains or blue plaques. Occasionally they are names indissolubly linked with the city like Dick Whittington's. All these features have fascinating but largely unknown stories behind them. Here, we recount a dozen of the most interesting of them in the hope that they will rescue their subjects from an unmerited, if understandable, neglect.

THE LIGHTS OF PICCADILLY CIRCUS

Piccadilly Circus, right in the heart of the capital, is a good place to start. This central hub is famous for its illuminated advertisements. The fronts of some buildings are now almost entirely covered by ever-changing walls of coloured lights spelling out the names of well-known products and even the temperature. But why are the lights there at all and why are they only in one part of the Circus?

Once upon a time Piccadilly Circus was a true circus, in other words a circular interchange linking Regent Street with Lower Regent Street and Waterloo Place. Then in 1886 a new road was created leading off from the north-east. To improve access into this road – Shaftesbury Avenue – buildings on the south side of what is now Glasshouse Street were demolished, leaving the buildings on the north side facing directly on to the Circus. The occupants of these buildings were suddenly presented with fantastic advertising possibilities. Taking advantage of the new technology of electrically illuminated advertisements, particularly the intermittent or flashing variety which attracted attention, some of them quickly put up large signs on the roofs of their buildings.

Vulgar additions
The London County Council disapproved of these vulgar additions to the London streetscape and succeeded in getting them taken down. But their clever opponents

countered by attaching the signs to the fronts of their buildings instead. The only way the Council could have them removed now was by invoking by-laws concerned with the safety of pedestrians walking on the pavements below. They did try to apply these by-laws, but the courts ruled that the signs presented no danger to the public and could therefore stay. Thus by 1910 famous names like Bovril and Schweppes shone forth in illuminated coloured letters 8 feet (2.4 metres) high and there was nothing that anybody could do about it.

Meanwhile, on the triangular Trocadero site, now occupied by **Madame Tussaud's Rock Circus** among others, the County Council was itself the freeholder so here it could apply not only by-laws but the clauses of its own leases to attack the new signs. The trouble was its leases had been drafted long before anyone had even heard of illuminated advertisements and their wording wasn't specific enough to deal with the new situation. So although they succeeded in getting Mr Hutter of the Piccadilly Restaurant on the top floor to take down a Gordon's Gin sign because its fixings damaged the façade of the building, they were powerless when the ingenious restaurateur simply constructed a steel frame protruding out over the roof parapet and hung the sign on it clear of the façade! By the early 1920s the battle of the lights had been won by the advertisers. Looking back, their victory would have been achieved much sooner had it not been for the austerity brought by the First World War.

If you go to Piccadilly Circus today, you will see that the lights – the subject of countless picture postcards – are mainly concentrated in one section of the Circus. The simple reason for this is that the freehold of the rest of the Circus is owned by the Crown Estate. Like the old London County Council, they were opposed to the signs, but they had the advantage of better leases which could be, and since have been, successfully enforced to prevent the erection of any signs they disapproved of. For this reason there have never been any illuminated advertisements on Crown buildings, and, according to recent pronouncements, there never will be.

THE STATUE OF EROS

Piccadilly Circus's other claim to fame is the Statue of Eros. This is a misnomer for two reasons. First, it is not a statue at all but a memorial fountain commemorating the great Victorian philanthropist, the Earl of Shaftesbury, after whom Shaftesbury Avenue is named. Secondly, the figure so delicately poised atop the fountain is not the God of Love but the Angel of Christian Charity. At least, that is what the experts say. The situation is confused somewhat by the words of the sculptor himself, Sir Arthur Gilbert, who said that the naked figure (formerly golden, now leaden and not the original) represents 'the blindfolded love sending forth … his missile of kindness'. It would seem therefore that Gilbert did indeed create the figure to represent love, but the love he had in mind was a religious sort, not the erotic type suggested both by the resemblance of the figure to Cupid and by the popular christening of the memorial 'the Statue of Eros' within a fortnight of its unveiling in June 1893.

Rancour

Given the nature of Lord Shaftesbury's work, it is extraordinary how much rancour his memorial managed to excite. Interference with the design by both the Memorial Committee and the London County Council led to squabbles between these two bodies and even more bitter arguments between them and the ultra-sensitive Gilbert. Gilbert was particularly incensed by the Council's insistence that he reduce the size of the main fountain basin. The memorial was also meant to function as a public drinking fountain and Gilbert claimed that, if the basin were made too small, drinkers would get soaked in their attempts to get a drink of water. After the unveiling (which he refused to attend) he was proved right and he was pilloried for it in the press even though he was in no way to blame. With his public reputation temporarily in shreds, he was also nearly bankrupt because the bronze had cost him a lot more than he had estimated. It comes as no surprise to find Gilbert admitting many years later that the Shaftesbury memorial affair traumatized his entire life.

Had the memorial been constructed to Gilbert's design, it would be a far more exciting structure than the rather dismal stump it is today. Not only would there be a large fountain playing into a wide basin at ground level, but the fountains at the top would form a shimmering globe of water, above which the graceful angel would appear to be hovering, completely unsupported.

There is one final intriguing mystery about Eros. Is the statue a clever pun on Shaftesbury's name? If you look at Eros's bow closely you will notice that it has no arrow in it and that it is pointing downwards. Are we meant to conjecture from this that the arrow or 'shaft' has been fired downwards and that it now lies 'buried' in the ground? There would certainly appear to be some kind of connection, but whether Gilbert ever intended it or not we shall never know for sure.

DRINKING FOUNTAINS

All over central London, in parks and gardens and by the sides of roads, you will find public drinking fountains. Many bear the name of one organization: the Metropolitan Drinking Fountain and Cattle Trough Association. Before this organization was founded in 1859, it was incredibly difficult – incredible in relation to our own experience today – for the vast majority of Londoners to get something so simple as a drink of water when they were out and about in the streets. Cart drivers and cabbies faced the additional difficulty of watering their horses. In fact the only places where horses could be watered were in the troughs some publicans placed outside their pubs. The water in these troughs was not free, however. It had to be paid for, either directly or by buying beer. 'All that water their horses here/Must pay a penny or have some beer' was one common sign erected above many public-house water troughs. With 50,000-plus horses on the streets at one time, horse-watering must have been a lucrative business for the average publican.

By the mid-1850s some improvements had been effected in the supply of drinking water to the capital, but distribution was still woefully inadequate. Into the breach stepped Samuel Gurney, MP and member of a well-known Quaker banking and philanthropic family. Through his efforts the Metropolitan Free Drinking Fountain Association was set up on 10 April 1859. Just 11 days later the first drinking fountain, incorporating its own filtration system, was activated in front of a large crowd of eager onlookers. The fountain, paid for by Gurney, was let into the wall of St Sepulchre's Church in Newgate Street and it can still be seen there today, complete with its two metal drinking cups (see page 146).

Bowls for dogs

Over the next couple of years more fountains were installed at the rate of nearly one a week. Before long, most incorporated small bowls for dogs. Then the Association decided to tackle the horse problem too: in 1867 it changed its name to include cattle troughs ('cattle' was used rather than 'horse' because the troughs were also intended for live cattle on their way to market) and started installing these all over London. The ones we see today are the solid granite variety introduced after the first metal ones had proved unsatisfactory. The Association continued installing troughs until the 1950s, when horse-drawn traffic was finally driven off the roads by motorized transport.

Today, the Association, based in Chislehurst in Kent, continues its work, installing modern drinking fountains in schools and playing fields and helping people in other countries, notably Africa, obtain their own supplies of fresh drinking water. Meanwhile its older fountains in London present a pretty sorry sight. Few work, and most are filled with rubbish. But that isn't the fault of the Association. The responsibility for maintaining them lies with the local authorities. However, they are hamstrung by a lack of resources, and in an age when most people can either turn on a tap or buy a bottle of mineral water, the renovation of derelict public drinking fountains is not a high priority.

CABBIES' SHELTERS

One inclement day in 1874 Captain George Armstrong, late of the army of the East India Company and now managing editor of the *Globe* newspaper, wanted to take a cab. Although there were cabs on the stand, none of the drivers was to be seen. After a bit of searching Armstrong discovered them in the local pub. They were naturally sheltering from the weather and at the same time enjoying some refreshment, primarily alcoholic. How much better it would be, he thought, if cabbies didn't have to go to pubs in bad weather. With their own refreshment rooms, they could get cheaper food and they would be protected from the temptations of drink. Victorian cabmen were notorious for their drunkenness.

So was born the Cabmen's Shelter Fund, an organization dedicated to building alcohol-free shelters for cab drivers complete with tables and benches and kitchens for cooking meals. Between 1875 and 1914, 61 shelters were built. Today 13 survive, five of them in Belgravia and Kensington, then as now smart residential suburbs and therefore the sorts of places where many cab journeys would start or end. The shelters look like rather grand garden sheds, a resemblance reinforced by their smart green livery. The Belgravia ones are in Grosvenor Gardens and Pont Street. The Kensington ones are in Kensington Road near the junction with Gloucester Road, Thurloe Place by the Victoria & Albert Museum, and Kensington Park Road just off Notting Hill Gate. Recently restored, these and the other surviving shelters are all still used by cab drivers. The Transport and General Workers Union administers the Cabmen's Shelter Fund and collects its small annual income from the licence fees paid by cab drivers.

THE COADE STONE LION

A London landmark no doubt well known to cabbies is the magnificent lion guarding the entrance to Westminster Bridge opposite the Houses of Parliament. This noble beast is not the stone sculpture you might think it is from a casual glance, but a piece of pottery made from a mould and fired in a kiln. It is, moreover, over 150 years old, yet it shows not a trace of its age, a testimony to the strength and weather-resisting property of the material from which it is made. This material is an artificial stone called Coade stone, named after its inventor, Eleanor Coade. Born in Exeter in 1733,

Coade came to London with her parents about 1760. Following her merchant father into business, she set up her own linen drapery before, in 1769, taking over an artificial-stone factory beside the Thames where the Royal Festival Hall now stands. There is some doubt as to whether she simply improved the existing artificial-stone formula employed at the factory or whether she did actually invent a completely new type of material. Whatever the truth, her own artificial stone was so superior to anything else on the market that it was soon much in demand for architectural ornaments and details of every kind, not only in Britain but also as far away as North America and Russia.

Secret of success

The secret of Coade stone's success lay both in the composition of the material and in the way it was fired. Just over half of it was raw clay. The rest, apart from flint and sand, was glass and ground-up pre-fired clay, known as grog. The grog meant that the stone did not shrink nearly as much as other artificial stones during firing. This was important when architectural details had to conform to precise measurements. The glass, which was the vitrifying or melting element, bound the whole material together in a way that made it a kind of half-porcelain and therefore extremely hard and weather-resistant. All these qualities were brought out to the full by the long and expensive firing at consistent high temperatures remarkable for the time: four days at about 2,000°F (1,100°C). At this temperature Coade-type material almost liquefies in the kiln so it is even more remarkable that the Coade factory was able to produce huge pieces the size of the South Bank Lion.

The lion was made in 1837, 16 years after Coade's death. The sculptor of the model, W. F. Woodington, inscribed both his initials and the exact date (24 May 1837) on one of the paws. It was painted red and erected, along with two smaller companions, over the gate of the Lion brewery next door to the Coade factory. During the Second World War the brewery was blitzed but miraculously the great lion survived. It was put here in 1966, roughly on the site where in 1799 Mrs Coade (she was not in fact married) had opened a gallery to display the incredible range of her products, nearly 1,000 pieces altogether.

Succumbing to competition from new materials like stucco, the Coade stone factory closed down in 1840, just three years after the making of the lion. Most people who know anything about the subject think that the secret formula died with the business and that it would not be possible to make anything out of Coade stone today. The truth, however, is very different. In the 1970s the British Museum Research Laboratory successfully worked out the composition of the stone. And in

1987, having postulated the probable firing time, a skilled kilnman produced a very respectable piece of Coade modelled by sculptress Mollie Adams.

THE BT TOWER

Where are London's highest restaurant and cocktail bar? In the unlikely setting of the BT Tower, that pencil-slim column of high-tech communications equipment soaring out of London near the Tottenham Court Road. The restaurant is the widest part of the Tower, near the top. The cocktail bar is immediately above. Actually, it's a little misleading to say they are the highest: 'were' would be more accurate since they have both been closed since 1980, mainly for security reasons. In 1971 a bomb exploded on the 31st floor causing damage which took two years to repair.

The closure was so long ago now that most people have forgotten that the Tower, then called the Post Office Tower, was once one of the capital's most popular attractions. You shot up to the top in a lift travelling at a 1,000 feet (300 metres) a minute and then either admired the view from the three public observation galleries where there was also a tea bar, or went on up to the smarter restaurant and cocktail bar for a drink and a meal. The thing about the restaurant was not just that it was 520 feet (160 metres) above the ground, but that it revolved while you were eating. In the space of an hour you would have gone through two and a half revolutions, giving you plenty of time to see the vista in every direction, provided you weren't too busy talking.

Television signals

Meanwhile the massive microwave radio station below, which is essentially what the Tower is, was pumping out television signals and telephone calls by the tens of thousands, and receiving them as well. The Tower was built in the first place because of increased demand for television and telephone cables. The Post Office, which then controlled telecommunications, had two alternatives: either dig up the streets and lay cables to a ring of microwave transmitters/receivers stationed on the high ground around London; or build a tower high enough for the microwaves to clear tall buildings in London and the high ground on both sides of the Thames valley. It chose the latter. It was a sensible decision on both practical and aesthetic grounds. Thirty years on the Tower remains a vital part of the country's telecommunications network, and it continues to look good too.

As you view it, the aerials, exposed to the elements to reduce microwave absorption, are directly below the restaurant and viewing galleries. Below the aerials are 16 apparatus floors enclosed in green anti-sun glass. These house the radio equipment with its batteries and power plant and other necessary bits and pieces. The whole thing weighs 13,000 tons and sits on foundations going down 24 feet (7.3 metres) to rest on the hard blue London clay.

Today you can visit the Tower only by special invitation. The public areas including the restaurant have been turned into a presentation suite used for TV and radio broadcasts, particularly for charity appeals such as the BBC's *Children in Need* project. In the 1980s they were used also as the control room for Richard Branson's much publicized attempt to cross the Atlantic by balloon. Plans to use them for a huge millennium charity party did not materialize.

MARBLE ARCH

At the other end of Oxford Street from the BT Tower, Marble Arch stands in the middle of an island around which traffic endlessly circulates. It is a particularly dismal setting for such a fine structure, but it is not a surprising one for the arch has never really been wanted by anyone. In fact, it has been a virtual orphan since the day it was born.

Regency architect John Nash conceived it as a national monument to the victories of Trafalgar (1805) and Waterloo (1815). It was to stand in front of Buckingham Palace (which in those days did not have its main front facing down the Mall) and it was to serve as an entrance for the exclusive use of the royal family.

The arch was indeed built at the entrance to the Palace, but right from the start it seemed to be jinxed. The foundations proved extremely difficult to lay because of the Tyburn river running underneath (see page 35). The sculpted friezes with which it was to be adorned were put up on the façade of Buckingham Palace instead. And an equestrian statue of George IV, which was to have topped off the arch, was thought to be more suited to Trafalgar Square (where it can now be seen in the north-east corner). Finally, the extension of the east wing of the Palace in the 1840s made the arch seem far too close. The decision was therefore taken to dismantle it and re-erect it somewhere else. The question was, where?

Cumberland Gate

Hyde Park's Cumberland Gate at the park's north-east corner was the answer. The existing gates were moved apart and the arch planted in the middle. Here at least it continued to function as a gateway. It also fitted into an architectural scheme by balancing Constitution Arch at Hyde Park Corner. And within a short time a use had been found for the three rooms in the arch (two small ones behind the sculpted panels and a large one at the top lit by skylights in the roof): the local police turned them into an observation post. During the Hyde Park riots in 1855 a large body of police hid inside the arch (which everybody supposed to be solid) and then sallied forth like Greeks from the Trojan Horse to take the rioters completely by surprise.

The police staffed the post until about 1950. Meanwhile a new traffic scheme had left the arch marooned on an island. There it stands today, its Ravaccione marble streaked with grime and its ironwork in parts broken and missing. Inside, the rooms are empty (apart from a big table and some benches in the top room) and the green-and-cream painted walls are peeling badly. Surely this famous London landmark deserves a better fate?

It is often claimed that one of the reasons why the arch had to be relocated was because Nash made it too small for the royal state coach to pass through. The gold state coach, a flamboyant affair made in 1762 and on show in the Royal Mews, is 8 feet 3 inches (2.5 metres) wide. The arch is at least 13 feet (4 metres) wide between the gateposts. There is therefore plenty of clearance and the charge against Nash is entirely without foundation.

CLEOPATRA'S NEEDLE

Marble Arch is a relatively modern copy of one relic of an ancient civilization: the Arch of Constantine in Rome. But down on the Thames is a real ancient monument, the Egyptian obelisk known as Cleopatra's Needle.

Two hundred years ago, this 180-ton monolith was lying in the sand at Alexandra on Egypt's Mediterranean coast. Then came the French, quickly followed by the British, who kicked the French out. The Turkish viceroy of Egypt offered the obelisk to the British as a memorial to their victorious campaign, but the army lacked the necessary equipment to handle it. So it was left prostrate in the sand and quietly forgotten.

Visiting Paris nearly 70 years later, General Sir James Alexander saw an obelisk which the French had succeeded in shipping from Luxor. He immediately began making enquiries about the British obelisk. The British government was not interested in financing its removal, but a wealthy surgeon friend of Alexander's, Erasmus Wilson, was, and John Dixon, a civil engineer based at Alexandria, was keen to manage the technical side of things.

Dixon's solution was to encase the obelisk in a cigar-shaped iron hull and tow it behind a steamer. All went well until the *Cleopatra* reached the Bay of Biscay in

September 1877. There one of the fierce storms for which the Bay is notorious blew up. After her ballast shifted, the *Cleopatra* began to list badly and her crew had to be taken off, a dangerous operation costing the lives of six of the towing ship's seamen. Eventually she had to be cut loose and abandoned to whatever fate awaited her.

Time capsule

Miraculously, she was found by another British steamer and deposited in a Spanish port. There she was picked up by a Port of London tug sent out specially for the purpose, and brought to the Thames in January 1878. At 3 p.m. on 13 September following, a week short of a year since the obelisk had set out on its eventful journey, it was lowered into position on the Victoria Embankment above a time capsule containing, among other things, the day's newspapers, a cheap razor, a box of hairpins, a copy of *Bradshaw's Railway Guide* and pictures of twelve of the prettiest Englishwomen of the day (history does not relate who they were).

The century or so that has elapsed since the obelisk's re-erection is a mere blip in time compared with its true age: about 3,500 years. Together with a companion now in New York's Central Park, it was originally ordered from the Aswan quarries by Thothmes III in about 1480 BC. Having been floated down the Nile to Heliopolis on the outskirts of Cairo, it was inscribed with the pharaoh's titles and prayers and offerings to the sun god and then set up at the entrance to the Temple of the Sun (in the Bible, the City of On). Two hundred years later Rameses II ordered details of his CV to be added to it. There they remain for anyone familiar with Egyptian hieroglyphics to read, provided London's polluted atmosphere has not damaged them too badly. One thing is certain: the obelisk has suffered more in a hundred years in London than in 3,000 in Egypt.

THE OXO TOWER

On the opposite side of the river and just a little way downstream from Cleopatra's Needle stands another Thames landmark, the Oxo Tower. The tower represents another amusing ruse for getting round the old London County Council's rooted objections to illuminated advertisements and sky signs.

In the 1920s, the Oxo meat company bought what had been the Post Office's private electricity-generating station and converted it into a warehouse and distribution centre for meat imports from South America. As part of the conversion a tower was added, mainly for the purposes of advertising the Oxo name (Oxo have always been imaginative in the marketing department). The initial design, prepared by architect

Albert Moore, featured the company's name spelt out in coloured lights at the top of the tower. Inevitably it was rejected. Moore's revised version incorporated what he called elemental geometric forms on each of the tower's four faces. These geometric forms just happened to be two circles and a cross arranged to spell Oxo! This time the planners had no option but to accept.

The Oxo name shone nightly through the illuminated magenta glass until the outbreak of the Second World War. It was visible, so it is claimed, as far away as Hampstead. Since the Tower was then the second highest commercial building in London, that is probably correct.

Now the Oxo name is shining forth again, though not because of any thing Oxo have done. After the war, the tower stood abandoned next to a large bombsite which in 1984 was bought by a local non-profit development company called Coin Street Community Builders. They have converted the old meat warehouse into flats with design studios below and a rooftop restaurant and brasserie, and a public viewing gallery, above.

THE LONDON UNDERGROUND MAP

The London Underground map is internationally regarded as a triumph of graphic design. Simple, clear and attractive, it performs its primary task of guiding passengers round the Underground system brilliantly, and it looks so good that it has been reproduced on whole shopfuls of tourist ware as an unmistakable symbol of London. Historically, the map pioneered a successful method of representing complex communications networks, a method subsequently adopted for the maps of most of the world's 80 other Underground systems. The unrecognized genius behind this achievement was Henry Beck, a charming, modest and witty man who died in 1974, aged 71.

In 1931, then a 28-year-old temporary draughtsman in the Establishment Office Drawing Section of the London Underground Group, Beck found himself laid off work yet again as part of the government's rigorous economy drive. With time on his hands, he fell to thinking about the Underground map. At that time it was a geographical representation superimposed on a lightly printed road map. The effect was messy and unclear. Taking a sheet of scrap paper (now in the Victoria & Albert Museum) he sketched out an alternative incorporating three revolutionary features: (a) replacement of the geographical map with a diagram; (b) limitation of the direction of the route lines to verticals, horizontals and 45° diagonals; and (c) enlargement of the central area in relation to the outlying areas for extra clarity.

Public seal of approval

Initially, his bosses in the publicity department were horrified by his departure from the traditional geographical approach, but after persistent badgering they were persuaded to print a trial run of 500 map folders. The new map was an enormous success with the public and by the end of 1933 the first of the posters with which we are now all so familiar appeared in booking halls, platforms and station entrances.

Beck later left London Underground and went to work for the London College of Printing, but he continued to labour freelance on his brainchild. Over the years he introduced many refinements, perhaps the most important of which was the white link line between circles to show interchange stations. Whereas the original concept of the map was produced very quickly, it took 16 years to come up with this tiny, and now apparently obvious, improvement.

Beck's last edition appeared in 1959. Thereafter development was taken out of his hands and his name removed from the map. This hurt him very much, even though he was not legally the copyright owner. Until 1990 or so other names appeared on the map, notably that of Paul E. Garbutt, a senior Underground official in the 1960s. In recent years, however, London Regional Transport have started to use their own corporate name rather than that of any particular individual, a change in practice which is partly intended as a mark of belated respect to Beck.

BLUE PLAQUES

More belated recognition might come Beck's way in the form of a blue plaque. In 1994 he became eligible for consideration for the first time, for 20 years had elapsed since his death. But somebody will have to propose him first and he will then have to wait his turn in the queue. All nominations are considered strictly in the order in which they are made.

Anyone can propose a candidate for a blue plaque. The only conditions are that the subject must have been dead for at least 20 years (or the centenary of their birth reached, whichever is the sooner) and that they must be considered eminent by their peers. Alternatively, they must have made an important contribution to human welfare or happiness, or be well enough known to be recognizable to the informed passer-by.

The people who decide on blue plaques are the English Heritage commissioners. They are advised by a committee made up of planners, architects, historians and general London luminaries. If the commissioners' decision on a submission is favourable, the householder is approached for consent to put up the plaque and the local authority's records searched to make sure the house is not due to be swept away by a motorway in the not too distant future. If no problems are encountered, a design of the plaque is made and sent off to either Mr and Mrs Ashworth in Blackheath, South London, or Tutbury Ceramics at Burton-on-Trent in Staffordshire, English Heritage's two plaque makers. Each plaque costs over £400 ($600) and about 12 are put up each year.

Choosing exactly where to place the plaque is achieved by shifting a little blue sticker about on a black-and-white photo of the house. This has proved to be the simplest and most effective method. With the plaque made and its position chosen, it is mounted and then unveiled at a small ceremony. For the person commemorated the moment of immortality has arrived.

DICK WHITTINGTON

One person who has already become immortal through his connection with London is Dick Whittington, the fabled hero of the old pantomime who rises from poverty and obscurity to become a wealthy merchant and thrice Lord Mayor of London. But, some people ask, did Whittington ever exist at all? And, if he did, how did he come by his legendary status? The short answer is that he was very much a real person, but the story of his life bears very little relation to the pantomime plot involving a cat, some rats and the boss's daughter.

Dick's father was Sir William Whittington, a landowner at Pauntley in Gloucestershire. Sometime after Sir William's death in 1358 Dick travelled up to London and enrolled at the Mercers' Company as an apprentice. Mercers were dealers in valuable imports such as silks and velvets which only nobles were allowed to wear. The court was therefore the major market and there were rich pickings to be had. Whittington proved skilful and adept at his trade and by the time he was about 40 had already made a substantial fortune. This was recognized in 1393 when he was made a City alderman and again in 1397 when the king appointed him to succeed the then Lord Mayor, who had died in office. Whittington was elected mayor at the next elections and later in life filled the office on two further occasions. He was thus Lord Mayor no fewer than four times.

As the richest merchant in London, Whittington naturally became an important banker to three successive English kings. But he also laid out large sums on public works: a library at Greyfriars' Monastery, a refuge for unmarried mothers at St Thomas's Hospital, a 128-seat public lavatory flushed by the Thames, and a new church of St Michael Paternoster next to his house in College Hill. These good works laid the foundations for Whittington's reputation as a public benefactor. Bequests made after his death in 1423 enhanced it. New works which he paid for posthumously included the rebuilding of Newgate Gaol, the building of the south gate of St Bartholomew's Hospital, a library at Guildhall, and, most important of all, a college of priests and a 13-person almshouse next to St Michael's Church. Known as Whittington College, the almshouse was the most important in London at the time and of course it guaranteed the survival of its benefactor's name.

Garbled version

Whittington's name may have survived intact, but the authentic facts of his life did not. Over the next two centuries the Whittington story was retold so many times as it was handed down from generation to generation that it became garbled and embroidered out of all recognition. By the time it appeared in print for the first time (in 1605) it had become in all major respects the colourful pantomime fable we know today.

What, apart from this fable, is left of Whittington today? The medieval St Michael's Church, where Whittington and his wife (they had no children) were buried, was destroyed in the Great Fire, but a modern one stands on the site. Further up College Hill, which is just behind Skinners' Hall, a plaque marks the site of Whittington's house. The ornate gateways here are remnants of the Mercers' School which occupied the old buildings after Whittington College moved out to Highgate in 1821. The new almshouse site was close to the Whittington Stone on Highgate Hill, intended to mark the spot where the panto Dick hears the church bells tolling 'Turn again, Dick Whittington, thrice Lord Mayor of London'. In 1965 Whittington College moved again, this time to a purpose-built village-within-a-village of 28 two-bedroom houses at Felbridge, near East Grinstead in West Sussex. The College is run by the Mercers' Company using income from the City estate left to the Company by Whittington for the purpose. This century, rapid growth in the value of the estate has made it possible for grants to be made to other institutions benefiting the sick and poor. In 1986 a major project was the establishment of a medical day centre for the elderly in Streatham run jointly with the hospital Whittington had supported in his own lifetime, St Thomas's. Thus nearly 600 years after his death, Whittington is still at work. No wonder he is a legend.

Chapter 5

WESTMINSTER

Three institutions lie at the heart of Westminster: the Palace of Westminster, otherwise known as the Houses of Parliament; Westminster Abbey; and Westminster School. The first two, particularly the Abbey, attract huge numbers of visitors, but there are still many features of both which most people are completely unaware of. As far as the third is concerned, despite the fact that it is one of England's oldest and most successful public schools, its existence here in the heart of London goes generally unrecognized – as, in consequence, does the fact that it can be visited. Here we will find what goes on behind the scenes in the Palace of Westminster, and go on a tour of Westminster School and the more unfrequented parts of the Abbey, revealing in the process the major part of the great medieval monastery of Westminster.

PALACE OF WESTMINSTER

The **Palace of Westminster** is one of the best-known buildings in the world – at least in outline form. Millions have also seen part of the sumptuous interior, either by watching debates in the two chambers or by going on an MP- or Peer-arranged 'Line of Route' tour. This takes in not only the two chambers, but also the principal sections of the Palace that are still under royal control, namely the Robing Room, Princes Gallery and Royal Gallery.

But what lies beyond the chambers, beyond the public face of the Houses of Parliament, beyond the central lobby and beyond the committee rooms on the first floor which, like the debating chambers, are also open to the public? The answer is a huge Gormenghast-like building constructed around 10 main internal courtyards, invisible from outside. Four are on the Westminster Abbey side. The other six, in a line and linked by a service road that runs right through the palace from one end to the other, are on the river side. Inside these courtyards the palace is not quite so impressive as on the outside. Whereas the external walls are all golden stonework covered with ornament and sculptures, inside they are very plain and bare and covered in sulphurous black grime.

Small town

Around these courtyards is an amazing warren of over 1,000 rooms, linked by 2 miles (3 kilometres) of corridors. These rooms provide not just the offices, meeting rooms and libraries you would expect, but a whole range of ancillary services, including a post office, police station, hairdresser, sales kiosk with the highest sales: space ratio of any retailing concern in Europe, Thomas Cook travel agency, miniature rifle range underneath the House of Lords, chess room (chess is the only indoor game officially allowed within the Palace precincts) and 14 bars and restaurants. Because of parliamentary privilege, the bars don't need an alcohol licence so it is possible to get a drink in the Palace at almost any time of the night or day.

There has to be this range of services because on a given day there is a community the size of a small town at work in the Palace. Besides the 1,000-odd MPs and Peers, there are 2,000 regular staff and then several thousand more people doing all kinds of different jobs. At the last count, nearly 10,000 passes were on issue.

Lord Chancellor's house

A handful of these people don't just work in the Palace, they live there as well. It's quite well known that the Speaker of the House of Commons has an official residence at the Palace. This is a splendid mansion at the Big Ben end, facing the river. Actually, it is far too splendid these days so the Speaker lives in a cosy top-floor flat and lets MPs use the grand reception rooms below for parties and functions. What is not nearly so well known is that the Lord Chancellor and three officials of the House of Lords also have homes in the Palace. The Lord Chancellor's magnificent residence, consisting of 29 rooms, is opposite the Speaker's House at the southern end of the Palace, also on the river front. Nearby are the official residences of the three House of Lords officers: the Gentleman Usher of the Black Rod, the Yeoman Usher of the Black Rod and the Staff Superintendent. Until recently quite a few more people lived in the Palace, but they have had to move out in the face of demands from MPs for office space (understandable when you remember the Houses of Parliament were originally built with no offices for MPs at all). Alternative accommodation has been found for them in nearby places like Parliament Street and Derby Gate.

With so many people working so closely together for so much of their time, a real community spirit has grown up within the Palace. But if this prompts thoughts of a sort of democratic free-for-all with everybody treating the place like home and greeting each other cordially by first names, you'd be wrong. This community is rigidly structured and hierarchic. At the top of course are the MPs and Peers – the club members, as it were. Everybody else is a 'Stranger'. But there are three classes of

Plate 12: *Site of Dick Whittington's house in College Hill in the City (see page 85). The real life original of the pantomime hero lived here in the early 1400s.*

Plate 14: *One of the two inconspicuous entrances into Marble Arch (see page 81). Inside are two small offices and the charge room shown in plate 13.*

Plate 11: *The Coade Stone lion on Westminster Bridge (see page 77).*

Plate 13: *The old police charge room inside Marble Arch (see page 81).*

Plate 15: *The 3,500-year-old Egyptian obelisk, otherwise known as Cleopatra's Needle, on the Embankment (see page 81). Given to the British in 1819 by Egypt's Turkish overlords, the obelisk was floated to London from Alexandria in 1878. It has a sister in Central Park in New York.*

Plate 16: *A cabmen's shelter in Kensington Park Road, Notting Hill (see page 77). Over 60 such shelters were built in the late 1800s and early 1900s for the benefit of London's hard-working cabbies.*

Plate 17: *The drinking fountain at St Sepulchre's Church, Newgate, the first public drinking fountain to be erected in London by the Metropolitan Free Drinking Fountain Association (see page 76).*

Plate 18: Westminster Abbey and School from the Abbey garden (see page 96).

Plate 19: *Courtyard of the Abbot's Lodging, Westminster Abbey (see page 97). Once the residence of the head of the medieval monastery of Westminster, the Lodging is the oldest house in London. The dining-hall is now used by Westminster School. Parts of the Lodging can be seen on tours of the Abbey and School.*

Plate 20: *The richly decorated library of the House of Commons (see page 88). After a disastrous fire, the Houses of Parliament were completely rebuilt in the mid-nineteenth century and are a triumph of picturesque Gothic colour and splendour. Sadly, few outsiders ever have the opportunity to see this great national treasure.*

Strangers, the third being us, the mere mortals whose hard-earned money provides the taxes that pay for the club. The two privileged Stranger classes are the 'officers' of either House and what one might call the 'other ranks', that is staff below the equivalent Civil Service rank of Higher Executive Officer.

Lords' Bar

Lots of rules define where the different classes may go and where they may not. For example, only MPs, Peers and officers are allowed on to the famous terrace on the river side of the palace (as some compensation the other ranks have access to a roof terrace with wonderful views near the Big Ben end of the Palace). There is in fact only one place where all the people in the Palace from the most noble Duke down to the lowliest clerk or cleaner may mix freely, and that is in the ironically named Lords' Bar. As you might guess, this is in the Lords' side of the building.

The division of the Palace into two sides – Lords and Commons – creates one of two axes which hold the whole vast agglomeration together. The Lords–Commons dividing line runs across the waist of the building from the public entrance of the Commons to the river on the far side. The other axis is the straight line running along the length of the building connecting the Speaker's Chair in the Commons with the Lord Chancellor's Woolsack in the Lords. They are on exactly the same level, dead opposite each other and a full 425 feet (130 metres) apart. The two axes cross in the Central Lobby.

Two floors below the Lobby is what must be the last working steam engine in London, performing the humble but essential role of relief sewage ejector. The number of MPs, let alone Strangers, who are aware of that can probably be counted on the fingers of one hand.

Record Office

Five other little-known features of the great Palace of Westminster deserve special mention. At the Lords' end, a large number of rooms are used as offices by the Lord Chancellor's Department, the only government ministry to have a base in the Palace. Also at the Lords' end, the huge Victoria Tower, 395 feet (120 metres) from ground level to the crown on the tip of its flagpole, is actually a record office containing, on 12 air-conditioned floors, all the priceless historical records of Parliament, including all original Acts passed since 1497 and the earliest journals of the House of Commons, handwritten and dating from 1547.

The medieval palace was started by Edward the Confessor about 1050 and slowly added to over the succeeding centuries. (One improvement made in 1351 was the

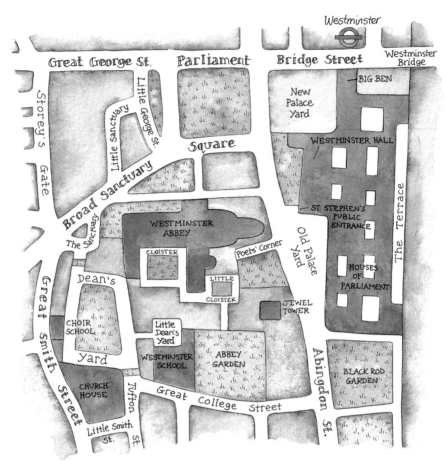

installation of hot and cold water taps for Edward III.) The Lords had always con-
vened in the Palace. The Commons moved in only in 1547 when they took over the
palace chapel of St Stephen's following the migration of the royal family to the newly
constructed Whitehall Palace just up the road. Over the following three centuries the
Palace was slowly transformed into the Houses of Parliament, hence its dual name
today. A lot more of the old Palace would have survived that transformation had it
not been for the great fire of 1834.

St Stephen's Chapel and Cloisters
It's usually said that, within the Houses of Parliament, Westminster Hall is the only
part of the original palace to survive the fire. It certainly is the most magnificent part

to survive, but it isn't actually the only one. Close to it are also the crypt of St Stephen's Chapel, and the very rarely seen Cloisters. Beautifully restored after the fire, the crypt chapel is probably the single greatest example of High Victorian Gothic art in the country. Members and officers use it for christenings and weddings. The two-storey cloisters, tucked away on the far side of Westminster Hall when viewed from the Abbey, were used by the dean, canons and vicars of the medieval College of St Stephen attached to the palace chapel. Ironically they were finished just a few years before Henry VIII closed down the College and all the other religious houses in the country. Today, the lower storey contains Members' private desks. The upper storey is the Members' main entrance to their lobby and the chamber beyond. Outside the Houses of Parliament, the medieval Jewel Tower also survived the fire.

Press Gallery

The Press Gallery is not, as its name suggests, a kind of balcony overlooking the debating chamber where journalists record details of the day's debates, although it does include such a gallery. It's actually a whole area of the palace set aside especially for the media. Spread over three floors, it consists of cramped and cluttered journalists' offices, rows of old-fashioned telephone booths dating from pre-fax and e-mail days, a library, an open-air patio overlooking Westminster Hall and of course a bar, cafeteria and dining-room. All these things are necessary when you have up to 250 journalists – hungry for news as well as refreshment – on the premises. It is all a far cry from the position 200 years ago when if a Stranger so much as doodled on a scrap of paper with a pencil stub he was immediately clapped into gaol for contempt.

Big Ben

Finally, we come to Big Ben. This is perhaps the best-known part of the palace, at least from the outside. What is not generally realized is that you can visit the clock tower, walk behind the illuminated clockfaces, watch the clock ticking in the clock room and go up to the open-sided belfry to watch the bells being struck. The hammers, outside rather than within the bells, are pulled slowly back as if by some unseen hand, and then banged down hard to make the chime. Contrary to Hunchback of Notre Dame-type stories, the great booming sound is far from deafening. The resonance penetrates right inside you, however, and the whole experience is profoundly moving.

On your way up the tower (you have to climb the stairs – there is no lift although there is a shaft ready for one) you pause for a breather in a bare room they call the Prison Cell. Here an MP in the 19th century and the suffragette Emily Pankhurst in the early years of this century were incarcerated for brief spells for various offences. It has not been used since.

Through the booming of Big Ben the Palace physically embraces a larger area of London than the 8 acres (3 hectares) of ground its foundations cover. Unbeknownst to most people, there is another bell which similarly extends the Palace's presence beyond the physical confines of its walls, though it does it in a rather more discreet – and less regular – way than its big brother. This is the Commons' division bell, the bell that sounds to alert MPs that a vote is about to be taken. Not only is it relayed to all parts of the Palace; it also goes to places outside that have subscribed to the division-bell service, which works over the phone lines. In the old days quite a few pubs and restaurants paid to be connected because it was good for business. Today it does not have quite the same draw and can actually be off-putting to non-Parliamentary customers. However, a few places frequented by MPs persist with it, notably the Royal Horseguards Hotel in Whitehall Court and the Red Lion pub in Parliament Street.

WESTMINSTER ABBEY

Every day 16,000 visitors tread the pavements of **Westminster Abbey**. What they see is the nation's church, the burial place of our early kings and queens, and the scene of every coronation since William the Conqueror's on Christmas Day 1066. Few think to ask why the Abbey is called an abbey and not, say, a cathedral. The fact is that for the first 500 years of its 1,000-year history, Westminster Abbey was a great medieval monastery, possibly, because of its special royal connections, the greatest in the land. And what's so exciting today is that, again because of those royal connections, much of that Abbey remains intact, embedded in the Westminster complex (which includes neighbouring Westminster School) and overlain by the history of the past 450 non-monastic years. Because of the destruction of the Catholic monasteries in England in the 1530s, such a survival is exceedingly rare in this country. In London, it may be unique. This little-appreciated but magnificent reminder of a lost era is a great secret of the otherwise so well-known Westminster Abbey. Not surprisingly, the Catholic monastic past of today's Anglican church is not stressed on tours of the Abbey, although just recently a few panels have been put in the cloisters area illustrating some aspects of the monks' lives.

Unfortunately, a tour of the Abbey as a monastery is not quite as straightforward as it sounds, mainly because a large part of the monastery is now part of Westminster School. However, it is possible to tour the school, though only during the Easter holidays, and you have to book in advance.

If you can't combine a visit to the Abbey with a tour of the school, the best day to come to the Abbey is Wednesday. In the summer this is the only day of the week on which both the Abbey garden – originally the monks' herb garden and a truly secret space deep in the heart of London – and the Abbey Library are open. The Library is the only completely original surviving section of the monks' massive dormitory.

Tomb of the Unknown Soldier

As you come in through the west door you will see the black marble slab surrounded by red poppies which marks the Tomb of the Unknown Soldier. Everyone has heard of the tomb, but few people know anything about how it came to be here.

The idea came from a man called David Railton who was a chaplain serving on the Western Front during the First World War. After the war he mentioned it to the Dean of Westminster. The Dean liked the idea and got the backing of the King, the Prime Minister and the military. Wheels were set in motion and, soon after, six working parties were sent to the battlefields of Ypres, the Marne, Cambrai, Arras, the Somme and the Aisne. Each exhumed one body and brought it back to an army hut at St Pol. The bodies were then examined to confirm that they were British. At midnight on 8 November, the director of the War Graves Commission in Flanders, Brigadier-General Wyatt, entered the hut blindfolded and touched one of the coffins.

Next day, 9 November, the chosen coffin began its journey back to Britain. It rested the night in the castle in the old town of Boulogne (where there is a plaque recording the fact) and at 8.33 p.m. the following evening reached Victoria Station in London. Having stayed on board the train that night, the next morning, 11 November 1920, the second anniversary of the armistice, it was laid to rest in the specially prepared grave in the Abbey. To symbolize the fact that all three of the main Western Front allies (Britain, France and Belgium) sustained huge losses of men, the English oak coffin was packed round with French soil and then (some time later) sealed with a slab of black Belgian marble. Other unknown warriors were buried on the same day in other countries. The Unknown Soldier was the last person to be buried in Westminster Abbey.

The Cosmati pavement

As you stand at the Unknown Soldier's tomb, facing the length of the church, look to the right and you will see a panelled gallery of carved oak known as the Abbot's Pew. This is accessible from the old Abbot's lodgings behind and in monastic days enabled the Abbot, the head of the monastery, to see directly into the nave of the

Abbey church from his lodgings. If he wanted to enter the church all he had to do was descend a flight of stairs and open the door you see directly beneath the gallery.

Moving into the Abbey down the left-hand aisle, you enter the part which includes the royal tombs and Poets' Corner. Carry on to the crossing and then turn right to stand under the Abbey's central tower. On your right now is the Quire where the monks sat during services. On your left, hidden beneath the carpet in front of the High Altar, is one of the Abbey's greatest treasures. Known as the Cosmati pavement, it is made from Purbeck marble (Purbeck is in the south-west of England) inlaid with red-and-green porphyry and glass. The inlay forms complex geometric patterns and inscriptions, one of which states (or used to state before it was worn away) that the floor was laid in 1268. The floor-layers were members of the famous Cosmati family from Rome, possibly the finest architects and decorators of their day. The Westminster floor is a superb example of their work and the only such pavement they ever created in Britain.

Normally it is covered by a carpet to protect it, but every few years the cover is taken off for a few days so that people can see it. I have to say that it is slightly disappointing because a lot of the inlay is missing and the colours have lost much of their vibrancy; but it is still an extremely impressive piece of work. In its original state it must have been as bright and colourful as the square ceiling of the central crossing point of the Abbey, directly above where you are standing now.

Carrying on down the left aisle of the church, keep an eye out for Henry III's tomb on the right. This also was the work of the Cosmati and it gives you some idea of what the floor looks like. Note how souvenir-hunters of former ages have stripped the mosaic pieces from the tomb up to arm's-reach height.

The Confessor's tomb

Henry III (reigned 1216–72) is an important figure in the history of the Abbey for it was he who ordered the demolition of Edward the Confessor's 200-year-old Abbey and the construction of the present building. But he was not denigrating the Confessor's work. On the contrary. The Confessor had been made a saint by the Pope and Henry's aim in rebuilding the church was to create a fitting house for the Confessor's tomb, by this time one of the most visited shrines in the kingdom. When you get to the Confessor's tomb note how the stones at the bridge end as you approach have been worn into hollows by the knees of thousands of medieval pilgrims. Catholics still come to pray here. It is the only important shrine in the country which is still in its original position and which still contains the body of its saint.

Later on, you will come to Poets' Corner in the south transept. When you get there, face the far end of the transept and look up to first-floor level. You should be able to see an arcade, lit from behind, with a large painted clock in the middle. To the right are some stairs, and to the left there are some more, descending to a ledge on which stands a bust. These stairs are another important relic of the old monastic Abbey, for they form part of the night passage that led from the monks' dormitory down into the Abbey. The passage was used by those unfortunates who had to get up in the middle of the night to conduct and attend services. Today, the dormitory is split into the Abbey Library and the main hall of Westminster School.

St Faith's Chapel

You now leave the Abbey church and enter the east side of the monks' cloister, which is still in a good state of preservation. The first entrance you come to leads into the Chapter House, a marvellous 13th-century chamber where the monks would meet to discuss their affairs and conduct any business needing their attention. It's surprisingly little visited. Even quieter is St Faith's Chapel, reached by a door to your left as you enter the Chapter House vestibule. Many are the times I have sat in here in welcome solitude.

The door opposite the entrance to St Faith's Chapel leads into a broom cupboard. Centuries ago it was the entrance to the Pyx where the monastery's valuables were stored. One day in the 1300s the treasury was robbed. After the thief had been caught and executed, his skin was pinned up like leather on the back of the door as a warning to others who might be tempted by the monastery's gold and jewels. Traces of that skin can still be clearly seen on the cupboard side of the door, a fact you may be able to verify for yourself if the English Heritage counter staff are in an obliging frame of mind.

Turn left out of the Chapter House vestibule, and continue along the East Cloister. The first door on the left is the entrance to the stairs leading up to the monks' dormitory, now the Abbey Library. To get an idea of the huge size of the dormitory you really need to see the school hall as well. But the old library, with its 17th-century shelves and leather-bound books, shows you how wide it was and also how high. What's more, it has part of the dormitory's original wooden roof, now nearly 500 years old. The school hall's roof was destroyed in the Second World War.

Pyx Chamber and Abbey Museum

After the library you come to the Pyx Chamber and the Westminster Abbey Museum. Together, these places form part of the undercroft to the monks' dormitory above. They are very ancient, as you can tell from their sturdy, rather primitive, architecture and, together with neighbouring passages and undercrofts, are the oldest part of the whole Abbey, having been part of the original structure built by Edward the Confessor in the 11th century.

The main feature of the museum is the collection of royal and noble funeral effigies, covering the late Middle Ages and the 17th and 18th centuries. The faces are made from death masks and the later ones are dressed up in magnificent original costumes. If you want to know what people like wily Henry VII, gay King Charles II with his plumed hat, and diminutive Lord Nelson really looked like, this is the place to come. Look carefully at Henry VII's rather ascetic face, and you will even see above his ears tufts of hair that got caught when the mask was peeled off. It is extraordinary how few Londoners know about this incredibly evocative collection and it remains, buried as it is deep in the Westminster complex, among the most precious of the city's secret treasures.

As you turn left out of the museum into the gloomy Dark Passage you are still in the oldest part of the monastery. Follow the sign to the garden and turn left. Under the skylight, the door on the left (opposite No. 8) leads into the Westminster School gym, which you see on the school tour. It is a relatively modern building and is not part of the original monastery, but it covers the site of the monks' cemetery.

College Garden

Carrying on you come to the hospital and old people's home section of the monastery. First you see the Little, or Infirmary, Cloister, where sick and aged monks lived and exercised. The houses around, at least their ground floors, date from the 1300s. On the far side of the Cloister are the remains (foundations only) of the infirmary chapel of St Katharine's. On the far right-hand corner of the cloister is the entrance to the infirmary garden. Here the monastery's physician grew the medicinal herbs with which he treated his patients. Today it is called the College Garden. The 18th-century boys' dormitory block runs down the right-hand side and, if you look through the gate to the right of it, you can see into the modern school yard. Only the original medieval Abbey wall separates the garden from Parliament and the outside world beyond, but it's amazing how few people, apart from those who live and work close by, know about it. The garden is perhaps the most secret space in central London to which there is nevertheless easy, free and regular public access. In the summer a band plays on Thursday lunchtimes.

Now retrace your steps back through the Little Cloister. As you pass through the Dark Passage look up through the windows on the left. The high wall you can see was part of the monk's refectory, one of the few buildings pulled down following the ejection of the monks. The space the refectory occupied now provides an enclosed garden for Ashburnham House, which you see on the Westminster School tour.

Nine Men's Morris

Carry on back along the East Cloister to the door into the Abbey and then turn left along the North Cloister where the brass-rubbing stands are. Facing south and protected from the cold north winds by the Abbey, this was the main living and working area for the monks. At the far end, on the stone seat on the right by another door into the Abbey, you can see where the novices – of whom there were only about half a dozen at any one time – have worn little hollows for their games of marbles and Nine Men's Morris.

Turn left here into the West Cloister. At the far end on the right is a recess containing a memorial to the Indian Civil Service. Originally this was the lavatorium where the monks washed their hands before proceeding on to their meals in the refectory through the door ahead (now leading to the Abbey Song School). They dried their hands on towels in the narrow recesses to the left of the refectory door.

Abbot's lodging

Turn right here and go through the archway. Just before you come out into Dean's Yard, look right through another archway. This leads into the courtyard of the Abbot of Westminster's house, the oldest residence in London. Today, the Abbot's successor, the Dean of Westminster, occupies the house. The living quarters are actually on the right. At the far end are the Jericho Parlour, a simple and austere 16th-century panelled room, and the more richly furnished late-14th-century Jerusalem Chamber, hung with tapestries and used for meetings by the Dean and Chapter. Henry IV died in this room in 1413. To the left is the Abbot's dining-hall, now the school dining-hall. The living quarters, Jericho Parlour and Jerusalem Chamber are never open to the public, but the dining-hall is included in the tour of the school.

As you come out into Dean's Yard, try to forget the modern square surrounded by buildings and imagine instead fields with animals and crops. These are what you would have seen 500 years ago, for here was the Abbey farm. Worked by the monks themselves, it was the main food supply for the Abbey community and any guests who happened to be staying. The Abbey guest house and the cellarer's house were in the old range to your left. Half-way along this side of the Yard a low stone archway, bearing all the signs of its great age, leads into what is now the main yard of Westminster School. Here the principal things you will see relating to the monastery are the main section of the monks' dormitory and the Abbot's 14th-century dining-hall.

WESTMINSTER SCHOOL

Hidden away in a quiet backwater deep in the heart of central London lies one of England's great public schools. It occupies an historic site next to Westminster Abbey and indeed for centuries was a part of the Abbey. It comes as a great surprise to many people to find that, for a few weeks every year, it is possible to go on a tour of the **school**. This provides a rare opportunity both to go behind the scenes of a quintessentially English institution, and to continue the tour of the medieval monastery of Westminster started in the tour of the Abbey.

The purpose of the tour seems to be less to explain how the school functions than to show the historic buildings which the school occupies. This is natural enough since many of them were part of the old Abbey and they are full of historical interest and associations. But it may be that the school and the way of life of the boys and girls interest you more than old buildings. If so, the guide will be happy to answer any questions you may have. One of the things he or she will tell you is that out of roughly 150 leavers each year, invariably half or more go on to Oxford and Cambridge universities. Westminster School is a real academic hothouse.

To find the school, you must make your way to Dean's Yard, a large enclosed quadrangle next door to Westminster Abbey. The entrance to the school is through a low medieval archway half-way along the eastern side (the one with all the old buildings in it). Passing through this archway, you come out into Little Dean's Yard, the main yard of the school, with boarding houses to the right.

Ashburnham House

The tour starts in Ashburnham House, the large elegant house to your left, slightly set back. Built in the 1660s for the, Ashburnham family, Ashburnham House incorporates the much older lodging house of the Abbey's prior, remains of which can be seen inside. Through the windows at the back of the house you can see the garden which was made out of the site of the monks' refectory. The refectory's north wall still stands to full height on the far side of the garden.

Ascending the house's wide staircase – its finest feature – you come to what is called the library floor, including the very handsome south-facing drawing-room-cum-reading room. Anyone could become a scholar with a place like this to work in. There are writing desks to write at and comfortable armchairs to read in. The walls are covered with old pictures of the school and the ornate ceiling and carved door jambs exude craftsmanship and quality.

The room is remarkably well preserved. That's probably because Ashburnham House has been used by the school only for the last century or so and during this time the boys have been relatively well behaved. In earlier times before the house became part of the school it was their custom to employ Abbey stonemasons to carve their names on every available smooth surface. All over the school (and occasionally in the Abbey too) you will find walls, doors and furniture defaced in this way.

'School'

The centrepiece of the tour is what at Westminster they call 'school'. 'School' is actually the school hall, a huge long high room with an organ at one end and walls covered in the brightly coloured coats of arms of illustrious old boys. Beyond the shell-shaped recess at the other end is the Abbey Library. In monastic times, the Library and the school hall formed the vast dormitory of the monks. After the monks had been kicked out by Henry VIII, the dormitory was given to the school for use as a classroom. In this room the whole school was taught for nearly 300 years, from 1599 to 1884. There were no individual classrooms. The only partition was a curtain across the middle of the hall dividing the lower school from the upper. You can still see the sturdy Tudor iron bar from which the curtain hung. At Westminster it is called the Greaze Bar. No one knows why exactly, but it's something to do with the ancient school custom, at least 250 years old, known as Greaze. On Pancake Day in February a pancake is tossed over this bar. A group of boys composed of one representative from each form then dive on the pancake and fight for the largest piece. The winner's reward – which seems rather prosaic compared with the violence of the contest – is a book token.

Dr Busby's library

As you come out of 'school', you pass a door on the left leading to Dr Busby's library, a room added in the 17th century to house the book collection of the then headmaster. The library, which is now used as a classics classroom, is not shown on the tour, but it contains one amusing school relic: the battered old school desk with two birch rods in the drawer. As at all public schools, there used to be a lot of thrashing at Westminster. When the rods stuck out twigs first, it meant a holiday. When the handles stuck out, which they did on most days, the boys knew they had better keep their heads down and their mouths shut!

Skipping the dormitory undercroft and the school gym (mentioned under Westminster Abbey), your guide will lead you through the cloisters of the Abbey into the Abbot's, now the Dean's, Lodging. This is actually a small courtyard completely enclosed by ancient buildings, one of which is the Abbot's original dining-hall. This was another of the rooms given over to the use of the school after the departure of the monks, and it's still used as a dining-hall by the school's 200 boarders. That means people have been eating here continuously for 600 years, something which is all too obvious from the mildly unpleasant odour of food that hangs about the place. Above, the 14th-century wooden roof is the work of Hugh Herland, the master carpenter who also constructed the roof in Westminster Hall just across the way.

Abbey farm

The tour ends outside in Dean's Yard. When this was the Abbey farm (see page 97), the almonry, where the monks distributed alms to the needy, stood over on the far side. The original Westminster School, a free school for the sons of local tradesmen, began in this almonry at least 600 years ago, and probably more. In 1461 it moved into the range of old buildings running down the side of Dean's Yard to your left. Then, after the ejection of the monks in 1540, it took over some of the main monastic buildings. You have already seen the Abbot's dining-hall, which became the school dining-hall, and the monks' dormitory, which became the school classroom. What you can't see because it no longer exists is the Abbey farm granary, which became the boys' dormitory. It was used until the 1720s and then replaced by the new building facing College Garden. The old granary stood to your left at the other end of Dean's Yard and they say that in dry weather you can still make out the faint outlines of its foundations in the parched grass.

Chapter 6

WHITEHALL

W hitehall (and its continuation, Parliament Street) is a broad thoroughfare linking Westminster with Trafalgar Square and the West End. Since the 16th century it has been a centre of government, and now virtually every building on both
sides of the street houses some department or other. Some of these buildings, even
the relatively modern-looking ones, contain fascinating historic interiors, with a few
dating right back to the days of Henry VIII and Whitehall Palace. Only one of the
buildings, however – the Foreign and Commonwealth Office (FCO) – can be visited, and even then under fairly onerous security conditions. Here I describe what you
see on the FCO tour and what you would see were you to be admitted to some of
the other buildings. Unfortunately I have had to pass over the Army's Horse Guards
building, the architectural centrepiece of the whole government complex, because it
is being completely refurbished.

FOREIGN OFFICE

The **Foreign and Commonwealth Office**, usually called the Foreign Office, or
just FO, has a superb set of Victorian interiors – all bright colours and intricate detail
– which experts reckon among the finest in London.

Designed by Matthew Digby Wyatt and Sir George Gilbert Scott in the 1860s and
1870s, the main rooms are in the ranges facing St James's Park on the side away from
Whitehall. These ranges are actually the original Foreign and India Offices. The
building was originally constructed for four different government departments: the
two just mentioned and the Home and Colonial Offices. Gradually, as its workload
has grown, the FO has come to occupy the whole of the enormous building, in the
heart of which is a huge courtyard, fully 4 acres (1.6 hectares) in extent.

The old India Office is at the King Charles Street corner of the present building.
Its main features are the Durbar Court and the Council Chamber. The Durbar
Court, taking its name from the Urdu word for a princely assembly, is the India
Office courtyard, floored with marble, roofed high overhead with glass and decorat-
ed with busts and colourful tiles to make an impressive covered reception area.

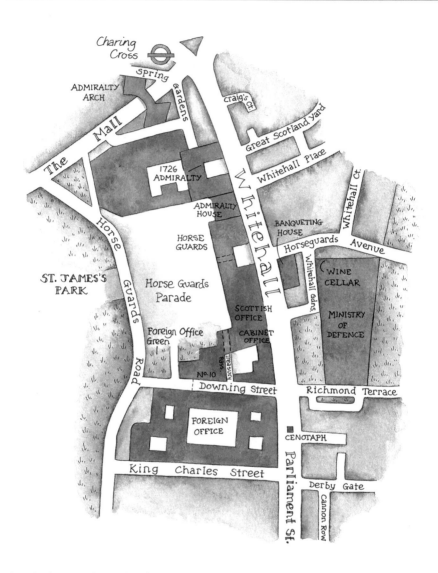

Overlooking it from the first floor, the Council Chamber is decorated and furnished in a rather more Georgian style. Indeed, the old mahogany chairs, portraits, chimney-piece and bookcases all date from the Georgian period and came from the original East India Company's office in Leadenhall Street in the City. From Leadenhall Street, the Company ruled British India from the early 17th century until the Indian Mutiny in 1857. After that the newly created India Office took control, and from this historic room decided the destiny of India for close on a century until independence in 1947.

Locarno Suite

The original Foreign Office section next to the old India Office encompasses the Grand Staircase, decorated with vast, slightly schmaltzy, murals illustrating themes from the history of the British nation, and the Locarno Suite, the grandest part of the whole building. Named after the famous European-borders treaty signed here in 1925, the Suite consists of three large reception rooms, the largest rising through two floors to a barrel roof. The walls are covered with brightly coloured stencilling, all the details and mouldings are picked out with gilding and the carpets are specially woven. There is also a mystery set of armorial bearings waiting for someone to unravel. The fireplaces and some of the furniture come from the first Foreign Office, a group of ramshackle 18th-century houses in Downing Street. The whole ensemble was designed not only to provide entertainment space for diplomatic assemblies of up to 1,500 people but also to impress the guests at those gatherings with the power of the British Empire, and of course with its high moral purpose. *Sic transit gloria mundi.* Not long after the Foreign Office was finished, the great British Empire collapsed and the once magnificent Locarno Suite disappeared behind shabby partitions introduced to create office space.

In the late 1980s, the FO began to make amends for its neglect – abuse, even – of its great interiors by launching an ambitious restoration programme. The result is a triumph, as you will see for yourself if you are fortunate enough to join one of the excellent guided tours of the office.

DOWNING STREET

The modern Foreign Office takes up the whole of the south side of late-17th-century Downing Street. American visitors will be pleased – and British readers surprised and perhaps disgruntled – to learn that the creator of the street, George Downing, was in fact an American. He was brought up in New England, where his father had emigrated to escape the increasingly authoritarian monarch in England, and he was one of the first students to graduate from the new Harvard University.

Imbued (not terribly deeply as it turned out) with republican sympathies, he came over to the old country and achieved high office as head of Cromwell's intelligence service during the Interregnum in the 1640s and 1650s. At the same time, he managed to acquire the Crown's interest in a tract of land abutting the south wall of royal

Whitehall Palace. Following the restoration of the monarchy in 1660, Downing underwent a miraculous conversion to royalism, and began building on his land once the last tenant of the existing buildings had died. Ironically, this was none other than the mother of one of the pillars of the revolution, John Hampden. (Mrs Hampden also happened to be the aunt of Oliver Cromwell.)

10 Downing Street

By 1684, when Downing himself went to his maker, 15 houses had been more or less completed. When Whitehall Palace burned down a few years later, some of these houses were taken over as offices, including the one now better known as No. 10. Here Treasury clerks were soon poring over their ledgers. In 1732 King George II handed over a large house behind No. 10 – built by Charles II for his illegitimate son the Earl of Lichfield – for the use of the First Lord of the Treasury. The holder of that office at the time was Sir Robert Walpole, the man who, by virtue of his total domination of the political process, created the office of Prime Minister. Ever since, No. 10 (linked to its much bigger 'rear annexe' by a long corridor) has been associated with the Prime Minister (officially still called the First Lord of the Treasury), and since 1877 it has been the home of every PM except one.

If you go round to Horse Guards Parade, you can see the Lichfield House annexe quite clearly: it is the large red-brick house with square windows on the corner looking out over the parade ground in one direction and the Downing Street garden in the other. The Cabinet room is here, as are Downing Street's historic first-floor state rooms: three drawing-rooms, a state dining-room and then a smaller dining-room, all filled with Adam and Chippendale furniture and 18th- and 19th-century prints and paintings.

11 and 12 Downing Street

No. 11 Downing Street was acquired by the government as an official residence for the Chancellor of the Exchequer in 1806. The Chancellor's study and sitting-room are on the ground floor off the entrance hall. The private apartments are on the first and second floors and extend over No. 12. This house was bought in 1803 for the Judge Advocate General but since 1879 its lower areas have been used as the office of the Parliamentary Secretary to the Treasury, the official title for the government Chief Whip, the person who whips government MPs into line for important votes in the House of Commons. Connecting doors link Nos. 10, 11 and 12.

There are three entrances to Downing Street. The main one is on Whitehall. Opposite, at the cul-de-sac end of the street by No. 12, is a flight of steps leading down to Foreign Office Green and St James's Park beyond. The third, little known, entrance is via Treasury Passage, a long narrow passage running from Horse Guards Parade undeneath the 18th-century silver-grey building known as Kent's Treasury, and so into Downing Street. All these entrances are gated, making Downing Street a secure little government enclave. You can see the Treasury Passage gateway quite clearly from Horse Guards Parade, though you have to look quite carefully.

CABINET OFFICE

A little way up Whitehall from Downing Street is the entrance to the Cabinet Office (No. 70 Whitehall). Had you been standing on this very spot 400 years ago, you would have been on the threshold of the recreational area of the great Tudor Palace of Whitehall. Behind you, on the other side of the road, would have been the state rooms, living quarters and domestic offices of the palace. In front were the sporting facilities built from the 1530s on by that great athlete Henry VIII: various courts for tennis and other games, a bowling alley, a tilt-yard for jousting (now Horse Guards – see map) and an arena for cock fighting known as the Cockpit. Various fascinating but almost totally unknown relics of these sports facilities, plus later and equally interesting historic structures, survive inside today's Cabinet Office (itself started in the 1820s and extended and refaced in the 1840s).

The most obvious is the bare brick upper storey of the two-storey passageway that ran from the road where you are now standing to the Cockpit, the largest of the sporting buildings. This upper storey, warmed from the fireplace, which still exists, formed a gallery from which royal spectators and courtiers could watch the games in the courts below. Today, the gallery looks out over a courtyard with a lawn and a large tree known as Treasury Green, but down to your right in the corner you can still quite clearly see the foundations of the so-called Little Close Tennis Court – in other words, the smaller of two covered tennis courts, probably like the one at Hampton Court.

Cockpit Gallery

Were you to enter the Cabinet Office now you would pass straight through the reception area and then climb some stairs into the Cockpit Gallery. Treasury Green is on the left, or south, side. On the other side are more evocative Tudor relics: a section of the wall of the large, five-bay Great Close Tennis Court and one of the four turrets that stood at each corner. The Great Close Tennis Court stood immediately to the right of the present Cabinet Office door up to the 1840s.

The Cockpit Gallery led directly into the gallery of the cockpit itself. In Charles II's time the old Cockpit, having been turned into a theatre and concert-hall, was demolished and replaced by a four-storey brick house. This in turn was knocked down in the 1730s and replaced by the silver-grey Treasury building through which runs Treasury Passage. Today, the Cockpit Gallery gives access to the first floor of this historic government office, designed by William Kent and used for meetings of the Treasury Board – usually with the king in attendance – until the later years of George III (reigned 1760–1820).

Treasury Board Room
The Treasury Board Room is the principal room in the building. Looking out over the garden of 10 Downing Street and St James's Park, it has hardly changed since the days when the 18th-century Treasury ministers, whose freshly cleaned portraits (including Walpole's) adorn the walls, gathered in the room to discuss the nation's finances. It is decorated in white with gold to pick out the fine plasterwork detailing, and much of the original furniture is still in place, including the royal throne and the meeting table with matching chairs. The only major change is the installation of a much larger table surrounding the old one, necessary to accommodate the greater number of people who attend meetings these days.

Besides the Board Room, Kent's Treasury incorporates a spiral staircase from the preceding four-storey brick house. Between the third and fourth floors, there is a formidable grille blocking the stair. Tradition has it that this barrier was placed here on the eve of the Bloodless Revolution of 1688 in order to confine the young Princess Anne, at that time a lodger in the house, to her quarters. While she was shut up, her father James II abdicated and fled the country, never to return. Later, following the death of King William and Queen Mary, she came to the throne as Queen Anne.

MINISTRY OF DEFENCE

Opposite the Cabinet Office on the other side of Whitehall, the huge Ministry of Defence building, completed in 1957, conceals more historic interiors: five grand Georgian rooms from two 18th-century mansions demolished to make way for the new building, and, most remarkable of all, a 16th-century vaulted wine cellar, once part of Whitehall Palace. There was a time when it was possible to see the cellar. It is a beautiful little building, 60 feet (18 metres) long, 30 feet (9 metres) wide and 20 feet (6 metres) high with four pillars down the middle, virtually identical to the one at Hampton Court. However, the security situation has put an end to that.

The story of the wine cellar goes back to the time of Cardinal Wolsey. After he became Archbishop of York in 1514, he extended York Place, the London residence of the York archbishops, building the wine cellar and a great hall above it in the process. When Henry VIII engineered the downfall of Wolsey and acquired York Place – renaming it Whitehall Palace – the cellar became his 'privy wine cellar' and the hall above, the royal guard chamber. A hundred and sixty years later, the great fire that swept through the Palace on this side of Whitehall left only the **Banqueting House** and the wine cellar standing.

Engineering feat

When, in the 1940s, the decision was taken to widen Horseguards Avenue and to build a huge new government office block, several old houses and the wine cellar were found to be in the way. The old houses were destroyed (apart from the few rooms already mentioned), but the wine cellar was saved, thanks to a challenging but impeccably executed engineering feat which involved bodily shifting the whole cellar to a new position.

First, the entire structure was cut away at foundation level and a concrete band inserted under its walls. Then it was placed on rollers – all 1,000 tons of it – and carefully rolled to one side. A large pit, 10 feet (3 metres) west of the original site and about 18 feet (5.5 metres) deep, was then dug and the cellar was rolled back and lowered into it. The new building was then constructed over it. Throughout the whole of this lengthy and delicate operation, no damage was done to the cellar and no new cracks appeared anywhere in its walls or roof.

Today, the cellar is in a large sub-basement beneath the Ministry of Defence. The basement completely surrounds the building so that you actually walk around outside it before stepping through the door into the interior. Simply furnished, its stone floor and walls proof against spillages and cigarette burns, it makes an excellent venue for office parties, so continuing an alcoholic tradition that goes back nearly 500 years.

SCOTTISH OFFICE

The Scottish Office ministers and civil servants are among the luckiest denizens of Whitehall, for their workplace is an 18th-century aristocratic town house full of the elegance and charm of that era. Opposite the Defence Ministry, between the Cabinet Office and Horse Guards, the Scottish Office – known also as Dover House after Lord Dover, who bought it in 1830 – has one of the most distinctive façades on the street: a grand pillared and porticoed entrance set in a windowless wall, with a shallow dome and the main block of the house rising behind.

Enter, and you find yourself in a light, graceful, circular entrance hall with stairs rising in front of you to the principal floor. Here, overlooking Horse Guards Parade, are to be found the grandest rooms of the house, now used as offices by the Scottish Secretary and his Minister of State. Directly below, on the ground floor, the junior ministers have their offices. With lower ceilings these are gloomier than those above, but their gorgeous decoration compensates. Originally these rooms were the private apartments of George III's son, the Duke of York, who lived in the house from 1787 to 1792.

On the top floor, above the Secretary of State's huge office, are a series of civil servants' rooms. Originally these were bedrooms and one, again overlooking Horse Guards and with an alcove big enough for a four-poster bed, belonged to Lord Byron's mistress Lady Caroline Lamb, wife of William Lamb (later, as Lord Melbourne, the Prime Minister). Here, it is said, the poet and Lady Caroline romped right under the nose of long-suffering William, though with all the desks, filing cabinets and computers crowding the room it is rather difficult to conjure up the scene.

Another Byronic legend current in the Office is that the rope stair-rail in the entrance hall was installed especially for Byron, who, you may remember, had a club foot.

THE ADMIRALTY

The Admiralty is, I believe, the oldest and certainly the least-known of all the historic government offices in Whitehall. Built in 1726 with all the appearance of a private house although designed specifically for the Admiralty, it stands midway between Horse Guards and Trafalgar Square, set back behind a screen added in 1760 by Robert Adam. The sculptures on the screen – showing a Roman prow on one side and the bow of a British man-of-war on the other – were executed by the Dutch sculptor Michael Spang: ironic, given the great naval wars between the Dutch and the English in the 17th century.

Behind the plain Admiralty façade – ornamented only with the Admiralty badge – the main feature of the office, as with Kent's Treasury, is the Board Room, the large meeting room where the Admiralty Board met throughout the years when Britain's Navy was establishing itself as the most powerful sea force in the world. On the first floor at the rear of the building and wood-panelled in the 17th-century style, the room is thought to have been taken out of the first Admiralty, built on this site in the 1690s. Despite severe damage during the Second World War, it still contains most of its original, specially made furnishings and fittings. The walnut-veneered grandfather clock is still in working order, as is the wind dial, connected to a metal vane on the roof. Either side of the dial are two superb Grinling Gibbons-style wood carvings featuring nautical instruments of the day, some of them with moving parts. These really are tremendous pieces of work and it is a great pity they cannot be seen more widely. The large mahogany meeting table has an unusual desk-type end with a hemispherical recess cut in it. This must have been designed for the Board secretary to take minutes at, though the story has grown up that it was tacked on in the 1870s for the convenience of a particularly portly First Lord of the Admiralty called George Hunt!

News of Trafalgar

It was at this recess that William Marsden, First Secretary to the Admiralty, was working late on the night of 6 November 1805. One o'clock had just struck and he was about to snuff out his candle and retire when a panting, travel-stained officer burst in. 'Sir,' he exclaimed epigrammatically, 'we have gained a great victory, but we have lost Lord Nelson.' The laconic Marsden later wrote:

The effect this produced on me it is not my purpose to describe. Lord Barham [First Lord of the Admiralty] had retired to rest, as had the domestics, and it was not until after some research that I could discover the room in which he slept. Drawing aside the curtains with a candle in my hand, I woke the old peer [he was 80] from a sound slumber. He showed no symptom of alarm, but calmly asked, 'What news, Mr Marsden?'

Having been told, Barham got up and sent on the news to the Prime Minister and the King. So were the tidings of the Battle of Trafalgar, Britain's greatest naval victory, and the loss of Nelson, her greatest seaman, received. Today, Nelson looks down from his full-size portrait as the Admiralty Board continues to direct the operations of Britain's much-diminished navy.

First Lord's house

The 1726 Admiralty included a residence for the First Lord, but it was quickly taken over for offices as the department expanded. In 1786, a new First Lord's house was built between Horse Guards and the Admiralty. With 30 rooms on four floors and in a relatively secluded position overlooking Horse Guards Parade, it was one of the most spacious and elegant of all government houses. The First Lord used the large first-floor library as his office until the new Admiralty extension was built along the north side of Horse Guards Parade from the 1890s. At that time, when Britain's Navy was at its largest and most powerful, the Admiralty empire extended all the way from the First Lord's house, through the old Admiralty, the extension and Admiralty Arch, across the Mall to Mall House, where the First Sea Lord (the senior naval officer) had his official residence. In 1964 the political appointment of First Lord of the Admiralty was abolished. Since then, Admiralty House has been divided up into apartments. In 1992–3 the Prime Minister used one while workmen were in No. 10.

THE SECRET SERVICES

Although not in Whitehall, the locations of the offices of the secret services – MI5, the internal security service, and MI6, the external security intelligence service – must be mentioned here because no self-respecting book on secret London would be complete without them.

In the mid-1990s, MI5 moved from 140 Gower Street to Thames House, Millbank, on the Westminster bank of the river between Lambeth Bridge and Millbank Tower. It is said that the building was acquired for £100 million ($150 million) in 1988 right at the peak of the 1980s property boom and that in the subsequent recession its value fell by as much as a half.

MI6 also moved in the mid-l990s, from Century House in Lambeth to a Terry Farrell-designed architectural extravaganza called Vauxhall Cross at the Vauxhall end of Vauxhall Bridge and conveniently close to MI5's Thames House. Behind the eye-catching façade – strange for a secret service – is a completely secure citadel constructed to unusually high specifications. There are no cheap plastic waste pipes, for example. Only copper, ten times more expensive, will do for MI6. No wonder the building is reputed to have cost £260 million ($390 million). You will see Vauxhall Cross right at the end of the Tyburn river walk (see page 36). MI6's recruitment is said to be handled from a comfortable house at 3 Carlton Gardens in the heart of London's 'old-boy' clubland.

GOVERNMENT ART COLLECTION

The pictures and other works of art decorating many of the rooms and offices mentioned in this chapter come from the **Government Art Collection**. Despite being one of the largest public art collections in the country, it is undoubtedly the least known. The main reason for this is that most of its works are in places inaccessible to the public – ministers' and senior civil servants' offices in Whitehall, and British embassies and missions around the world. But the traditionally secretive attitude of the government does not help. When I was researching the first edition of this book and asked for information about the collection, I was told that all there was was a press release relating to a small exhibition of 24 works that had taken place some years before, and that is was not possible to mention individual works for security reasons.

The egregious nature of this typical piece of Whitehall obfuscation is highlighted when contrasted with the attitude of the people who actually curate the collection. It is clear they would like to publicize the collection far more and that it is only lack of resources that prevents them. So niggardly was their funding in the past that they had to get Christie's – the famous auctioneers – to sponsor the publication of five separate embassy catalogues, starting with Bonn and Paris, which really we the tax-payers, through the government, should have underwritten. (The existence of these catalogues, incidentally, made the government's statement that individual works could not be mentioned for security reasons even more absurd.) Since then, things have improved a little. In 1997 a catalogue of the 20th-century works in the collection was published, but there is still no complete catalogue of the whole collection.

British culture and history

The collection has a history going back to 1898, but it is really a post-Second World War creation. Today it contains about 11,500 items, mainly paintings, drawings and prints, but also sculptures and tapestries. Its overt aim – at least overseas – is to spread knowledge of British culture and history through the works of British artists, but it has no major works by such quintessential figures as Gainsborough and Reynolds, Constable and Turner, mainly of course because they are too expensive. It does, however, have many other fine things, including 17th- and 18th-century landscapes, marine paintings and topographical views of country houses; Second World War pictures by official war artists; 20th-century pictures by Duncan Grant, Paul Nash, Lawrence Gowing, Walter Sickert and others; historical portraits; and some abstract works by people like John Piper, Augustus John, David Hockney and Graham Sutherland are also represented. The Treasury has always taken the utilitarian view that the Government Art Collection's paintings and prints are more wall-coverings than art, and certainly not cultural ambassadors for Britain. Nevertheless it still came as something of a shock in 1993 when Treasury officials suggested that the collection be sold off. Fortunately, wiser counsels have prevailed since then and the collection remains intact in public hands.

Chapter 7

ST JAMES'S

S t James's is an historic district lying between Piccadilly Circus and St James's Palace, from which it takes its name. Two features stand out for the seeker of secret London: the gentlemen's clubs in their anonymous clubhouses, and the hidden passages and mews leading off the main thoroughfares.

THE SECRET WORLD OF THE CLUBS OF ST JAMES'S

Rivalling Whitehall in their concern to keep all but insiders out, the traditional clubs of nearby St James's form a cosy little world all of their own, strictly out of bounds to all but members and their guests. Human nature being what it is, the aura of exclusivity, not to say secrecy, surrounding these clubs excites a lot of interest and speculation, and people in the real world outside are always keen to know what the clubs are like on the inside, who the members are and what they get up to.

The truth is that the clubs are all much of a muchness, any differences between them being of detail and degree rather than substance. By and large they all look like, and for the most part have the atmosphere of, places designed by and for conservative gentlemen of advanced age addicted to smoking, drinking and bridge, leavened by a little hunting or reading. Leather armchairs, 19th-century prints and cartoons, ancient club trophies and miscellaneous antiquarian artefacts like Captain Cook's magnifying glasses (Army and Navy), Charles Dickens's chair (Athenaeum) and Napoleon's death mask (Brooks's) abound.

Of late years the dry, stuffy atmosphere in many of the clubs has been lightened somewhat by the creation of special areas for lady members. These tend to be much more fresh and attractive, with brighter colours and loose covers on the chairs, and there are probably many male members who secretly prefer to read their *Daily Telegraph* or *Financial Times* in the Ladies' Sitting Room rather than in the drab old library or smoking-room.

Having been rather critical, it is only fair to point out some of the attractions of these clubs, attractions which are, after all, powerful enough to keep the clubs in existence long after the kind of society which gave rise to them has vanished. Put simply, in the old clubs of London today, you can eat and drink well in spacious, elegant – indeed unique

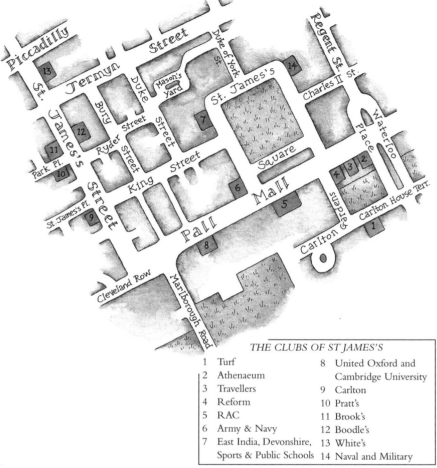

THE CLUBS OF ST JAMES'S	
1 Turf	8 United Oxford and
2 Athenaeum	Cambridge University
3 Travellers	9 Carlton
4 Reform	10 Pratt's
5 RAC	11 Brook's
6 Army & Navy	12 Boodle's
7 East India, Devonshire,	13 White's
Sports & Public Schools	14 Naval and Military

– surroundings for prices well below what you would pay in the nearest equivalent: the very best London hotels. Throw in the history and traditions, the company and the social cachet, the personal service and all the facilities available (libraries, swimming-pools, squash courts, cheap central London bedrooms) and you probably have an unbeatable package, at least if you are a club-type person. So, while one may make jokes about these dinosaur-like institutions, one would not want them to disappear. London would not be the same without them.

Short of joining the staff, becoming a member or finding a member to invite you as their guest, the only way to see inside a traditional London club is to take advantage of a very little known opportunity, which is that the **Travellers Club** – alone among the 14 clubs in the St James's area – admits visitors for guided tours. The Travellers tour is described in the appropriate place in the following short walking tour of the St James's clubs, in which I point out which clubs are which (they most certainly do not advertise themselves on the outside) and tell you a little bit about their history and character.

Turf and Athenaeum Clubs

Starting in Carlton House Terrace near the Duke of York's memorial, No. 5 is the Turf Club, founded in Piccadilly as the Arlington Club in 1864 and established here in 1965. It is an aristocratic sort of place (in recent years it had no fewer than 16 dukes on its membership list) and its main claim to fame is that it codified the rules of whist.

Round the corner in Waterloo Place, its entrance marked by the golden statue of the goddess Athene, is the Athenaeum (107 Pall Mall), a club with an intellectual reputation and popular with bishops. Author and civil servant John Wilson Croker founded it in 1824. The strikingly elegant clubhouse, with a frieze copied from the Parthenon, was designed by Regency architect Decimus Burton to match the Institute of Directors (formerly the United Services Club) opposite. Inside, the club has an excellent library and a 100-foot (30-metre) long drawing-room where the 19th-century novelist Anthony Trollope was fond of working.

Travellers Club

Turning left along Pall Mall, next to the Athenaeum is the aforementioned Travellers Club (106 Pall Mall), founded in 1819. Members were originally required to have journeyed at least 500 miles (800 kilometres) from London, a relatively uncommon thing in those days. Now you only have to have travelled abroad once, though the Club particularly likes it if you have also lived abroad.

On the ground floor you see the two morning-rooms which form the ladies' area, and at the back, overlooking the garden, the splendid smoking-room. The vestibule in between is the only place in the club where members may talk business.

Upstairs are the coffee-room and the library. The coffee-room, overlooking Pall Mall, is actually the club dining-room and, despite its name, is the only room in the club where coffee may *not* be drunk! Note the 'solo' tables, complete with book stands, for misanthropic members. Companionless but companionable members can always find company on the Club Table.

Above the smoking-room and also overlooking the garden, the library is the finest room in the club. Having been discovered by location hunters, it is also in frequent demand as a setting for films and photo shoots, perhaps to the chagrin of literary members. Group tours normally end in a civilized fashion here with a fortifying glass of sherry, served in a generous club measure.

Upstairs again, in a part of the club not shown to visitors, are the club bedrooms. Three members of staff (the housekeeper, the porter and the trainee house manager) live in. Until his death in 1998 aged 96, they were joined by Monsignor Alfred Gilbey, who moved to the Travellers from the Athenaeum in 1966 and acted as a sort of unofficial chaplain to clubland. He was one of a small (and no doubt shrinking) band of elderly gentlemen for whom the clubs of St James's are not just a home from home, but home itself.

Reform, RAC, and Army and Navy Clubs

One on from the Travellers is the Reform Club (104 Pall Mall), its house in Italian palazzo style like the Travellers, but much bigger. Inside, the richly decorated rooms are grouped around an impressive central hall, rather gloomy despite its skylight. Drinks and nibbles are served here before dinner and coffee after. As its name suggests, the Reform was founded for people with radical political leanings, 'radical' in those days (1836) meaning people who supported the 1832 Reform Act which reduced aristocratic control of the House of Commons. Until the Reform was founded, Brooks's, which we shall come to in a minute, was the only 'radical' club, but then as now it was rigidly upper class and no place for up-and-coming commercial men with wealth but no breeding.

Continuing along the left-hand side of Pall Mall, we come to the RAC Club (No. 89), its entrance marked by a grand portico and lamps on curly iron brackets. Founded in 1897 'for the Protection, Encouragement and Development of Automobilism', the Royal Automobile Club is the newest of the St James's clubs. It is also possibly the largest, the least class-conscious, the best equipped (no other club has a swimming-pool and a rifle range), and the only one with an associated country club (at Epsom).

Opposite the RAC is the new building put up in 1968 for the Junior Carlton Club. Members never felt comfortable in it and in 1977 the club merged with the Carlton, which we shall come to in a minute.

Opposite the ex-Junior Carlton, on the other side of the entrance to St James's Square, is another modern clubhouse. Opened in 1963, this is the home of the Army and Navy Club (36 Pall Mall), founded well over a century before in 1837 as London's third general military club. Its nickname, 'the Rag', comes from an early member's derogatory comment about the club food being 'a rag and famish affair'. Things have improved since.

East India, Devonshire, Sports and Public Schools Club

Looking up the side of St James's Square beyond the Rag, near the top (with flag-poles protruding) is the East India, Devonshire, Sports and Public Schools Club (16

St James's Square), an amalgam of four different clubs. The original East India Club was founded in 1849 for servants and officers of the East India Company who had travelled in the east. The white stucco clubhouse was opened the following year. In 1938, the club swallowed a fellow St James's Square institution, the Sports Club. Thereafter, while the Indian element faded away, the sporting tradition prospered. Until 20 or 30 years ago, English rugby and cricket teams were always chosen at Sunday meetings at the club. Two further clubs – the Public Schools and Devonshire – were absorbed by the East India in 1972 and 1976, respectively.

Naval and Military Club

Opposite the East India Club at 4 St James's Square is the Naval and Military Club. Founded by five army officers in 1862, for well over a century it was based at a former aristocratic town house in Piccadilly before moving to these impressive premises in the late 1990s. Nicknamed the In and Out club because of the lettering on the gateposts leading into the forecourt of its former clubhouse, the Naval and Military is particularly notable for the number of clubs it has absorbed over the years – at least eight. One is the Portland Club, founded in 1816. This famous old club laid down the rules of bridge and still arbitrates when disputes arise over the how the game should be played.

United Oxford and Cambridge University Club

Carrying on along Pall Mall from the RAC, you come to the United Oxford and Cambridge University Club at No. 71. Founded as the Oxford and Cambridge Club in 1830 to soak up the waiting list for the United University Club, it did a kind of reverse takeover in 1971 when the United University Club fell on hard times. Strictly for graduates of Oxford and Cambridge universities, it has a library to rival those in the Athenaeum and the Travellers, and, above its main windows on the street front, a series of relief panels with blue backgrounds showing literary and other greats: from left to right, Homer, Bacon, Shakespeare, Apollo and Athene with the nine Muses, Milton, Newton and Virgil.

Carlton Club

Go to the end of Pall Mall and follow the road round to the right into St James's Street, keeping to the left-hand side. At No. 69, two down from St James's Place, is the Carlton Club. The most famous of all the political clubs, the Carlton was founded in Pall Mall in 1832 as a centre for opponents of the Reform Act of that year. (That this one Act of Parliament should have led to the creation of two London clubs shows what a seismic piece of legislation it was.) Gradually it evolved into a club for Conservative Party MPs and for half a century before the Conservative Party Central

Office was set up was effectively the party's headquarters. The IRA bombed the club in the 1980s, hence the security cameras outside.

Pratt's

Continue on up St James's Street to Park Place. Round the corner, the first door on the left-hand side (No. 14) is Pratt's, perhaps the oddest of all the St James's clubs. Whereas all the others have large country house-type clubhouses and are open all day, Pratt's by contrast meets in a small town house and opens only in the evenings. But then it is more of a private dining club than a traditional gentlemen's club, and in this sense it continues to reflect the unusual circumstances in which it was founded. One night in 1841, bored with his usual haunts, the Duke of Beaufort, accompanied by some friends, dropped in on his steward, William Pratt, at this house here in Park Place. Having enjoyed themselves so much drinking and gambling in Pratt's kitchen, the Duke and his friends returned again and again until the informal gatherings became a regular club. Today, there is still a duke in charge, but it is the Duke of Devonshire rather than the Duke of Beaufort.

Brooks's

You have probably already noticed the elegant plain-brick building on the corner of St James's Street and Park Place, opposite Pratt's. This is Brooks's Club. Brooks's is one of a small coterie of clubs at this top end of St James's Street (the others being White's and Boodle's) which are by far the oldest of all the clubs in St James's and which, partly for that reason, are also the most exclusive socially (Brooks's is actually so exclusive that it doesn't even have a street number). A characteristic they all have in common is that they are named after the tradesmen who originally ran them. This in itself is a sign not only of antiquity, but also that these clubs were set up for no particular purpose other than to allow members to eat and drink (and gamble) in congenial company. That said, White's and Brooks's did become identified with, respectively, Tory (conservative) and Whig (aristocratic liberal) politics at the end of the 18th century and White's is still the old Tory landowner's club *par excellence.*

Brooks's, however, can probably claim to be the most famous of all London's clubs, partly because of all the stories about the incredible gambling that went on there in the old days, especially in the 1770s when rich young aristocrats like Charles James Fox and the Earl of Carlisle played for hours, even days, on end and lost thousands of guineas, if not whole estates, on a single throw of the dice. Fox in particular was noted for gambling and drinking all night and then wandering down to the House of Commons to deliver astonishingly clever speeches.

The club was founded in Pall Mall in 1764 and moved, under William Brooks's direction, to this purpose-built clubhouse in 1778 (the lead water cisterns-turned-flowerpots outside the entrance are dated just two years before this). The clubhouse was designed as a small country house and still today an open fire in the hall greets members when they come in from the street on a cold winter's day.

Boodle's
Across St James's Street from Brooks's, the clubhouse with the prominent Venetian window with white plasterwork above belongs to Boodle's (28 St James's Street), founded in 1762 and based here since 1783. Tip-top service has always been a tradition at Boodle's and it used to be the case (though no doubt isn't now) that coins were boiled before being passed on as change so as not to sully members' hands! Boodle's was started by Edward Boodle, son of a Shropshire innkeeper. It is not the only central London enterprise owing its success to this family. In 1767 Edward's nephew, another Edward, joined a Mayfair law firm a few streets away, rising in the course of time to become its senior partner. Now called Boodle Hatfield, the firm is still practising in Mayfair and, having been founded around 1720, is almost certainly the oldest law firm in London. Right from the very beginning its biggest client has been the Grosvenor estate.

White's
Carry on up St James's Street, crossing the junction with Jermyn Street. At No. 37, one down from Piccadilly on the right-hand side, you come to White's. White's' strangely modest façade which, unlike Brooks's' or Boodle's', merges into the streetscape making it easy to miss, belies the club's significance as the father of all London clubs. Evolving out of a St James's Street chocolate house started by Francis White in 1693, it was already a fully fledged club by the time it moved to this site in 1753. Having celebrated its tercentenary in 1993, it is securely enough established (with a membership list that reads like *Burke's Peerage*) to look forward with some confidence to its next 300 years.

Exploring the hidden courts and passages of St James's

After 300 years of constant building and rebuilding, St James's is honeycombed with a network of hidden passages, alleyways, courts and mews. Exploring them on foot is the best way of getting to the heart of this exclusive and fascinating little enclave. This fairly short walk starts and finishes at Piccadilly Circus and goes in an anti-clockwise direction, touching St James's Palace with its Chapel Royal (open for Sunday services) at its furthest point.

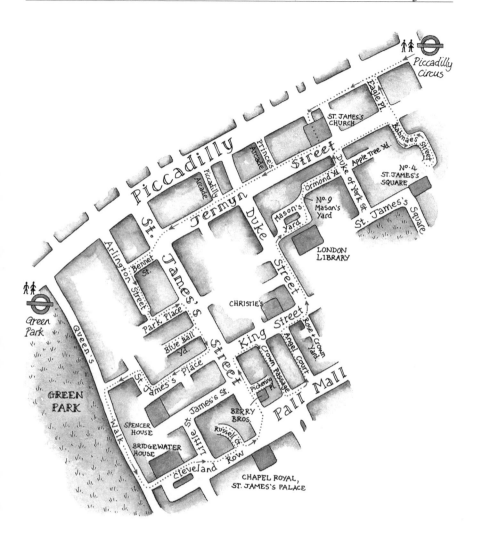

Start/Finish: Piccadilly Circus Underground (Bakerloo and Piccadilly Lines)

Length: 1⅓ miles (2 km)

Time: 45 minutes

Food: Numerous pubs and sandwich bars *en route* for refreshment, but Crown Passage at the half-way stage makes an ideal stopping point. Here you will find the best pub in the area – the Red Lion – and a good selection of sandwich bars and wine bars.

119

Sights: Piccadilly Circus, Wren's church of St James's, Jermyn Street for shopping, the **Alfred Dunhill Museum**, Royal Over-Seas League, Pratt's Club, Brooks's Club, **Spencer House**, Green Park, St James's Palace and **Chapel Royal, Christie's**, London Library.

Walk along the south side of Piccadilly away from the tube station until you come to St James's Church. Turn left through the gates into the paved churchyard and enter the church. Continue on through the vestibule doors until you come out the far side in Jermyn Street. Here, by the entrance to the Aroma café, turn right and walk along the street, passing the entrance to Prince's Arcade. Cross Duke Street St James's (one of the lesser-known attractions of **Dunhill's** on the corner is its upstairs museum) and continue on along Jermyn Street, passing the Piccadilly Arcade.

Royal Over-Seas League

At the end of the street cross St James's Street into Bennet Street, turning left at The Blue Posts pub. This looks like a cul-de-sac, but there is a way out at the far end where some steps lead down to Park Place. Descending, you get a good idea of the steepness of the slope on which St James's is laid out. On the right at the bottom is the entrance to Over-Seas House, home of the Royal Over-Seas League, a club founded in 1910 to promote the idea of world comradeship under the aegis of the British Empire. The club occupies two

fine historic houses (Vernon House and Rutland House) which you can visit on weekdays during office hours. Every September there is an open exhibition at the League for professional artists up to the age of 35. This is also open to the public.

Blue Ball Yard

Turn left in Park Place and go to the end (Brooks's Club is on the left and Pratt's Club – at No. 14 – on the right). Here, turn right back on to St James's Street. Fifty yards (45 metres) down on the right is the arched entrance to Blue Ball Yard. It doesn't look much from the street, but when you get inside you see on the left a picturesque range of traditional mews cottages and garages. Built in 1741, they were originally coach houses, with rooms for coachmen and grooms at the top, and large cellars and wine vaults underneath. Today they make an unusual annexe to the Stafford Hotel, the entrance to whose bar and restaurant you can see at the end of the yard. Above are bedrooms. Down below one of the ancient brick-vaulted cellars has been turned into an atmospheric subterranean dining-room. The others are used for storing the hotel's 20,000 bottles of wine.

Plate 21: *Looking down the north side of Horseguards Parade towards Admiralty House, built in 1786 as the official residence of the First Lord of the Admiralty (see page 109). In the left foreground is a corner of the ivy-covered Second World War Admiralty citadel (see page 45). Horse Guards Parade is the former jousting field of King Henry VIII's Whitehall Palace.*

Plate 22: *The truly sumptuous Grand Reception Room in the Foreign and Commonwealth Office's Locarno Suite (see page 103). The Suite dates from the 1870s and was built at a time when Britain's overseas empire looked set to last a thousand years. History, however, had other things in mind.*

Plate 23: The west front of Spencer House in St James's (see the St James's walk, page 121).

Plate 25: The Athenaeum Club's entrance in Waterloo Place (see page 114). The golden figure represents the Greek goddess Athene.

Plate 24: Berry Bros. & Rudd's wine cellars beneath St James's Street (see the St James's walk, page 123).

Plate 26: *The severely elegant eighteenth-century clubhouse of Brooks's in St James's Street (see page 117). Brooks's is one of the most aristocratic of London's traditional gentlemen's clubs.*

Plate 27: *A dining-room at the Stafford Hotel converted from an old wine vault beneath Blue Ball Yard (see the St James's walk, page 120).*

Plate 28: *The Dowgate Hill entrance to Skinners' Hall, home to one of the 'Great Twelve' livery companies in the City (see page 133).*

Plate 29: *The Adam-designed 18th-century boardroom inside the 20th-century, hi-tech Lloyd's building (see page 128).*

Plate 30: *One of the magnificent rooms inside the Bank of England (see page 128). The Bank also has its very own section of Roman mosaic floor.*

Plate 31: *The porter's lodge in Ely Place (see page 146).*

Spencer House

Come back out on to St James's Street and turn right. At the next right, turn into St James's Place. On the left, by the red pillar box, a little courtyard gives access to the secluded Duke's Hotel, formerly chambers for wealthy bachelors. Further on and still on the left, **Spencer House** is the former town house of the late Princess of Wales's family. At the moment, it is on long lease to Lord Rothschild. He has recently spent several million pounds restoring it and opened the main rooms to the public (on Sundays). The rest of the house has been turned into offices for his various investment companies. Follow the road round to the right, go past the 80-year-old Stafford Hotel on the right and then turn left (between Nos. 22 and 23) into a gated passageway which dips and then climbs up to Queen's Walk in Green Park. Here turn left and walk down the hill passing the garden front of Spencer House. Technically the rams' heads on the frieze are classical architectural ornaments but I prefer to think of them as an allusion to the great flocks of sheep on the Northamptonshire uplands which made the Spencers so much money in the 15th and 16th centuries.

Bridgewater House

Beyond Spencer House is the much larger Bridgewater House with urns along its balustraded top. At the corner of its garden turn left into another gated path (don't be afraid of the sign saying it is not a public right of way and that it is liable to close without notice – it is here only for legal reasons). You come out in Cleveland Row, with the entrance to Bridgewater House on the left and Selwyn House on the right. Bridgewater House, a vast town house built in 1846 for Lord Ellesmere, heir to the vast Bridgewater estates with all their canal wealth, is today both home and office to wealthy Greek shipowner and banker Captain John Latsis. Selwyn House, named after a family which lived in an older house on this site in the 18th century, is the London office of Pilkington's glass company.

St James's Palace

Cleveland Row brings you to St James's Palace: if you look down the barred and police-guarded road to the right you can see the guards with their bear-skin hats standing outside Clarence House, the home of the Queen Mother. Go past the entrance to Little St James's Street on the left and carry on along the side of the palace. Russell Court on the left is a dead end, but as a cobbled mews of relatively traditional character – especially its little cottages right at the far end – it is worth a peep. As you enter, you can see in the stained-glass windows of a masonic hall reversed lettering reading PROVINCE OF EAST ANGLIA NORFOLK SUFFOLK CAMBRIDGE.

Coming out of Russell Court and turning left, carry on down Cleveland Row with the Palace on your right. St James's Palace is the only royal palace in London which is completely closed to the public – or so most people think. There is in fact a way to see part of it, although it means coming on a Sunday and only during the winter season from October through to Easter.

The Chapel Royal

St James's Palace has two chapels. One, the Queen's Chapel, is outside the palace in Marlborough Road. The other, the **Chapel Royal**, is inside the palace. On most Sundays *in the winter season* only, services are held in the Chapel Royal which the public are free to attend. Times are published the day before in *The Times* and *Daily Telegraph* newspapers.

A feature of these services is the singing by the Chapel Royal choir. This consists of six Gentlemen choristers and ten Children choristers. The latter go to the City of London School where they are called the Queen's Scholars because the Queen pays two-thirds of their fees. Dressed in their scarlet and gold state coats, they make not only a beautiful sound but a picturesque and colourful sight. Historically, they are continuing a Chapel Royal tradition of fine church music stretching back a thousand years. Strictly speaking, the Chapel Royal is not a building but a department, an

organization, a team of priests and singers charged with meeting the spiritual needs of the sovereign. In medieval times when the Court moved about a good deal, so did the Chapel Royal, ferrying its vestments and service books about in panniers on two packhorses. In 1415 it went to France with Henry V and sang mass before the battle of Agincourt. As the Court gradually settled down, the Chapel Royal ceased its wanderings and settled down with it. With its royal associations, the Chapel has always been able to attract the finest musicians. Tallis, Byrd and Purcell – big names in the 16th and 17th centuries – were all Chapel Royal organists. Handel was a specially appointed Composer in the 18th century. Today, musical historians describe the Chapel as nothing less than 'the cradle of English church music'.

The Holbein ceiling

The Chapel Royal organization has been at St James's Palace since 1702, but the actual chapel building forms part of the original Palace put up in Henry VIII's time. It has been changed a good deal since then, particularly by the Victorians, but the richly decorated Tudor ceiling, said to have been painted by Holbein, survives. Designed in the first half of 1540 when Henry was married to Anne of Cleves, the ceiling is mainly covered in royal coats of arms and initials. These are to be expected. But there are two oddities. One is the series of vignettes incorporating the names of the Cleve family estates on the continent. A possible explanation for this is that perhaps it was the Flanders Mare's dowry that paid for the chapel. The second unusual feature is the single instance in the north-west corner of Henry's arms combined with those of Catherine Howard, his next wife after Anne. Since he divorced Anne and married Catherine in July 1540, the same month he divorced Anne, Holbein must have been putting his finishing touches to the ceiling at that very time. So does the famous story of Henry VIII and his six wives help date one work at least in Holbein's *oeuvre*!

Outside the Palace, you can spot the location of the Chapel by looking to the right of the gatehouse: the double row of narrow windows is in the Chapel's north wall (unusually for a Christian church it is laid out on a north–south rather than an east–west axis). If you come to a Sunday service, you reach the Chapel by going through the police barrier mentioned earlier into Stable Yard; then you turn left into Ambassadors Court (ambassadors to the UK are still officially accredited to the Court of St James's); from there you pass through a surviving archway from the medieval leper house-cum-convent which preceded the Palace. This brings you into Colour Court, the Tudor section of the Palace behind the gatehouse. The Chapel is on the left.

Berry Bros. & Rudd

Returning to the walk, when you reach Pall Mall cross to the far side of St James's Street on the zebra crossing and walk up the right-hand side of the street. Berry Bros. at No. 3 is just the sort of old-established, up-market wine merchant you would expect to find in St James's. With its battered (but of course carefully preserved) shop front, it looks every bit the long-lived, well-established business it is. But like every commercial concern it still has to operate in a competitive market and its future, for that reason, is by no means guaranteed.

Luckily, however, it has two things to help it survive. One is 'Cutty Sark' whisky, a global seller created by the firm and a healthy generator of profits. The other is what might be called Berry Bros.' very own secret weapon: its huge subterranean storage area. This enables it to supply instantly, from what looks to be just a small shop, any wine on its extensive price list – in quantity if required. No other wine merchant in central London can match this level of service, which is why no other wine merchant in central London – including those like Justerini and Brooks which are nearly as old – has quite the same name as Berry Bros. If you go into the shop (living antique is the only term for it) and place an order (one bottle will do), an assistant will go to a raised trapdoor against the wall on the right-hand side. This is the entrance to the original shop cellar, and

still the main entrance to the vastly
expanded network of cellars which the
moles of Berry Bros. have been burrow-
ing for the past 300 years. The latest
addition came in the early 1980s when
the firm acquired the cellars under
Rothmans next door. These are actually
on two below-ground floors. Kept at a
constant and fairly cool temperature by
the damp London clay, these huge vaults
are capable of storing 18,000 cases of
wine – that's 216,000 bottles. Most of
them are for sale, but some are laid down
to mature. And tucked away in various
nooks and crannies are the firm's choic-
est and oldest selections, strictly for private drinking only: Cognac from the
1830s, Lafitte from the 1860s, and of
course port. According to the cellar
manager, who has personally tippled
both (strictly in the line of duty), the
1863 Cockburn's is superb but the 1820
Croft's is disappointing. To get some idea
of the scale of these secret vaults, stand
outside the shop to the left of the
entrance to Pickering Place (this,
incidentally, is where the Widow
Bourne established the original business
– then a grocer's – in the 1690s; William
Pickering was her son- in-law). Looking
down St James's Street towards the
Palace, the cellars come right out under
the pavement and extend as far away
from you as the corner of Pall Mall (the
pavement on the corner is right above
the tasting area). Now go into Pickering
Place (it is public property), the prettiest

little courtyard in St James's. Berry Bros.
have the houses on three of the four
sides (they were built in the garden of
Widow Bourne's house in the 1730s)
and the cellars extend under the courtyard right to the back of the house. It
should be clear now how Berry Bros.
can produce so much wine from what
appears to be just one small shop.

Crown Passage and Angel Court
Turn right out of Pickering Place and
continue on up St James's Street. A little
further on you pass Lock's the hatters,
here since 1764, and then Lobb's the
boot- and shoemakers, relatively new
arrivals in the 1850s. Lobb's' shoes, incidentally, take up to six months to make
and they have 30,000 lasts stored on
ceiling-high racks in the basement, filed
in alphabetical order of customer. At
King Street, turn right and then when
you get to Crown Passage, turn right
again. Crown Passage – probably taking
its name from a lost pub – is exactly
what it should be, a lively little 'village'
street full of useful shops and services,
including an ironmonger's, for workers
and residents in the surrounding streets.

Go down to the end of Crown
Passage, passing the Red Lion pub on the
way, and turn left along Pall Mall. After a
few yards, turn left into Angel Court.
Like Crown Passage, Angel Court is
probably also named after a former pub,
but there the resemblance ends. Where
Crown Passage is full of life, Angel Court

is completely dead. There is absolutely nothing at street level to interest the passing walker, and the only sound to break the otherwise dead silence is the hum of air-conditioning systems in the towering office buildings on either side. The only good thing to say about it is that no attempt has been made to create a kind of instant sham community so beloved of property developers with big ideas and no soul.

King Street

Angel Court brings you back on to King Street. **Christie's** world-famous auction house, founded in 1766, is directly opposite: the galleries are open every weekday for viewing and it's quite all right for you just to wander in off the street and take a look around – the sort of thing you always mean to do if you work in the area but somehow never quite get round to.

From Angel Court turn right along King Street. Rose and Crown Yard on the right is a dead end and not very interesting to look at. From the yard, cross King Street and walk up the right-hand side of Duke Street St James's: Princes Place, a short dead end, is on the left. Between Nos. 12 and 13 walk on the right through the archway into Mason's Yard. This was originally built as a stableyard for St James's Square in the 1660s. The centre of the yard has always been built on, the site today being occupied by an electricity sub-station. Keep this to your left and walk to the end.

London Library

Here look right and you will see a back wall of the London Library, the famous members-only lending library conceived by historian Thomas Carlyle in 1841 and based in St James's Square since 1845. Apart from the fact that you can borrow books from it for extended periods, the beauty of the library is that readers are free to browse among the shelves in the warren of old-fashioned bookstacks lying behind the elegant St James's Square façade – provided you don't mind the occasional electric shock, that is. All the shelves and stairs in the stacks are made of metal to reduce the fire risk, and you used to get a small charge when you put your hand on a banister. Re-wiring in the late 1990s dealt with the problem, so depriving elderly members of their traditional boost as they climbed from London Topography Quarto in the basement to Periodicals and Societies on the sixth floor!

From your vantage point in Mason's Yard, you can see part of the library's new extension, completed in 1992, with some of the bookstacks clearly visible through the upper windows. Behind the windows at first-floor level lies the spacious reading-room with its main window looking onto St James's Square. In the mid-1990s, the library was extended again back to Duke Street.

Babmaes Street

Turn left round the corner of the sub-station and head for the far-right corner of the yard. Here, by the Directors Lodge Club, is a passage marked 'No. 9 Mason's Yard'. In existence probably since the building of the yard and certainly since 1720, this eventually brings you out in Ormond Yard. Here, besides a couple of clubs, is Briggs's barber shop, a favourite resort for club and business types in the surrounding streets. Go to the end of the yard. Opposite, you can see to the far end of the uninteresting Apple Tree Yard.

Turn left here up Duke of York Street, and then right at the top into Jermyn Street once more. Carry on along the right-hand side of the street until you get to Babmaes Street.

A long dead end with two dog-legs, Babmaes Street is really a mews penetrating as far as some of the grand houses on the north-east corner of St

James's Square. The big gates on the right at the far end lead to the rear of No. 4 St James's Square, a mansion with no fewer than 77 rooms, servants' quarters, its own private courtyard garden, garaging for six cars, and to the left, at 7/9 Babmaes Street, its own little coach house last used as such in 1942. The house is now home to the Naval and Military Club. Babmaes Street's curious name is a corruption – via Babmay's – of Baptist May, the name of an adviser to the aristocratic family responsible for developing so much of the St James's area in the late 17th century.

Retrace your steps out of Babmaes Street, cross Jermyn Street and enter Eagle Place. This brings you back on to Piccadilly once more. Turn right and you arrive back at the start of the walk at Piccadilly Circus.

Chapter 8

THE CITY

The City is like an old garden which has been dug over for centuries. So rich and fertile is it now that every square inch has something interesting to reveal, particularly to the hunter-out of London secrets.

Below ground is a good place to start, for the City is not just what you see on the surface. It also extends downwards through the 20 feet (6 metres) or so of what the archaeologists call 'made' earth, the spoil that has accumulated since the Romans arrived two millennia ago. Many Roman and medieval remains still lie buried in this constantly worked-over stratum. Some others have been excavated and preserved, though they may not necessarily be generally accessible.

Roman bath-houses

For example, in the basement of a modern office block at 100 Lower Thames Street opposite the old Billingsgate fish market is a complete **Roman bath-house** with walls standing up to 3 feet (1 metre) high and all the various rooms – hot, warm and cold rooms, vestibule and adjoining house – clearly visible. (Funds permitting, this may open to the public one day.) Further up-river underneath 85 Queen Victoria Street is an even larger bath-house but this one has been buried beneath concrete foundations and is completely invisible. In the basement of a shop at the corner of Leadenhall Market (90 Gracechurch Street) there is a section of the wall of the Roman basilica, and at the **Bank of England** and beneath a Georgian merchant's house at 11 Ironmonger Lane are fine Roman mosaic floors. Underneath the Guildhall complex is an amphitheatre which will almost certainly be open to the public one day.

City wall

By far the biggest relic of Roman and medieval London is the City wall. Some sections have been revealed and linked together to form a 1¾-mile (3-kilometre) walk routemarked by special information panels. Although the walk is hardly 'secret', it takes you into some pretty out-of-the-way places and so is well worth doing for that reason. (Buy the Museum of London's *London Wall Walk* before setting out.) Other sections of the wall, though excavated, are not generally accessible and are known to only very few people. There is, for example, a section underneath the Old Bailey. At one time it was possible to arrange a visit to see it, but not any longer for security reasons. Nearby is another buried section of the wall. About 10 feet (3 metres) high with an intact Saxon bastion at one end, it is in a specially constructed chamber under the Merrill Lynch building at the corner of Giltspur Street and Newgate Street. Until the late 1990s this was the van park of the old post and sorting office in King Edward Street and the wall was one of the highlights of a tour of the office which also incidentally included the Post Office's own Underground railway (see page 49).

Rare interiors

Above ground, there are some very special and rare interiors which few people ever see. For example, the Great Eastern Hotel at Liverpool Street Station, the only hotel in the City, has a magnificent masonic meeting hall. The **Bank of England** has some splendid official rooms (not to mention, of course, stacks of gold bars in the vaults – the Underground railway, however, which is supposed to link the Bank to the main clearing banks, is completely mythical). High up on the eleventh floor of Richard Rogers' high-tech Lloyd's building is a chaste neo-classical boardroom designed in the 18th century by Robert Adam for a country house in Wiltshire. A long stone's throw away, the **Mansion House**, official home of the Lord Mayor, is one of the great unrecognized palaces of London. And inside St Paul's Cathedral, seen only by scholars, is a beautiful galleried library with exceptional stone carvings by William Kempster and other masons who worked on the building of St Paul's.

CITY MARKETS

Most of the key institutions of the City are rarely seen by outsiders. There was a time just a few years ago when it was possible to see at least four of the City's famous exchanges at work: the Stock Exchange, Lloyd's insurance market, the London International Financial Futures and Options Exchange (LIFFE) and the **London Metal Exchange**. Now with greater security pressures only the last one admits visitors and even then usually only those involved in the business in some way. Still, it's always worth a try.

London Metal Exchange

The London Metal Exchange is perhaps the most remarkable of all. In its dealing-room in Plantation House, Fenchurch Street, the traders sit in a circle about 15 feet

(4.5 metres) wide. As trading begins, they are quite polite, talking quietly to each other, nodding and flourishing sheaves of paper. But gradually the pace and volume pick up until by the end of the session – which lasts just a few minutes – the traders are literally bawling at each other, gesticulating madly and stamping their feet. Suddenly a bell sounds and they all rush off to the phones dangling on wires round the room to relay their deals back to their offices. Shortly afterwards the whole process starts again, with a different metal on the floor.

THE LIVERY

The largest and perhaps to the outside world the least-known of all the City institutions is the livery. The livery is a unique and powerful network, actively and benevolently involved in many aspects of both City and national life. It consists of 23,000 liverymen split up into 100 livery companies, each representing a different trade or profession. The oldest of these companies were founded in the Middle Ages when the City was a self-sufficient town, not the specialized financial district it is today. The job of the companies was to regulate the trades practised in the City, and to look after the interests of members. Members wore the livery or uniform of their company, hence the name 'livery company'.

KEY TO MAP OF THE CITY (OVERLEAF)

Note: The Carpenters', Cutlers', Drapers', Grocers', Leathersellers', Mercers' and Saddlers' halls all appear on one or other of the two City Walks maps on pages 137 and 145.

1	Billingsgate Bath-house		LIVERY HALLS	29	Goldsmiths' Hall
2	Huggin Hill Bath-house	15	Skinners' Hall	30	Haberdashers' Hall
3	Roman basilica wall	16	Fishmongers' Hall	31	Innholders' Hall
4	Roman mosaic floor: Ironmonger Lane	17	Apothecaries' Hall	32	Insurers' Hall
		18	Armourers' Hall	33	Ironmongers' Hall
5	Roman mosaic floor: Bank of England	19	Bakers' Hall	34	Master Mariners' Hall
		20	Barbers' Hall	35	Merchant Taylors' Hall
6	Guildhall amphitheatre	21	Brewers' Hall	36	Painter Stainers' Hall
7	London wall: Old Bailey	22	Butchers' Hall	37	Pewterers' Hall
8	London wall: Merrill Lynch	23	Clothworkers' Hall	38	Plaisterers' Hall
		24	Coopers' Hall	39	Salters' Hall
9	Great Eastern Hotel	25	Dyers' Hall	40	Stationers' Hall
10	Lloyd's	26	Founders' Hall	41	Tallow Chandlers' Hall
11	Mansion House	27	Girdlers' Hall	42	Vintners' Hall
12	St Paul's Cathedral	28	Glaziers'/Scientific	43	Wax Chandlers' Hall
13	Stock Exchange		Instrument-Makers'		
14	London Metal Exchange		Hall		

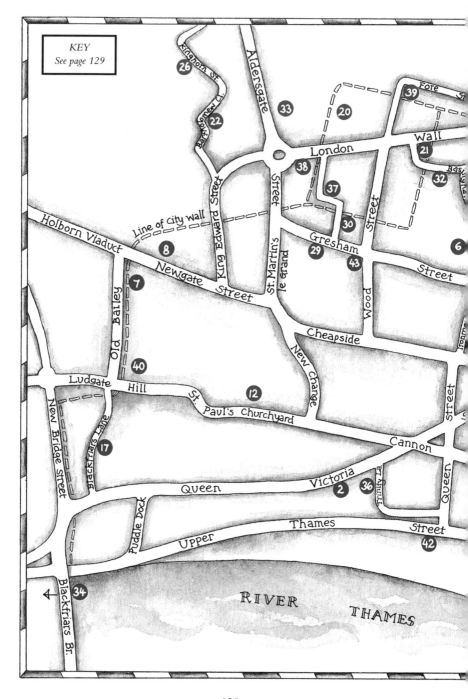

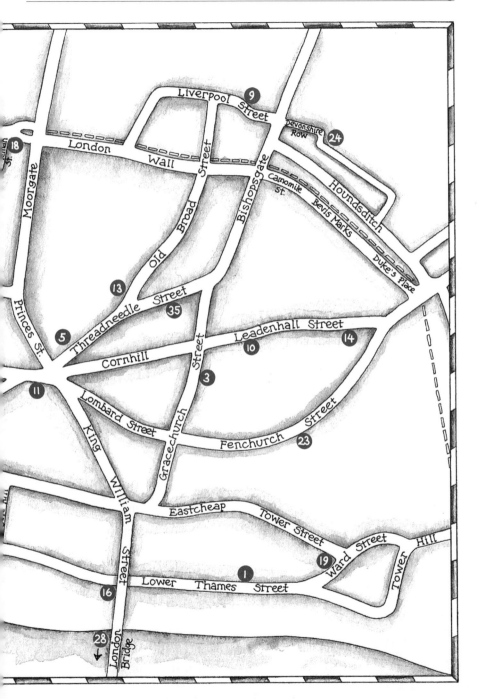

Some companies – notably the Apothecaries, Farriers, Fishmongers, Goldsmiths, Gunmakers, Saddlers and Vintners – are still involved in their historic function of trade regulation. For example, the Fishmongers' Company inspectors, known as Fishmeters, still inspect fish every day at Billingsgate fish market in Docklands to ensure that it is 'wholesome for Man's Body'. Other companies – like the Turners – no longer control their trade, but remain connected with it through their livery members and by supporting education, training and research through grants and prizes. A few companies, whose industries have died out, have adopted new ones. The Horners, for example, are now connected with the plastics industry; the Salters have adopted the chemical industry; and the Fan Makers represent the heating and air-conditioning industry, surely a wonderful case of adapting to changing circumstances.

Livery schools

Last but not least are the companies like the Skinners who have no connection with their original trade – furs – but who continue to do good work for the community through their charitable and educational activities. In the Skinners' case, Tonbridge School in Kent is their main educational establishment. The best-known livery school in London is St Paul's, a Mercers' Company foundation dating from 1509. It was originally based next door to St Paul's Cathedral, but moved out to more spacious premises in west London in 1884. A less-well known one is the Leathersellers' Colfe's School in Lee, SE12, founded in its present form in 1652.

Between 1709 and 1930 no livery companies were established, but since 1947, 21 new companies have been formed, the latest being the Information Technologists. These people have been of vital importance since the City went over to a computerized share-dealing system in 1987. Inevitably, the modern companies have close links with the industries and professions they represent and so, in a sense, are much closer to the original idea of livery companies than some of the older ones which have lost touch with their original trades. These modern companies include two which seem particularly far removed from not just City life, but urban life in general: the Farmers' Company (granted livery 1952) and the Guild of Air Pilots and Air Navigators (granted livery 1956).

Livery halls

Within the modern Square Mile the livery companies have both a political and physical presence. Politically, they occupy an important position in the City's constitution in that it is the liverymen who elect annually the Lord Mayor and the City's two sheriffs. Physically, the companies' headquarters include some of the finest and most historic buildings remaining within the City. They are called 'halls' because, besides offices and other facilities, they include large dining-halls where hundreds of livery-men at a time can assemble for banquets, elections and other functions. From the earliest days, the social side of livery has been very important.

Today there are 36 halls in the City (this number does not include the Watermen and Lightermen's Hall at 18 St Mary-at-Hill because, although an old-established company, the Watermen have not been granted livery status). By and large, these halls are almost completely unknown to all but liverymen because none of them is open to the public on a regular basis. However, a few open for guided tours on a handful of days a year and it is well worth taking the trouble to get tickets for at least one of them. Tickets are obtainable from the **City Information Office** on the south side of St Paul's Cathedral. Since the livery companies fix their open days and deliver their tickets to the Centre at the beginning of the year, it is advisable to contact the Centre around that time, say the last week in January or the first week in February. If you leave it any later, you may find that all the tickets have been taken.

In recent years, the number of halls offering guided tours has shrunk owing to growing security pressures in the City. However, the Vintners', Skinners', Fishmongers', Tallow Chandlers' and Goldsmiths' have kept the ball rolling, and they will probably continue to open in future years.

The Skinners' and Fishmongers' are two of the finest halls, though they are very different in character, the former being intimate and homely and the latter grand and stately and slightly impersonal.

Skinners' Hall

The handsome 18th-century stuccoed façade of Skinners' Hall stands out on the west side of Dowgate Hill, next to Cannon Street Station. The office entrance is at No. 8 and the arched entrance to the pretty little courtyard and hall beyond is one – or rather half – down at 8½. The Hall is actually much larger than it appears from the street; you can see large sections from nearby College Street.

The tour takes in the main hall, the outer hall, the old court-room and, upstairs, the panelled court-room (where the directors of the Company meet) and the little library, more a kind of cosy sitting-room. The hall contains a series of 15 large paint-ed panels by Frank Brangwyn and a collection of superb Company plate, the centrepiece of which is a loving-cup in the form of a golden cockerel made for the Company in 1602. There are four more of these and the set is worth £2.5 million ($3.75 million).

In other rooms you see portraits and Company treasures such as an antique rent chest, illuminated medieval manuscripts from the Company's archives and an ancient bell presented by the Hughes family of Whitechapel Bell Foundry (see page 158). The Hughes are senior members of the Skinners' livery.

Great Twelve

The Skinners are members of the 'Great Twelve', the top 12 livery companies in order of precedence. When precedence began to be important, the Skinners disputed sixth position with the Merchant Taylors, so in 1484 the Lord Mayor ruled that the two companies should occupy the sixth and seventh positions in alternate years and invite each other to dinner each year. The ruling, including the dinner clause, is still in force. The dispute allegedly gave rise to the expression 'at sixes and sevens'.

The Skinners have been on this site since the late 1200s. In those days, the Walbrook river (see page 22) ran down the hill here into the Thames. The furs which the wealthy merchants of the Skinners' Company sold to the upper classes (only top people were legally entitled to wear fur in ancient times) were cleaned in the river by an exploited class of operatives known as 'tawyers'. It is significant that there is no Tawyers' Hall today. It is the merchants' companies which have tended to survive in the City rather than the poorer and less powerful labourers' companies.

For 200 years or more the Skinners have had little or no contact with the trade from which they grew, but even so nearby Great St Thomas Apostle Street remained until literally the last few years a centre of the fur trade. When this book was first written, many doors of empty buildings in the street – which has now been re-developed – still bore the names of defunct or relocated fur and skin dealers.

Fishmongers' Hall

Fishmongers' Hall is a landmark riverside building on the upstream side of London Bridge. On the downstream side is the old Billingsgate market, until just a decade ago London's main fish market and of course the scene of Fishmongers' Company inspections. The Hall was built in the Greek Revival style in the 1830s at the same time as London Bridge and the main entrance is from the approach road to the bridge, quite some height above ground level.

On the tour you see the lower halls and the court-room, and, on the principal floor, the palatial dining-room, drawing-room and banqueting hall. The latter, overlooking the London Bridge approach and capable of accommodating with ease 200 guests at a sit-down meal, is particularly impressive. The rooms on the river front all have the fine views you would expect.

A feature of the drawing-room is Annigoni's famous 1954 portrait of the Queen. Apparently when the artist, then little known outside his own country, received the letter from the Fishmongers' Company asking him to paint the portrait of the newly crowned Queen of England he thought somebody was playing him a huge practical joke! Another prized possession of the Company is the dagger with which Sir William Walworth, then head of the Company and Lord Mayor of London, is reputed to have stabbed Wat Tyler, leader of the Peasants' Revolt, in 1381. A lifesize wooden statue of Walworth, carved in 1684, commands the main staircase of the Hall.

Doggett's rowing race

Among all the various tasks that the Fishmongers have acquired over the past seven centuries, perhaps the most curious is overseeing an annual sculling race on the Thames known as Doggett's Coat and Badge Race. Thomas Doggett, an Irish theatre manager and comedian, established the race in 1716 as an incentive for London's young watermen apprentices. Now said to be the oldest annually contested event in the British sporting calendar, it is usually held in July, over a 4½-mile (7-kilometre) course between London Bridge and Chelsea. The contestants come from the Watermen and Lightermen's Company and the winner receives a scarlet coat and silver badge, which he wears to a special lunch at Fishmongers' Hall held in his honour.

Goldsmiths' Hall

There is one livery hall which you can see without having to apply to the City Information Centre for tickets. This is **Goldsmiths' Hall**, where every year the Company, which is still active in its trade, holds jewellery and silverware exhibitions. Two are regular events: the Goldsmiths' Fair in the autumn, when over 70 designer-makers display and sell their pieces to the public; and the Passing Out Exhibition in December, a degree-work show by jewellery and silversmithing students. The other exhibitions (usually two in number) are generally one-man shows or retrospectives featuring the work of individual designers or design houses.

OFF THE BEATEN TRACK

If there is a secret City below ground and another one behind closed doors, there is a third out on the streets in the shape of what a Yorkshireman would call the City's snickelways, in other words its lanes, alleyways and passages.

Despite the two great rebuildings following the 1666 fire and the 1940 Blitz, the medieval street layout has survived virtually intact. One of its main features – and the one that gives the City its peculiar and ineradicable charm – is the maze of narrow lanes, alleys and passageways connecting the main thoroughfares. In the following two walks we set out to explore them and in the process get right to the heart of the built-up area. One of the walks covers the City east of St Paul's, the other and shorter the City west of St Paul's. Along the way you see many other City sights, enumerated in the introductions. While you do the walks, keep an eye out to see how successful the City Corporation is being in its attempts to green the City. Its aim is to have a tree or some shrubs (or at least something green and growing) visible from every street corner. The objective is clearly well on the way to being met, but there is still a little way to go.

The City – East of St Paul's walk

Start/Finish: St Paul's Underground (Central Line)
Length: 3 miles (5 km)
Time: 2½ hours
Food: No shortage of places of all kinds throughout the walk, but two to look out for in particular are Talbot Court about a third of the way round (restaurant, pub and sandwich bar/cafe) and Priest's Court towards the end (sandwich bar and cheap restaurant).
Sights: City institutions like the **Mansion House**, the **Bank of England**, Lloyds and the Stock Exchange; the 202-feet (61-metre) high **Monument** to the Great Fire of 1666 and the rather taller International Financial Centre; the livery halls of the Carpenters', Drapers', Grocers', Mercers' and Saddlers' companies; numerous City churches including the least altered of Sir Christopher Wren's; Britain's oldest synagogue (the **Spanish and Portuguese**).
Notes: (a) This walk should be done between Monday and Friday during office hours. Not only is it during the working day that the City is at its liveliest and most exciting, it is also when the greatest number of places – including some of the passages which are an integral part of the walk – are open.
(b) This is quite a long walk for such a dense place as the City so you might prefer to do it in two goes. A natural half-way break at Fenchurch Street is indicated in the text.

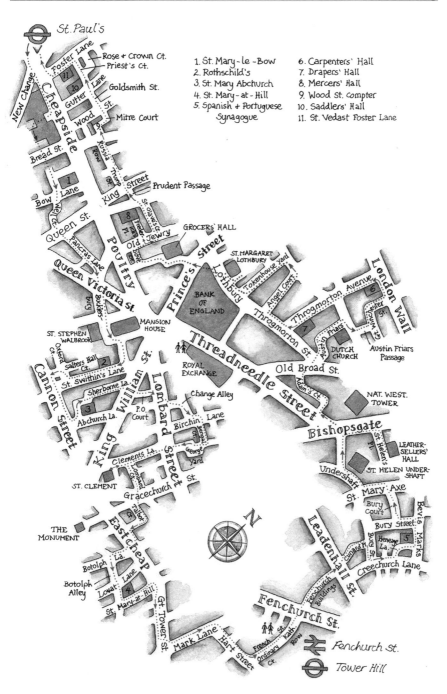

St. Paul's

Rose + Crown Ct.
Priest's Ct.
Goldsmith St.
Mitre Court

1. St. Mary-le-Bow
2. Rothschild's
3. St. Mary Abchurch
4. St. Mary-at-Hill
5. Spanish + Portuguese Synagogue

6. Carpenters' Hall
7. Drapers' Hall
8. Mercers' Hall
9. Wood St. Compter
10. Saddlers' Hall
11. St. Vedast Foster Lane

Foster Lane
New Change
Cheapside
Gutter Lane
Wood St.
Russia Row
Trump St.
Bread St.
Bow Lane
Distaff Lane
King Street
Prudent Passage
Queen St.
Pancras Lane
Poultry
GROCERS' HALL
Prince's Street
ST. MARGARET LOTHBURY
Lothbury
Tokenhouse Yard
Angel Court
Throgmorton Avenue
London Wall
Queen Victoria St.
Bucklersbury
BANK OF ENGLAND
Throgmorton St.
Austin Friars
Foster St.
MANSION HOUSE
ST. STEPHEN WALBROOK
Oxford Ct.
Salters Hall Ct.
St. Swithin's Lane
Sherborne La.
Abchurch La.
P.O. Court
Cannon Street
King William St.
Lombard Street
Birchin Lane
Change Alley
DUTCH CHURCH
Austin Friars Passage
Old Broad St.
Adam's Ct.
NAT. WEST. TOWER
ROYAL EXCHANGE
Threadneedle Street
Bishopsgate
St. Helen's Pl.
LEATHER-SELLERS' HALL
Undershaft
ST. HELEN UNDER-SHAFT
ST. CLEMENT
Clements La.
George Yard
Sheep St.
Gracechurch St.
St. Mary Axe
Bury Court
Bury Street
Bevis Marks
Heneage La.
Bury St.
THE MONUMENT
Eastcheap
Botolph La.
Botolph Alley
Lovat Lane
St. Mary-at-Hill
Gt. Tower St.
Leadenhall St.
Creechurch Lane
Cunard St.
Fenchurch Buildings
Mark Lane
Hart Street
Fenchurch St.
French Ordinary Ct.
Kath. Row
Fenchurch St.
Tower Hill

137

Take Exit 2 from St Paul's station and turn right towards Cheapside and Bow Church. Cross New Change and enter Cheapside. Beyond the first terrace of shops, turn right on to the forecourt with the flowerbeds and go through the central archway between the two banks. In the courtyard (this is an extension of the Bank of England) turn immediately left through another archway and go down the steps and across the road into a passage with a Japanese fast-food restaurant at the entrance. This brings you out into a garden area, formerly the churchyard of St Mary-le-Bow. St Mary's has a crypt restaurant which is now about 20 feet (6 metres) below ground level. In Roman times it was the street level.

Colony of Virginia

In the middle of the garden stands a statue of Captain John Smith, a City man and one of the founders of the colony of Virginia in 1606. A Corporation board explains in more detail why exactly the statue is here. Keep the statue to your left and carry straight on down the alley behind the church. Turn right into Bow Lane – a narrow pedestrian-only street thronged with office workers at lunchtime – and then almost immediately left through the archway into Well Court, no doubt taking its name from a well that was once here. Follow this round to the right into the court proper and turn

left. Cross Queen Street – Guildhall to the left, Southwark Bridge to the right – into Pancras Lane. St Pancras Church was here until the Great Fire of 1666. Its churchyard is now a small, rather scruffy, garden, often used as a bicycle park. A little further on is the site of another church destroyed in the Great Fire – St Benet Sherehog. From its name (a 'shere hog' is a ram castrated after its first shearing) you can tell this church stood in the heart of the medieval City's wool district.

At the end of Pancras Lane, cross Queen Victoria Street – Royal Exchange to the left, exposed remains of the Roman Temple of Mithras to the right – into Bucklersbury. Walk on down here (crossing the course of the Walbrook river in the process) towards the **Mansion House** and the church of St Stephen Walbrook. Chad Varah, founder of the Samaritans, is rector of the church. The Lord Mayor is one of the churchwardens.

Go into the alley between the two buildings and follow it round to the left past St Stephen's churchyard. When you meet the road, turn right and then at the T-junction (St Mary Woolnoth on the left) go right again into St Swithin's Lane. On the right there are two large courts leading off this narrow lane. The first – New Court – has been the home of Rothschild's merchant bank since 1804. The second was the Hall of the Founders' Company until they moved to Smithfield in 1987. It is now let as offices.

Near the bottom, just after the Bankers Books bookshop, turn right through the parking area into Salters Hall Court, home of the Salters' Company until bombed out in 1941. They had come here 300 years previously when they bought Oxford House, hence the name Oxford Court you can see on the garden wall. The garden is the old churchyard of St Swithin's London Stone, destroyed in the same blitz as the hall.

The London Stone

Turn left out of the court and then left again on Cannon Street. Here you will find, set into the building on the left, the 'London Stone' from which the church took its name. The plaque tells you more about it. Continue on. Having crossed St Swithin's Lane, you come to Abchurch Lane. Here turn left and then left again across the churchyard of St Mary Abchurch. It's worth having a look inside this church. This one in addition has a large painted dome and rich dark woodwork, and is the least altered of all Sir Christopher Wren's City churches. It was built in 1676.

'Shitteborwe' Lane

Go round the corner of the church into Sherborne Lane, where if the windows are open you can hear dealers trading in an office somewhere up above. In other parts of the country – Dorset for example – Sherborne is a perfectly innocuous name meaning 'clear stream'. Here, however, it has slightly less lyrical connotations. Apparently it is a corruption of Shitteborwe (presumably pronounced 'shitborough'), a medieval colloquialism for 'public lavatory'!

At the end of the lane go straight over King William Street into Post Office Court, site of the General Post Office in the 18th century. This completely covered passageway brings you onto Lombard Street, the traditional centre of the banking community, hence the old-fashioned signs hanging outside the various branches. Coutts' on the right occupies the site of Lloyd's Coffee House, the 17th-century precursor of the modern Lloyd's insurance market.

Cross Lombard Street diagonally right and enter Change Alley, short for Exchange Alley and so called because of its proximity to the Royal Exchange, whose green gates you can see at the far end. Take the first turn on the right. At the crossing, a blue plaque on the left marks the site of the Kings Arms Tavern where the first meeting of the Marine Society was held in 1756. Founded to promote careers at sea, particularly for poor boys, the Society continues its maritime work from its current headquarters in Lambeth.

Naval officer killed

Carrying straight on, Change Alley brings you to Birchin Lane. Turn left and then right here into a narrow passageway called Bengal Court. (A modern plaque at the entrance commemorates a naval officer killed during the Second World War while trying to stop a gang of jewel thieves.) At the end of Bengal Court, the entrance to the ancient George and Vulture restaurant is on the left, while George Yard is on the right. Take the right turn and walk through the yard to Lombard Street. To the left you see the tower-block office of Dresdner Kleinwort Benson, another old-established merchant bank. Cross Lombard Street into Clements Lane, leading to the church of St Clement at the bottom. Walk down to the church and take a look into Church Court with its well-kept but unfortunately seatless churchyard (and the plaque at the entrance recording the residence in 1784 of the first Serbian Minister of Education) before retracing your steps a short distance back up the lane and turning right into Lombard Court. This brings you to Gracechurch Street. Cross over – the **Monument** to the Great Fire is the major landmark to the right – into Talbot Court, one of the places mentioned at the beginning as a good place to stop for something to eat or drink. As you can see, it's got a nice pub, the Ship, and round the corner is a good sandwich bar with seats.

St Mary-at-Hill

Emerging on Eastcheap – 'cheap', as also in Cheapside and in place names like Chipping Norton, means market – turn left and then first right into Botolph Lane. Half-way down turn left into Botolph Alley. At Lovat Lane cross over and go down the alley on the right-hand side of the church. At the next lane, St Mary-at-Hill, also the name of the church, turn left up the hill. The doorway on the left marked 'Entrance to Church' leads to the tiny little churchyard as well as to the church. The latter has been rebuilt in a plain dignified manner following a disastrous fire in the 1980s.

Continue on up the hill and turn right onto the main road, heading for All Hallows Church and, in the distance, the Tower of London. Cross where you can and turn left into Mark Lane and then right into Hart Street. Having passed the Ship pub and St Olave's Church with its Samuel Pepys and naval associations, turn left just before the bridge into French Ordinary Court. The French Ordinary was an eating-house catering for French Protestant refugees in the 17th century ('ordinaries' served simple meals at fixed prices). The cavernous court takes you under Fenchurch Street railway station and brings you out into St Katherine's Row, next to the old churchyard of St Katharine (*sic*) Coleman, demolished in 1926.

At Fenchurch Street – St Botolph Aldgate to the right – cross over and go into Fenchurch Buildings. At Leadenhall Street, cross diagonally left into Cunard Place and then turn right into Bury Street and left into Creechurch Lane. As you turn left, a plaque on the right-hand corner marks a seminal spot: the site of the first synagogue built after the re-admission of Jews to England during the Commonwealth Interregnum. They had been kicked out 350 years before following vicious persecution.

Turning left off Creechurch Lane into Heneage Lane and following the latter round to the right you come to the back of the second synagogue built after the re-admission (the **Spanish and Portuguese Synagogue**). This one has fortunately managed to survive and is now the oldest such structure in Britain. At the end of Heneage Lane, turn left on to Bevis Marks. A little way along you can see the front of the synagogue through the gates, the date of its construction (1701) clearly visible above the door. Immediately after the synagogue, turn left into Bury Street and then right into tiled Bury Court. On St Mary Axe, turn left towards the new Lloyd's building and then right into Undershaft (the 'shaft' was a medieval maypole). Where the road divides, bear right to stay close to St Helen's Church and its pretty church-yard, unusually open for the City.

Carry on past and out into Bishopsgate. Here turn right and walk up to St Helen's Place, a private gated road owned by the Leathersellers' Company who have their Hall at the far end on the left. Feel free to go into the road for a look – the gates are for cars, not people.

When you have finished, retrace your steps back down Bishopsgate. At the lights turn right into Threadneedle Street (corruption of 'three needles' – no doubt a shop sign, perhaps of a haberdasher's) and then turn right again through the gates at No. 40. Passing under an archway you come to a quiet courtyard garden with the International Financial Centre rising high above. Turn left down some steps into Adam's Court and then go straight over Old Broad Street into Austin Friars.

The enclave of which this narrow winding lane is the main thoroughfare covers the site of the main Augustinian monastery in medieval England. After the dissolution the nave of the friars' church was given to Protestant refugees from Holland for use as a Dutch church. As you can see, after 450 years the Dutch are still here, though their present house of worship is a 1950s' rebuild.

Carpenters' and Drapers' road

Go right round the end of the church and then left into Austin Friars Passage. At the road turn left and follow it round to the right to London Wall.

Here turn left and then left again into gated Throgmorton Avenue. The arms on the gates belong to the Carpenters' Company, who have their Hall on the left of the entrance. They also own the first section of the avenue, hence the little coats of arms stuck on the fronts of the buildings.

Where the road widens out and the tarmac turns to granite setts, the ownership changes to the Drapers' Company. It's now their coat of arms you see on the lampstands and by the drainpipe half-way up the building on the left. Keep going straight down the avenue and you come to Drapers' Hall with its little garden. Though perhaps large by current City standards, the garden is a mere fragment of what it used to be when the drapers dried and bleached their clothes in it.

Throgmorton Avenue brings you out on to Throgmorton Street by the Stock Exchange. Turn right and then right again into Angel Court, where a comprehensive redevelopment has obliterated all traces of whatever may have been here before. There is an interesting inscription, however, which says that the land is owned by the Clothworkers' Company (their Hall is elsewhere) and that part of it was bequeathed to them by a 16th-century master, Thomas Ormiston. It is rare to find such explicit statements of land ownership in London.

Go to the left of the inscription and turn left, carrying straight on by the

phone box when the road bends to the right. Where the sign says No. 1 Telegraph Street, turn left into the unnamed passage. You come out in Tokenhouse Yard, the site of an office where in the 17th century special business tokens were issued at times of coin shortage. Go down to the end of the yard and turn right on Lothbury. Have a look in St Margaret's Close behind the church of St Margaret Lothbury before crossing over to the **Bank of England**, by the statue of the bank's architect, and walking along to the corner.

Cut left through the colonnade here and cross the road to the vehicle barrier barring the entrance on the far side. You are now on Grocers' Company land. Go through the barrier into the courtyard in front of Grocers' Hall and walk along in front of the Hall, turning right at the far end into another yard. Near the end turn right into Dove Court and then right again into Old Jewry, London's medieval Jewish quarter before the great expulsion of 1291. Frederick's Place on the left is an attractive little cobbled cul-de-sac savouring of the old, pre-Blitz, City. Mercers' Hall is at the end. The blue plaque on the big house on the left relates to the time when, as a young man, Benjamin Disraeli, later novelist and Prime Minister, worked here as an articled clerk in a solicitor's office.

Forgotten prison

Just beyond Frederick's Place, named after a 17th-century Lord Mayor, turn left into St Olave's Court leading to the converted church of St Olave Jewry and its tiny churchyard garden. At the end turn left and right into white-tiled Prudent Passage – derivation unknown – and then cross King Street into Trump Street, which becomes Russia Row. At the end of Russia Row go straight on into the entrance of Mitre Court. Besides covering the yard of an old inn called the Mitre, this also conceals the site of one of the old City prisons, the Wood Street Compter (pronounced 'counter'), demolished in 1816. In the middle, steps lead down to one of the old prison dungeons, now used as a storeroom by the adjacent Four Vintners wine merchants. The manager is happy to show people around provided he has an assistant to look after the shop. Continue on past the steps and out of the court into Goldsmith Street. Straight ahead now is Saddlers' Hall. Just to the right of the Gutter Lane street sign is the easily missed entrance to a passage with railings

on the right and also a plaque relating to old Broderers' Hall. Having lost their Hall in the Blitz, the Broderers, or Embroiderers, sold up and moved out to a new address near Hampton Court). Go down the passage to Priest's Court, which links up with Rose and Crown Court to make a little island block where there is a cheap restaurant, ideal for lunch. Go straight on through Priest's Court and turn left on Foster Lane. On the left the first door you come to gives access to a pretty little courtyard attached to the adjacent church of St Vedast Foster Lane. If the door is open you are welcome to go in. At the far end is the parish hall. This end is the rectory with roof-garden and first-floor gallery leading to the church. A relatively recent occupant was the late Canon Gonville ffrench-Beytagh, the brave Dean of Johannesburg expelled from South Africa in the 1970s for helping channel funds to the African National Congress.

Now carry on to the end of Foster Lane. Here once more is Cheapside and, to the right, St Paul's Underground, where the walk ends.

The City – West of St Paul's walk

Start/Finish: St Paul's Underground (Central Line)
Length: 2 miles (3 km)
Time: 1½ hours
Food: Pubs all along the route and nests of sandwich bars on Fleet Street (half-way) and in the Carter Lane area near the end, but a special

place to look out for is Ely Place a third of the way along. Here you will find the ancient Olde Mitre pub and at St Etheldreda's Church, a cafe serving lunch and afternoon tea 12.00–14.30 and 15.00–16.30 Monday to Friday.

Sights: Postman's Park and the heroes' memorial, **Dr Johnson's House**, a medieval crypt and hall, a private road which is part of Cambridgeshire, the Newgate execution bell, the **Central Criminal Courts (Old Bailey)**, London's hardest-to-find pub and the **St Bride Printing Library**.

Note: See note (a) to the City – East of St Paul's walk.

Take the main exit from St Paul's Underground station and turn left at the top of the stairs, heading north along St Martin's le Grand towards the tree on the left at the far end. Nomura House to your left was built about a century ago following the demolition of three earlier buildings, as the blue plaques indicate. At the tree turn left into Postman's Park and walk towards the building in the middle with the tiled roof. This is an extraordinary monument, a memorial to 53 men, women and children who gave their lives to save others from disaster: fires, drowning, out-of-control trains and other everyday catastrophes. It was the inspiration of Victorian artist G. F. Watts. He had been struck by the story of Alice Ayres, a 26-year-old live-in maid who had rescued her employer's three children from a fire and then lost her own life while attempting to jump to safety from an upstairs window. Watts felt that such people deserved some permanent memorial so, after due

negotiations, he began this wall of plaques. His wife added a few after his death but the idea never really caught on so even now there are still some blanks to be filled up.

Cutlers' Hall

Go straight on past the memorial and out of the park, cross the road and turn left beside the Merrill Lynch building. At the far end is an archway with a plaque on it. Turn right into the gated path to the left of the archway and follow it round to the left between the remains of Christ Church Greyfriars (bombed in the Blitz) and its former churchyard. On Newgate Street turn right and then left into Warwick Lane. On the right now the red-brick building with the terracotta frieze showing craftsmen forging metal is the livery Hall of the Cutlers' Company, No. 18 in the order of company precedence and chartered since 1416. Cutlers, of course, make knives and forks and other eating implements.

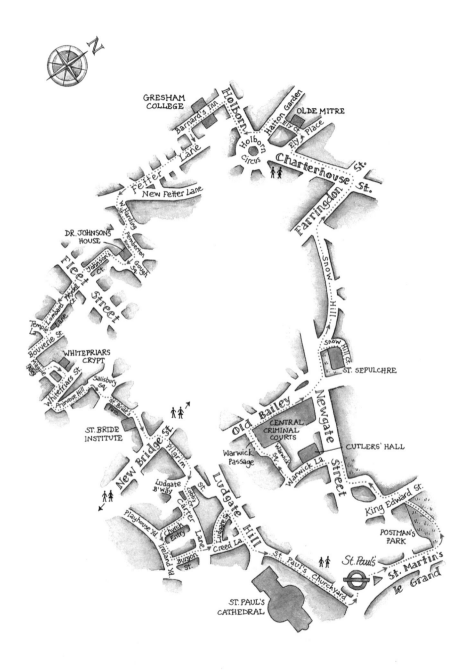

Beyond the Hall turn first right into Warwick Square, site of the London home of the Earls of Warwick in the 15th century. In the far corner go left into Warwick Passage. This takes you under the **Central Criminal Courts** and out on to Old Bailey. Turn right towards the lights and cross over Newgate Street to the corner of St Sepulchre's churchyard. Here you can see the first drinking fountain installed by the Metropolitan Drinking Fountain and Cattle Trough Association mentioned on page 76. To the right is the Merrill Lynch building beneath which is preserved in a special chamber the Roman wall and bastion mentioned on page 128.

For whom the bell tolls

Turn away from the yard along the side of the churchyard to the junction with Snow Hill. Snow Hill Court behind the church, reached by a gate outside the west door, is worth a quick look. Formerly the parish hall, it now serves as the Snow Hill Medical Centre. In the church itself is a poignant relic of Newgate Prison, precursor of the Central Criminal Courts. At midnight on the eve of an execution the bellman of St Sepulchre's used to rouse the prisoners in the condemned cell with a handbell and exhort them to make their peace with God while they still had the chance. The practice died out over two

centuries ago but somehow the old bell has survived. It is now in a glass case mounted on a pillar in front of the pulpit. There is a similar bell in the Whitechapel Bell Foundry (see page 158). Could one be an imposter?

Make your way down Snow Hill, passing first the police station on the site of the old Saracen's Head Inn (where Wackford Squeers meets Nicholas Nickleby in Dickens' novel of that name) and then a rather run-down part of Smithfield market. At the bottom of the hill turn right into Farringdon Street and then at the lights left into Charterhouse Street. Walk up the hill on the right-hand side and at the top turn right into Ely Place. This is a private road belonging to the Crown, hence the gates and the gatekeeper. Another curiosity is that, though within the bounds of the City, the road is technically part of the county of Cambridgeshire. This strange anomaly arises from the fact that for centuries Ely Place was the town house of the Bishops of Ely (Ely being in Cambridgeshire). Attached to the episcopal palace was an ancient church dedicated to St Etheldreda. When the bishops moved to the more fashionable West End in 1772 Ely Place was built over with the elegant terraces you see today, but the church, half-way down on the left, was preserved. Today it is used for Roman Catholic worship and has a convent attached next door. The crypt chapel beneath the main church is the oldest centre of Roman Catholic worship in London.

Hidden pub

Before you get to St Etheldreda's turn left opposite No. 33 into narrow Ely Court. This leads to what must be the most out-of-the-way pub in London, the Olde Mitre (mitres being the hats that bishops wear). Bishop Goodrich started it in 1546 for the use of his London servants and it has been here ever since. It has small dark rooms and old wooden furniture and the stump of an ancient cherry tree around which Queen Elizabeth I is said to have danced.

Carry on to the end of Ely Court, cross Hatton Garden (famous for diamonds) and turn left. At Holborn cross to the far side of the road and turn right. After a while you will come to a doorway with the words 'Barnard's Inn' over it. Turn in here. At the end of the tiled passage you come to the only surviving buildings of the original Inn, namely a small 18th-century house on the left, and, to the right, a beautiful little 15th-century hall which has miraculously survived 500 years of bombs and rebuilding. Barnard's Inn was one of the Inns of Chancery. These were colleges associated with solicitors and attorneys and similar to the Inns of Court which were for barristers or advocates. Having lost their

educational function, the Chancery Inns finally died out in the 19th century. Barnard's Inn was bought by the Mercers' Company for their school, which moved here from Whittington College in 1892 (see page 86) and stayed until 1959. Then in 1991 the Inn became the base of another old-established City educational institution, Gresham College.

Free lectures

Gresham College is unique in London and probably in the country. As established by public-spirited City merchant Sir Thomas Gresham in 1597 it is essentially a public lecture foundation. The College appoints eminent scholars to professorships in seven ancient disciplines – astronomy, divinity, geometry, law, music, physic and rhetoric – and since 1985 one modern one (commerce) and pays them to deliver free lectures to the public. Originally the aim was to convey the new learning of the Renaissance to the mass of illiterate people. Today, besides giving their lectures, usually in the old hall, the professors also do research and hold seminars, and prepare reports and studies on pressing contemporary issues. In short, the College has become a kind of university, but with several important differences. There is no formal teaching, the students (i.e. the public) do not have to turn up for lectures and there are certainly no exams! The funding for the whole exercise comes from income generated by Gresham's estate. He bequeathed it jointly to the City Corporation and his own livery company, the Mercers, and they now administer it through the augustly named Joint Grand Gresham Committee. Go straight on through the archway by the hall into the courtyard and then through another archway. Now bear left and exit on Fetter Lane. Turn right here and walk down to the junction with New Fetter Lane, where stands the statue of John Wilkes, an 18th-century Lord Mayor of the City and MP. The inscription calls him 'the champion of English freedom' because he stood up to a brow-beating government that first tried to muzzle his satirical newspaper, the *North Briton*, and then to deprive him of his seat in Parliament. He succeeded in the first but not in the second and of course made him a martyr and popular hero in the process.

Dr Johnson's House

Cross New Fetter Lane here and turn right past the plaque on the left commemorating the Moravians, a Protestant sect from Germany who sought refuge in England in the 18th century. (Their original burial ground still exists behind a high wall at World's End in Chelsea.) On the right you pass the eastern boundary of the Bacon

estate, mentioned on page 67, and the former Public Record Office before turning left into West Harding Street and its continuation (bearing right) Pemberton Row. Follow the signs to **Dr Johnson's house** in Gough Square. Here the Doctor compiled his great dictionary, published in 1755. The adjoining curator's house is said to be the smallest in the City: one can easily believe it. Carrying on past the house into Johnson's Court you eventually come out on Fleet Street (St Paul's to the left). Cross straight over into Pleydell Court (and so into the Radnor estate – see page 67) and continue down Lombard Lane towards the river.

Medieval crypt

At the bottom turn left into Temple Lane, right into Bouverie Street and then left into Magpie Alley. This brings you to the back of 65 Fleet Street, the offices of Freshfields, one of the top law firms in the City. It looks normal enough, but if you peep over the railings into the glass-walled basement you will see a most extraordinary thing: a complete little medieval building encased within the modern structure above and around it. This is the modern way of preserving and displaying archaeological remains – of which there are many in the City – and it seems to work very well. The crypt, for that is what it is, is the only surviving building from the medieval monastery of **Whitefriars**. For centuries it lay hidden beneath a house in Britton Court, serving as a coal cellar. When Britton Court was swept away it was unearthed and incorporated in this new building, still in its original position. It has now stood here for something like 700 years. If you would like to take a closer look, there are steps down on the left. Continue on into Ashentree Court. Turn right on Whitefriars Street and then left into Primrose Hill and follow it round to the left up past the back of the Harrow pub. At the end under the office block climb the steps up to Salisbury Square and turn right. In the middle stands a memorial to yet another freedom-loving Lord Mayor and MP, this one being Robert Waithman, a self-made man and a powerful advocate of parliamentary reform and other radical causes in the early 19th century. He just lived to see the passing of the Reform Act in 1832.

Printing library

Go past the obelisk into St Bride's Passage, a sort of raised courtyard with St Bride's Church on the left and the **St Bride Foundation Institute** and printing library ahead. Go down the steps by the library entrance and turn right at the bottom. At New Bridge Street, cross over (you may have to use the lights, left) into Pilgrim Street and go up the steps. Carry on at the top

and take the first right into Ludgate Broadway followed by an immediate left into Cobb's Court. Follow this round to the right and cross Carter Lane into Church Entry. Church Entry follows the exact line of the crossing between the nave and chancel of the great church of the Blackfriars Monastery which at one time sprawled over this whole area. After the dissolution the nave was turned into the local parish church of St Ann Blackfriars, the little churchyard of which survives on the right as a garden. Church Entry leads into Playhouse Yard where, in 1600, Richard Burbage, Shakespeare's friend, opened the Blackfriar's Playhouse in one of the old monastic buildings. Turn left into Ireland Yard. Haberdasher William Ireland lived here in one of the monastery gatehouses before Shakespeare bought it in 1613. Walk along past the second little church garden (the actual site of the church of St Ann Blackfriars) and take the second left into Burgon Street. At Carter Lane cross over into Creed Lane and turn immediately left into Ludgate Square. This curving street (not a square at all) brings you out on the main thorough-fare of Ludgate Hill. Here turn right. Cross over to the forecourt of St Paul's Cathedral and make your way round its left-hand side, staying outside the railed churchyard. St Paul's Underground station, where the walk ends, is at the far end on the left.

Chapter 9

SPECIAL COLLECTION

L ondon must be as well endowed as any other city with museums, galleries, historic buildings and other attractions which are regularly open to the public. It probably also compares pretty well when it comes to places which are not regularly open but which still admit visitors, usually on guided tours. Some of these places have been mentioned elsewhere in the book: the livery halls in the City for example, or the Foreign Office in Whitehall. Here I describe a further seven of them, including a beautiful roof garden in Kensington, a 600-year-old bell foundry in the East End and a refuge for homeless women in Soho. All the places are little known and all reveal yet more of the many hidden faces of London. The chapter concludes with two classic, but unique, establishments where you can find food and drink. By this time you will no doubt be in need of some refreshment!

KENSINGTON ROOF GARDENS

Among all the private roof terraces and roof gardens in London, there is none quite like the **Kensington Roof Gardens**. Covering 1½ acres (½ hectare), making them the largest in Europe, they are laid out on top of a department-store building in Kensington High Street. Because the store for which they were originally constructed, Derry & Toms, has been closed for many years, their existence has been largely forgotten. The gardens are divided into three themed areas, two on the north side overlooking the High Street and a larger one on the south side. The larger one is the English woodland garden, an informal area of curving lawn and trees up to 40 feet (12 metres) high, through which runs a stream crossed by two little bridges. At one end of the stream a little lake is home to a pair of pink flamingos and a dozen or so clipped-wing ducks, the latter often sought out as mates by lustful mallard flying in from Hyde Park. Walking past the lake you come to the Tudor garden, a series of three little walled courtyards with creeper-covered walls, floors made of bricks laid in a herringbone pattern, and old roses overflowing in a rustic, higgledy-piggledy sort of way from the flowerbeds. In the centre a fountain plays, fostering the illusion of a rural idyll far from the madding crowd.

From the Tudor garden, a paved walk through a series of roughly carved Tudor arches salvaged from some unidentified stately home leads to the *pièce de résistance* of the whole garden: the formal Spanish garden with its clipped lawns, neat paths lined with coloured tiles, palm trees and whitewashed, red-tiled mock convent complete with campanile and well. The Spanish garden is much more open and feels more spacious than the other two and on a sunny day looks quite stunning, the white walls setting off the colours of the trees and shrubs and flowering plants. The spire of St Mary Abbots rising gracefully into the sky beyond makes the whole scene even more picturesque.

Sun Pavilion

The gardens date from the 1930s. Conceived by Trevor Bowen, head of the Barker's Stores empire, they were begun in the summer of 1936 and completed two years later at a cost of £25,000. Ralph Hancock, a leading gardener of the day, was responsible for the landscape design. Barker's in-house architect, Bernard George, designed the central Sun Pavilion, now a nightclub. This is a marvellous sanatorium-style 1930s building with a curving glass façade on the south side to catch the rays. Here shoppers used to take a cup of tea or coffee before strolling through the gardens and admiring the views from the balconies around the outer edge. Sadly the balconies are now all closed but there are still some places (such as the portholes on the south side) where you can glimpse a panorama. The gardens were laid out over Derry & Toms, a famous Kensington store which had been taken over by Barker's in 1920. Barker's itself was taken over by House of Fraser in 1957. In 1973 Derry & Toms was shut down and the gardens passed into other hands. Since 1981 they, and the nightclub in the middle, have belonged to Richard Branson's Virgin group. Virgin have generously opened them to the public when the club is not in use. The ground-floor entrance is at the bottom of Derry Street on the right-hand side. Take the lift up to the top floor, turn left and there you are, in a mature garden with lawns, trees, shrubs and a stream 100 feet (30 metres) above the noisy bustle of one of west London's most fashionable shopping streets. The sensation is really quite strange.

TYBURN CONVENT

A little over 200 years ago the Marble Arch traffic interchange was the site of Tyburn Tree, London's main place of execution. A plaque on the traffic island at the junction of the interchange with the Edgware Road marks the approximate site of the gallows. Between the 12th century and 1783, when the gallows were moved to Newgate

Prison in the City, an estimated 50,000 people lost their lives here. One hundred and five of that number were Catholic martyrs executed during the Protestant Reformation of the 16th and 17th centuries. The first to go, in 1535, was John Houghton, Prior of the London Charterhouse (see page 156). The last, in 1681, was no less a figure than the Primate of all Ireland, the Blessed Oliver Plunket. He had been accused of complicity in the Popish Plot. Following the rehabilitation of Roman Catholics in Britain in the 19th century, pressure built up for the construction of a shrine to the Tyburn martyrs. Eventually in 1902 a house was bought for the purpose in Hyde Park Place close to the site of the gallows. The following year it was handed over to a homeless order of French nuns. They quickly established the **Tyburn convent** and the shrine to the martyrs and they have been collecting relics and praying for the souls of the martyrs ever since. The shrine is a simply furnished chapel in the basement of the convent. On the walls there are pictures and relics of the martyrs. Over the altar stands a large reconstruction of the Tyburn gibbet, a triangular affair from which up to 20 victims could be suspended at one time. The nuns who show you round know the stories of all the martyrs and will happily answer any questions you have about them.

Haven of tranquillity

Above the shrine is the main chapel of the convent, open to the public all day and accessible direct from the Bayswater Road. Silent and pristine and always occupied by at least one or two nuns fulfilling the order's commitment to constant prayer and contemplation, it is a haven of peace and tranquillity just a few minutes' walk from the hustle and bustle of Oxford Street. The 25 Tyburn nuns belong to the sisters of the Adoration of the Sacred Heart of Jesus of Montmartre. This is an enclosed Benedictine order, which means that the nuns never leave the convent, not even to visit relatives. Once enrolled they spend all their time in study and prayer, apart from just one hour a day when they relax, talk, play games and take exercise in the convent garden. Snooker and scrabble are their favourite indoor pursuits. Outdoors they like to hitch up their habits, skip and play netball and badminton. In the early 1990s they put their fondness for games to good use when they held the first Nuns' World Snooker Championship and a sponsored skip to raise money for urgent building repairs. The Tyburn shrine is the finishing point for the Tyburn Walk, an annual event on the last Sunday in April when a silent procession led by a Catholic bishop walks from the site of Newgate Prison in the City, following the exact route taken by the martyrs and all the other unfortunates who suffered the extreme penalty at Tyburn. The walk is about 3 miles (5 kilometres) long and

Plate 32: The mock Spanish convent in the Kensington Roof Gardens (see page 150).

Plate 33: *The replica 17th-century goldsmith's shop inside Coutts' Bank (see page 155).*

Plate 34: *Casting bells in the Whitechapel Bell Foundry in east London (see page 158). The Foundry has been in existence for over 400 years, and on its existing site for over 200. There are occasional tours of the works.*

Plate 35: *Front door of the 18th-century House of St Barnabas-in-Soho (see page 153), an emergency refuge for homeless women. Guided tours of the refuge are an interesting and unusual experience.*

Plate 36: Charterhouse: former school buildings, now offices (see page 156). Once a medieval monastery, Charterhouse became a school and almshouse four centuries ago. It is still an almshouse today and can be visited on Wednesday afternoons in summer.

Plate 37: The medieval Wash House Court, a tranquil corner of the old Carthusian monastery of Charterhouse (see page 157).

takes roughly two hours, starting at 3 p.m. There is a special martyrs' service in the shrine on arrival.

HOUSE OF ST BARNABAS-IN-SOHO

Cycling around Berkeley Square at dusk with house lights on and the windows still uncurtained, I invariably look up to catch a glimpse of the richly decorated gold and blue ceiling of the principal first-floor room of No. 44 on the west side of the square. This ceiling and the rest of the sumptuous interior led architectural critic Sir Nikolaus Pevsner to dub the house, built about 1744 for royal maid of honour Lady Isabella Finch, the finest terrace house in London. Elsewhere in the West End there are many other houses, externally unexceptional but with remarkable interiors representing three centuries of changing tastes in design and architecture. Home House at 20 Portman Square, for example, is Robert Adam's finest London town house. 20 St James's Square, designed by him two years earlier in 1771, is a close runner-up. 16 Carlton House Terrace, headquarters of the Crown Estate Commissioners, is a magnificent ornamental extravaganza designed by Robert Owen, author of the influential *Grammar of Ornament* published in 1856. 1 South Audley Street, dating from 1878, is an equally magnificent exercise in the high Victorian 'artistic' manner. 46 Grosvenor Street nearby, the 1910 home of German-born banker Sir Edward Speyer, perfectly evokes the opulence, the vulgarity almost, of the Edwardian plutocracy.

Refuge for the homeless

All these houses and many more similar ones not mentioned have long since passed out of private hands into commercial or institutional use. While the organizations that occupy them now might well respond favourably to a request for a visit, with one exception none of them is open as such to the public. The exception, which very few people are aware of, is **1 Greek Street** in Soho, an 18th-century corner house fronting both Greek Street and Soho Square. Built about 1746, it is a classic example of a well-to-do domestic interior of the period and the last remaining house to preserve the interior decorations which all the houses in Soho Square once boasted. An added attraction for visitors is that the house is home not, like so many, to some wealthy company, but to a simple, hardup emergency refuge for homeless women, so any money you put in the collecting box (there is no admission charge even though the charity is entirely dependent on voluntary contributions) is going to a good cause. On the tour you see the main staircase and principal rooms, all ornamented with fine plasterwork; the courtyard, on which Charles Dickens modelled the house of Dr Manette in *A Tale* *of Two Cities*; and the little chapel copied from a medieval French original near Arles. You also hear about the work of the charity, which was founded in 1846 and has been here since 1862, and pass through some of the common rooms used by the 29 guests, who may stay here for up to one month while they find their feet and decide what to do. Some find work; others return to their friends and relatives; a number go to homes for the elderly or the mentally handicapped. Altogether about 400 women pass through the house in an average year, enjoying for a few weeks at least warmth, good food, clean surroundings and the privacy of their own cubicle. All in all a visit to St Barnabas is a refreshingly unusual experience and it brings you closer to life in London than visiting any number of museums, galleries and the usual tourist attractions.

COUTTS & CO AND THE PRIVATE BANKS

The City may be the centre of international banking and commerce, but the 1½-mile (2.5-kilometre) long thoroughfare formed by Fleet Street and the Strand is *par excellence* the territory of the private bank. Originating from goldsmiths' shops in the 17th century, the **private banks** deal with wealthy individuals rather than *hoi polloi* like the high-street retail banks. The irony is that with one exception all the private banks are today owned by the high-street banks and are allowed to retain their customs and traditions and their separate identities only because of their commercial importance as brands.

Child & Co.

Child & Co. at 1 Fleet Street is the oldest bank in Britain. Founded in 1559 by the Blanchard family, it was inherited by Francis Child and established on this site in 1673. The Childs went on to amass great wealth, and built themselves a country house at Osterley Park in west London now owned by the National Trust. Today, Child's is the private banking arm of the Royal Bank of Scotland. The Royal Bank also owns Drummond's, an 18th-century bank on the south side of Trafalgar Square. Both Drummond's and Child's have cases of muskets in their banking halls, acquired after the Gordon Riots of 1780.

Gosling's

A little further on from Child's at 19 Fleet Street is the Gosling branch of Barclays Bank. Founded about 1650, Gosling's could easily be a private banking arm, but it is not. Something is made of its history, however. Its Three Squirrels street sign is the original 17th-century pewter one. Inside, a board lists all the Goslings involved in the bank from the earliest days up to 1965.

Hoare's Bank

Continuing on down Fleet Street you come to Hoare's Bank at the sign of the Golden Bottle, now No. 37. Founded by Richard Hoare in 1672 and still run by the Hoare family, this is the only surviving independent private bank. It's been on this site since 1690 and in this historic building since 1829. Inside nothing much has changed in the old-fashioned banking hall with its panelled walls, stone-flagged floor and high mahogany counter topped off with a decorative brass rail. The cast-iron stove in the centre, however, no longer pumps out heat. That function has been taken over by a more up-to-date system. Should the frock-coated doorman allow you into the hall for a quick look, you will see through the window at the back a courtyard surrounded by more buildings. Here present-day Hoares still have rooms, for the bank has maintained its tradition of always having at least one partner on the premises day and night for the benefit of its valued customers.

Coutts & Co.

The largest private bank – and possibly the best-known because of its connection with the Queen – is Coutts & Co., at 440 Strand opposite Charing Cross Station, founded in 1692 by Scotsman John Campbell. The Coutts family married into the bank in 1755, and until the 1990s there were still members of the Coutts family on the board. Today the bank is back in Scottish hands as part of the Royal Bank of Scotland group. The royal connection dates from the 18th century when Thomas Coutts, the key figure in the bank's history, acquired the Privy Purse account. Today it is the sole account handled by the Villiers branch, one of five little branches inside the 440 Strand building. Traditionally, correspondence on the account travelled between Buckingham Palace and 440 Strand by means of horse and carriage, but this picturesque custom had to be stopped in 1993 after one too many collisions with cars in this always congested part of London.

When Coutts celebrated their 300th anniversary in 1992 they created some exhibits to bring their long history to life for staff and customers. One of them can be seen in the impressive garden court atrium hall at the top of the escalator. Behind the screen is a beautifully reconstructed late 17th-century goldsmith's shop with the bank's founder, John Campbell, seated at a desk conversing with an early customer, fellow Campbell the Duke of Argyll. In the window, an apprentice sits working at his jewellery. The scales, taper holder, account book and other exhibits come from the bank's own museum collection. Also in the atrium are some family portraits and display cabinets featuring pictures and documents from the bank's archives relating to former distinguished customers.

Chinese wallpaper

Upstairs is the large square boardroom, the main feature of which is its hand-painted Chinese wallpaper. This was given to the bank by Britain's first ambassador to China in 1794. The paper is very unusual because it was produced for China's domestic market, not for export. It is extraordinarily lucky to have survived because it has been moved twice in its 200-year life: once when Coutts moved to this site from 59 Strand in 1904, and again in the 1970s when this building (originally a John Nash creation of the 1830s) was completely reconstructed internally. Down in the bank's vaults is the main part of its historical collection. Besides records and artefacts associated with the bank itself, it includes a unique collection taken out of forgotten customers' deposit boxes, what the bank calls its Customer Oubliette (*oublier* is French for 'to forget'). In the 1980s 3,500 of these forgotten boxes, some of them left with the bank in the 18th century, were opened, revealing a treasure trove of letters, papers, gold, silver, jewels and other valuable and historic items. Where possible, things were returned to astonished descendants of the original depositors. But much remains, in particular a beautiful guitar in a green leather case. It was deposited a few days before the Battle of Waterloo and still awaits collection.

CHARTERHOUSE

What with the Great Fire of 1666 and the Blitz of 1940–41 very little of old London is left for us to enjoy today. One forgotten corner is the old Carthusian monastery of **Charterhouse** in an unfrequented part of London north of Smithfield market. Step through the old archway past the great oaken gate and you find yourself in a world within a world, one with all the peace and tranquillity that seems to be naturally associated with ancient things. The monastery was founded in 1370 by Sir Edward Manny, one of Edward III's most famous knights. After the dissolution (when its prior became the first Catholic martyr of the Reformation – see page 152) it was turned into a royal tent store and then a nobleman's mansion. In 1611 City merchant Thomas Sutton bought it and endowed it in his will so that it could be run as a school and an almshouse. The school developed into the well-known boys' public school of Charterhouse before it moved out to its present site at Godalming in 1872. The almshouse, somewhat reduced in size, continues meanwhile.

Impoverished pensioners

The 40 inmates are all impoverished male pensioners, from various walks of life. They each have their own room in the main courtyard, furnished with their own things if they choose, and they take their meals together in the Great Hall, looked down on by figures from the past in gleaming old portraits. Should they fall ill or become incapacitated there is a fully equipped infirmary with a resident matron where they can be properly cared for. The tour of the almshouse, which takes place on Wednesday afternoons between April and July, includes the Great Hall and the Master's or main courtyard. You also see the medieval Wash House Court, the monks' refectory, now the Brothers' Library, the chapel, the steel-doored treasury in the tower above, now a sort of archive room though it needs doing up a bit, and the tapestried and gilded Great Chamber where James I was proclaimed king and and where he dubbed 133 knights in 1603. From the vestibule of the Great Chamber you step out on to the roof walk above a section of the old cloister. This gives you a good view of the original Charterhouse enclave. To the left, old school buildings have been let out as offices to add to the house's income. To the right, the Great Cloister lawn is now part of the medical school of St Bartholomew's Hospital in nearby Smithfield. St Bart's is an even more ancient foundation than Charterhouse.

THE ROYAL INSTITUTION OF GREAT BRITAIN

At first sight there would appear to be little connection between the fashionable quarter of Mayfair and the world of science. Yet this playground of playboys is in fact home to one of the most historic scientific institutions in the world and the place where Michael Faraday made the discoveries in electromagnetic induction which laid the foundation of today's electrical industries. With its grand premises off Piccadilly and its televised Christmas lectures, you might think that the **Royal Institution of Great Britain** would be famous up and down the land. But the truth is that it is one of the great unknown scientific shrines. Part of the problem lies in its excessively grandiose name which says so much about its status but so little about its activities. The Royal Society is in fact a learned society specializing in science. It would be much better called something like the Royal Scientific Society. The Institution was founded in 1799 by the American Count Rumford with the twin aims of carrying out scientific research and raising the public understanding of science. Faraday, who lived and worked at the Institution for 50 years, was pre-eminent at both. Besides being possibly the greatest experimental scientist who has ever lived, he was also a gifted communicator: in fact it was he who started the Christmas lectures for children way back in 1826. The acoustically perfect lecture theatre where Faraday delivered his lectures and where the modern televised lectures are given, is one of the highlights of a tour of the Royal Institution build-ing. You also see the library, conversation room and some other beautiful Georgian spaces dating from the time when the building was a private house. Also on show are two collections of fascinating scientific apparatus. Upstairs, the Ambulatory houses, among other things, early versions of the safety lamp for miners invented by Faraday's predecessor, Sir Humphry Davy. Downstairs in what used to be the ser-vants' hall and cellars are Faraday's magnetic laboratory (recreated in modern times on its original site) and a collection of his personal and scientific possessions. What you do not see (for obvious reasons) are the extensive laboratories operated by the Institution. Under the supervision of an eminent scientist who lives in the direc-tor's special second-floor flat, the Institution continues to carry on scientific research just as it has always done. In fact, at any time up to 40 scientists and PhD students are beavering away behind the scenes on state- and industry-funded cut-ting-edge research. A more incongruous activity in the heart of London's art and *haute couture* district would be hard to imagine!

WHITECHAPEL BELL FOUNDRY

For a business employing 35 people to have neither sales force nor marketing depart-ment seems, in these intensely competitive times, quite extraordinary. But then, if you have customers who have been with you for 400 years and only one other competitor, perhaps you can afford to dispense with what any other company would regard as vital necessities. The **Whitechapel Bell Foundry** is the business that finds itself in this for-tunate position. Wimbledon Parish Church and Westminster Abbey are its oldest cus-tomers, and Taylors of Loughborough are its only rival. Between them the two firms share a steady trade for cast bells of all kinds and sizes, from great big bells for cathedral belfries to tiny little bells for grandfather clocks. Big Ben, weighing 13½ tons (13¾ tonnes), is the biggest bell ever cast at Whitechapel. The huge template frames the entrance to the foundry's antiquated premises in the Whitechapel Road. Billiter Street, from the old French word for 'bell founder', was the traditional centre of bell-found-ing in medieval London. But around 1420 Robert Chamberlain set up his bell-found-ing business a little to the east in Aldgate. Here it stayed until 1738 when his succes-sors moved it a little further east still to a former inn on the Whitechapel Road. This is the site of the foundry today. The present owners are the Hughes family, one of whom acts as the guide on the fascinating foundry tour. If you are at all practical or interested in how things are made, the tour is without doubt one of the best things you can do in London.

'Liberty Bell'

Having had an introduction to the history and technique of bell-founding, you pass through the old inn yard to the bell-moulding shop. Here the moulds are prepared and the bells cast. Each bell has two moulds, an inner and an outer one, and the molten bell metal (77 per cent copper, 23 per cent tin) is poured into the space between. All the work is done by hand. The American 'Liberty Bell' was cast here in 1752. Two centuries later the 1976 Bicentennial Bell, a gift from Britain to the USA, was cast in the very same pit. To give you some idea of what bells cost, a ½-ton bell cast from new metal would cost about £4,500 ($6,750). Most bells are in fact made from old ones melted down. In the back foundry beyond the moulding shop, the metal bell frames are assembled and the bell-clappers made. Upstairs, in a warren of small rooms and attics, the small bells are turned and tuned and fitted, if necessary, with leather handles. Here also the great bell wheels, around which the bell-ropes pass in grooves, are constructed out of oak, ash and ply. The last process you see is the tuning of the big bells. They are cast sharp and then flattened down to the correct pitch. Once this was done by tuning fork and human ear, but now a sophisticated electronic method is used, a reminder that while Whitechapel may have a craft tradition stretching back behind it nearly 600 years, it is not afraid to look forward and embrace any new technology that improves the bell-making process.

FOOD AND DRINK

If you want to see what a genuine Victorian grocer's shop looks like you don't have to search for a preserved interior in one of London's thirty-odd local history museums. You just take a trip to **W. Martyn** in Muswell Hill Broadway in north London. Sandwiched between a Sue Ryder charity shop and an Our Price music store, the exterior looks plain enough. But step inside and you travel back in time to the era of Queen Victoria's Jubilee in 1897. This was when the shop was opened by the Martyn family. They have continued to run it ever since, with the result that everything inside is just as it was a century or so ago. The floorboards are still bare, the walls are still lined with the original wooden shelving, the old mahogany counter still runs down the full length of the shop, and people still serve you instead of you helping yourself and taking your things to a central till. All that's changed in fact is the food. Martyn's started out as a general grocers, but has evolved into a tea and coffee specialist and a fine foods store. Not for nothing is it known locally as the Fortnum & Mason of Muswell Hill. You won't find much fresh food here but you will find lots of pickles, preserves, mustards, spices, nuts and hand-made biscuits. Their brightly coloured packaging makes a gay display set off against the dark brown of the old wooden fittings.

The Hoop and Grapes pub

On the eastern edge of the City in Aldgate High Street is the Hoop and Grapes pub, conspicuously old-fashioned and picturesque. Of course it was not designed to be thus, but when a building has been in existence for nearly 400 years it is rather hard for it to look anything else. Constructed early in the 17th century, the Hoop and Grapes escaped by a whisker when the City was destroyed by the Great Fire in 1666. Untouched also by Hitler's bombs, it is now the only surviving timber-framed building in the City. In many other towns and cities elsewhere in England a building like the Hoop and Grapes would be a commonplace, but here in London it is a rarity.

By a stroke of great good fortune the pub occupies a prominent corner site opposite the Aldgate traffic interchange so you can stand well back in the centre of the interchange (accessed by subway) and really appreciate its pleasing scale and appearance in contrast to the more modern buildings all around. Up close there is also much to engage the eye: from the cock-eyed front door and battered stone posts carved with grapes outside, to the stone-flagged floor and exposed timber frame inside. Down in the basement there is said to a smugglers' tunnel linking the pub with the Thames. Of course the tunnel is sealed off now so its existence cannot be verified either way, but if there was such a tunnel in this part of London this would surely be the place for it.

ACKNOWLEDGEMENTS

Many people and organizations have helped me with the research for this book. Some of them – such as the authors of London books and the staff of libraries like the Guildhall Library – have been unwitting assistants. Others have been more knowingly involved. My thanks go to all of them, whether they realized they were helping or not. For special mention I would like to single out English Heritage, London Underground, Thames Water, Chris Pond of the House of Commons, Peter Goddard of Westminster School, Kate Crowe of the Foreign Office, Michelle Bennet of the Cabinet Office, John Harding and Maggie Hughes of the Ministry of Defence, Cathy McGoldrick-Scott of the Scottish Office, David Baldwin of the Chapel Royal, Ian Campbell of Berry Bros. and Rudd, Simon Wedgewood of the Travellers Club, Emma St John-Smith of Westminster Abbey, James Clare of the Corporation of London's Department of Building Services, Roz Sherris of the Museum of London, Joan South of the Leaseholders' Enfranchisement Association, PC James Charman of Marylebone Police Station and, last but not least, Roger Morgan of Subterranea Britannica who kindly checked the chapter on subterranean London.

Among my friends, Jeremy Finnis answered the call as always and gave me a hand with pictures, Toby Helm and Henrietta Rolston took me backstage in the House of Commons, and Duncan Budge, Sarah Elliott, Helena Beaufoy, Wendy Palmer and Robert Terry all came up with valuable snippets of information which played an important part in building up the overall picture.

OPENING TIMES, ADDRESSES AND FURTHER INFORMATION

Many of the places listed here have no special visitor facilities so, if you have a physical impairment of any kind, you would be well advised to ring in advance of your visit to check the exact position.

Hundreds of normally inaccessible places in London, including several mentioned in this book, can be seen on one or two days a year as a result of two special annual access schemes. The **National Gardens Scheme** arranges for private and institutional gardens all over London to be open on selected days in summer to raise money for charity. For details see the yellow *National Gardens Scheme* booklet distributed to public libraries from the spring onwards or ring the Scheme's Hon. County Organizer, Mrs M. Snell, on 01932 864532. **London Open House** arranges for buildings of architectural interest to be open one weekend in September as part of the nationwide Heritage Open Days event. For details see the *Open House* booklet distributed to public libraries from mid-August, write to London Open House at Linton House (Unit C1), 39–51 Highgate Road, London NW5 1RS, or visit their website at www.londonopenhouse.demon.co.uk.

CHAPTER 1

Thames Barrier Visitor Centre
Unity Way, Woolwich SE18.
Tel: 020 8854 1373.
Open 10.00–17.00 Mon–Fri, 10.30–17.30 Sat–Sun.
Admission charge.
Trains: Charlton (from Charing Cross).

St Paul's Cathedral
EC4.
Tel: 020 7246 8348.
Open for sightseeing 08.30–16.00 Mon–Sat.
Admission charge.
Underground: St Paul's (Central Line).

Ice House Gallery
Holland Park W8.
Tel: 020 7602 3316.
Open during exhibitions Apr–Oct 11.00–19.00 Mon–Sun.
Admission free.
Underground: Kensington High Street (District and Circle Lines).

Commonwealth Institute
Kensington High Street W8.
Tel: 020 7603 4535.
Open 10.00–17.00 Mon–Sun.
Admission charge.
Underground: Kensington High Street (District and Circle Lines).

Chelsea Hospital
Royal Hospital Road SW3.
Tel: 020 7881 5204.
Open 10.00–12.00 and 14.00–16.00 Mon–Sat, 14.00–16.00 Sun.
Admission free.
Underground: Sloane Square (District and Circle Lines).

Buckingham Palace
Buckingham Palace Road SW1.
Tel: 020 7799 2331.
Open Aug–Oct 09.30–17.30 Mon–Sun.
Admission charge.
Underground: Green Park (Piccadilly, Victoria and Jubilee Lines), St James's Park (District and Circle Lines).

Queen's Gallery
Buckingham Gate SW1.
Tel: 020 7839 1377.
Closed till 2002.
Underground: Green Park (Piccadilly, Victoria and Jubilee Lines), St James's Park (District and Circle Lines).

Mount Pleasant Sorting Office
Tour Manager, Mount Pleasant Sorting Office EC1.
Tel: 020 7239 2313.
Tours by arrangement Mon–Thur from 14.00.
Admission free.
Underground: Farringdon (Circle, Hammersmith & City and Metropolitan Lines; also connects with trains from London Bridge, Moorgate and King's Cross).

Clerks' Well
14–16 Farringdon Lane EC1.
Tel: 020 7527 7960.
Open by appointment with Finsbury Public Library. Library is open Mon–Sat but closed Wed and Fri p.m.
Admission free.
Underground: Farringdon (Circle, Hammersmith & City and Metropolitan Lines; also connects with trains from London Bridge, Moorgate and King's Cross).

CHAPTER 2

Cabinet War Rooms
Clive Steps, King Charles Street SW1.
Tel: 020 7930 6961.
Open Apr–Sep 09.30–18.00 Mon–Sun (opens 10.00 Oct–Mar). Last admission 17.15. Liable to close at short notice for state occasions.
Admission charge.
Underground: Westminster (District and Circle Lines).

Mail Rail
See Mount Pleasant details under Hidden Landscape.

Abbey Mills Pumping Station
Abbey Lane, Stratford E15.
Thames Water Customer Services.

Tel: 0845 9200800.
Admission free.
Underground: Stratford (Central Line; also trains from Liverpool Street).

Crossness Pumping Station
Belvedere Road, Abbey Wood SE2.
Crossness Beam Engine Trust.
Tel: 020 8311 3711.
Tours by arrangement Tue and Sun.
Admission: donation requested.
Trains: Abbey Wood (from Charing Cross).
Note: Thames Water are happy to arrange visits to their major water and sewage works. Contact the Customer Services, number under Abbey Mills above.

House of Detention
Clerkenwell Close EC1.
Tel: 020 7253 9494.
Open 10.00–18.00 Mon–Sun.
Admission charge.
Underground: Farringdon (Circle, Hammersmith & City and Metropolitan Lines; also connects with trains from London Bridge, Moorgate and King's Cross).

CHAPTER 3

Dulwich Picture Gallery
College Road, Dulwich SE21.
Tel: 020 8693 5254.
Open 10.00–17.00 Tue–Fri, 11.00–17.00 Sat, 14.00-17.00 Sun, closed Mon.
Admission charge.
Trains: North Dulwich (from London Bridge), West Dulwich (from Victoria).

Crown Estate
16 Carlton House Terrace SW1.
Tel: 020 7210 4377.
Publishes an annual report and has a website at www.crownestate.co.uk

Grosvenor Estate Office
70–72 Grosvenor Street W1.
Tel: 020 7408 0988.
Underground: Bond Street (Central and Jubilee Lines).

Smith's Charity Estate
The estate is managed by Cluttons, Chartered
Surveyors, 48 Pelham Street, SW7.
Tel: 020 7584 3651.
The Wellcome Trust, the new owners, can be con-
tacted on 020 7611 8888.

Linley Sambourne Museum
18 Stafford Terrace W8.
Tel: 020 7937 0663.
Open Mar–Oct 10.00–16.00 Wed, 14.15–16.15
guided tours only Sun.
Admission charge.
Underground: Kensington High Street (District
and Circle Lines).

CHAPTER 4

Rock Circus
London Pavilion, 1 Piccadilly Circus W1.
Tel: 020 7734 7203.
Open 11.00–21.00 Mon, Wed, Thur and Sun.
12.00–21.00 Tue, 11.00–22.00 Fri and Sat.
Admission charge.
Underground: Piccadilly Circus (Bakerloo and
Piccadilly Lines).

CHAPTER 5

Palace of Westminster
SW1. Public Information Office.
Tel: 020 7219 4272.
Security is very tight and there are no general
tours of the Palace. To see any part of it you will
have to do one or more of the following:
1. Turn up for access to Lords and Commons
debates and select committees most days when
Parliament is in session. Ring the Public
Information Office on the above number for
details. As you go into the Commons you will see,
but not go into, Westminster Hall.
2. Book a 'Line of Route' tour through your MP
or a peer. This includes both chambers, the Royal
Apartments and Westminster Hall. Overseas visitors
should apply in writing to the Deputy Education
Officer, House of Commons, London SW1A 0AA.
3. Book a visit to Big Ben through your MP. The
Palace works department, which conducts the

tours, is usually very busy doing more essential
work and may not be able to fit you in for some
time to come.
4. The only way you will be able to see other
parts of the Palace is by having a personal contact
inside. Even then what you will see will depend
on the status of your contact. Obviously MPs,
senior officers or journalists with full passes are
best, though even with one of these you probably
still won't be able to see either the Lord
Chancellor's House or the Speaker's House.
Admission: all visits to the Palace are free.
Underground: Westminster (District and Circle
Lines).

Westminster Abbey
Broad Sanctuary SW1.
Tel: 020 7222 5152.
Abbey: 09.30–15.45 Mon–Fri (also 18.00–19.00
Wed), 09.30–13.45 Sat, closed Sun.
Chapter House, Pyx Chamber and Museum:
10.30–16.00 Mon–Sun.
Garden: 10.00–18.00 Tues–Thur (closes 16.00
Oct–Mar). Band plays Jul and Aug 12.30–14.00
Thur. Closed Thur before Good Friday (Maundy
Thursdays).
Library: May–Sep 11.00–15.00 Wed.
Admission: charge.
Underground: Westminster (District and Circle
Lines).

Westminster School
Little Dean's Yard SW1.
Tel: 020 7963 1010.
Tours by appointment during the school holidays
(generally last week in Mar, first two weeks in
Apr, Jul, Aug, and last two weeks of Oct). Groups
of 10–20 preferred.
Admission charge.
Underground: Westminster (District and Circle
Lines).

CHAPTER 6

Foreign and Commonwealth Office
King Charles Street SW1A 2AF.
Tel: 020 7210 3865.
The FCO's Historical Branch organizes tours
by appointment, usually only for groups with
satisfactory accreditation.

Admission free.
Underground: Westminster (District and Circle Lines).

Banqueting House
Whitehall SW1.
Tel: 020 7839 8918.
Open 10.00–17.00 Mon–Sat. May close at short notice for government functions.
Admission charge.
Underground: Charing Cross (Bakerloo, Jubilee and Northern Lines), Embankment (Bakerloo, District, Circle and Northern Lines), Westminster (District and Circle Lines).

Government Art Collection
No visits.
Tel: 020 7580 9120.
For more information about the Collection, the magazines *Country Life* and *Apollo* (9 November 1989 and November 1989, respectively) contain articles about its history, development and contents, and the National Art Library at the Victoria & Albert Museum has the Paris and Bonn catalogues and a series of annual acquisitions lists starting in 1979. A catalogue of 20th-century works in the collection was published in 1997. For information on possible forthcoming exhibitions containing works from the collection, contact the Culture, Media and Sport Department on 020 7211 6000.

CHAPTER 7

Travellers Club
106 Pall Mall SW1.
Tel: 020 7930 8688.
Guided tours by appointment Mon–Fri.
Admission charge.
Underground: Green Park (Jubilee, Piccadilly and Victoria Lines), Piccadilly Circus (Bakerloo and Piccadilly Lines).

Alfred Dunhill Museum
48 Jermyn Street SW1.
Tel: 020 7838 8233.
Open 09.30–18.00 Mon–Fri, 10.00–18.00 Sat.
Admission free.
Underground: Green Park (Jubilee, Piccadilly and Victoria Lines), Piccadilly Circus (Bakerloo and Piccadilly Lines).

Spencer House
27 St James's Place SW1.
Tel: 020 7499 8620.
Guided tours Feb–Jul and Sep–Dec 10.30–17.30 Sun. Tours leave every 20 minutes 11.15–16.45.
Admission charge.
Underground: Green Park (Jubilee, Piccadilly and Victoria Lines), Piccadilly Circus (Bakerloo and Piccadilly Lines).

Chapel Royal
St James's Place SW1.
Tel: 020 7930 4832.
Sun services, from first Sun in Oct until Good Friday, are usually at 08.30 (Holy Communion) and 11.15 (Sung Eucharist or Sung Morning Prayer). For up-to-date times check in preceding Saturday's *Times* or *Daily Telegraph* newspapers. There are also public services on Prayer Book Saints' Days (Holy Communion 12.30), Ash Wednesday (Sung Evensong 18.00), and Ascension Day (Sung Eucharist 17.45). The 1662 prayer book is used for all services.
Underground: Green Park (Jubilee, Piccadilly and Victoria Lines), Piccadilly Circus (Bakerloo and Piccadilly Lines).

Christie's
8 King Street SW1.
Tel: 020 7839 9060.
Viewing galleries open 09.00–16.30 Mon–Fri, 14.00–17.00 most Suns with late-night viewing on Tue till 20.00.
Admission free.
Underground: Green Park (Jubilee, Piccadilly and Victoria Lines), Piccadilly Circus (Bakerloo and Piccadilly Lines).

CHAPTER 8

Billingsgate Bath-house
100 Lower Thames Street EC3.
Tel: 020 7332 1772.
Access by arrangement with the Historic Buildings Officer, Department of Buildings and Services, Corporation of London, Guildhall EC2.
Underground: Tower Hill (District and Circle Lines).

Bank of England Museum
Bank of England, Threadneedle Street EC2.
Tel: 020 7601 5545.
Open 10.00–17.00 Mon–Fri.
Admission free.

Underground: Bank (Central and Northern Lines).

Mansion House
Walbrook EC4.
Tel: 020 7626 2500.
Group tours by written application 11.00 and 14.00 Tue, Wed and Thur.
Admission free.
Underground: Bank (Central and Northern Lines).

London Metal Exchange
56 Leadenhall Street EC3.
Tel: 020 7264 5555.
Visits to the viewing gallery by appointment.
Admission free.
Underground: Monument/Tower Hill (District and Circle Lines).

City Information Office
St Paul's Churchyard EC4.
Tel: 0207 332 1456.
Open Apr–Sep 09.30–17.00 Mon–Sun;
Oct–Mar 09.30–17.00 Mon–Fri, 09.30–12.30 Sat.
Underground: St Paul's (Central Line).

Goldsmiths' Hall
Foster Lane EC2.
Tel: 020 7606 7010.
Ring for dates of silversmiths' fair and degree show.
Admission charge.
Underground: St Paul's (Central Line).

Monument
Monument Street EC3.
Tel: 020 7403 3761.
Open 10.00–18.00 Mon–Fri, 14.00–18.00 Sat–Sun (last admission 17.40).
Admission charge.
Underground: Monument (District and Circle Lines).

Spanish and Portuguese Synagogue
Off Bevis Marks EC3.
Tel: 020 7626 1274.
Open Sun, Mon and Fri 11.30–13.00, Tues 10.30–16.00, Wed 10.30–13.00.
Admission: donation requested.
Underground: Aldgate (Circle and Metropolitan Lines).

Dr Johnson's House
17 Gough Square EC4.
Tel: 020 7353 3745.
Open 11.00–17.30 Mon–Sat (closes 17.00 Oct–Apr). Last admission 16.45. Closed Sun and Bank Holidays.
Admission charge.
Underground: Blackfriars (District and Circle Lines), Chancery Lane (Central Line).

Central Criminal Courts
Old Bailey EC4.
Tel: 020 7248 3277.
Courts open 10.30–16.00 Mon–Fri with adjournment for lunch (children under 14 and cameras, recorders, bags and packages not allowed).
Admission free.
Underground: St Paul's (Central Line).

Gresham College
Barnard's Inn Hall, Holborn EC1.
Tel: 020 7831 0575.
Write or ring for details of free public lectures.
Underground: Chancery Lane (Central Line).

Whitefriars Crypt
Freshfields, 65 Fleet Street EC4.
Tel: 020 7936 4000.
Crypt visible from outside at all times. For an appointment to see inside, contact the Premises Manager at Freshfields.
Admission free.
Underground: Blackfriars (District and Circle Lines).

St Bride Printing Library
Bride Lane EC4.
Tel: 020 7353 4660.
Open 09.30–17.30 Mon–Fri.
Admission free.
Underground: Blackfriars (District and Circle Lines).

CHAPTER 9

Kensington Roof Gardens
99 Kensington High Street W8 (entrance in Derry Street).
Tel: 020 7937 7994.
Open 09.00–17.00 Mon–Sun provided the club is not in use. Ring first to check.
Admission free.
Underground: Kensington High Street (District and Circle Lines).

Tyburn Convent
8 Hyde Park Place, Bayswater Road W2.
Tel: 020 7723 7262.
Guided tours of the shrine 10.30, 15.30 and 17.30 Mon–Sun. 'Monastic Afternoon' (comprising talk on the martyrs, tea, tour of the shrine, slide show on the life of the nuns, and vespers) first Sun of each month 14.00–17.00. Chapel open for prayer 06.30–20.30. Mass 07.30 Mon–Sun.
Admission free.
Underground: Marble Arch (Central Line).
For information about the Tyburn Walk contact The Guild of Our Lady of Ransom, 31 Southdown Road, Wimbledon SW20. Tel: 020 8947 2598.

1 Greek Street (House of St Barnabas-in-Soho)
1 Greek Street W1.
Tel: 020 7437 1894.
Open for short guided tours 14.30–16.30 Wed, 11.00–12.30 Thur (ring first to check). For parties of 10 or more, write for an appointment to the Guide, c/o the Warden's Office.
Admission free but donations are appreciated.
Underground: Tottenham Court Road (Central and Northern Lines).

Private Banks
Child's: 1 Fleet Street EC4.
Tel: 020 7353 4080.
Drummonds: 49 Charing Cross SW1.
Tel: 020 7839 1200.
Barclays (Gosling branch): 19 Fleet Street EC4.
Tel: 020 7441 5800.
Hoare's: 37 Fleet Street EC4.
Tel: 020 7353 4522.
Coutts & Co.: 440 Strand WC2.
Tel: 020 7753 1000.
All the banking halls are open at least 09.30–15.30 Mon–Fri.

Underground for Fleet Street banks: Temple/Blackfriars (District and Circle Lines). Underground for Coutts and Drummonds: Charing Cross (Bakerloo, Jubilee and Northern Lines).

Charterhouse
Charterhouse Square EC1.
Tel: 020 7253 9503.
Guided tours Apr–Jul 14.15 Wed.
Admission charge.
Underground: Barbican (Circle, Metropolitan and Hammersmith & City Lines).

The Royal Institution of Great Britain
21 Albemarle Street W1.
Tel: 020 7409 2992.
The Faraday Museum is open Mon–Fri 10.00–18.00 (admission charge). The rest of the building is open during the British Association-sponsored National Science Week in March and the London Open House event in September. Otherwise group tours by appointment throughout the year. Non-members may obtain tickets to the annual Christmas lectures (charge) and to the occasional public lunchtime lecture (free).
Underground: Green Park (Jubilee, Piccadilly and Victoria Lines), Piccadilly Circus (Bakerloo and Piccadilly Lines).

Whitechapel Bell Foundry
32 & 34 Whitechapel Road E1.
Tel: 020 7247 2599.
Tours by appointment 10.00 Sat.
Admission charge.
Underground: Aldgate East (District and Hammersmith & City Lines).

W. Martyn
135 Muswell Hill Broadway N10.
Tel: 020 8883 5642.
Open 09.30–17.30 Mon, 09.30–13.00 Thur, 09.00–17.30 Sat.
Underground: Highgate (Northern Line).

Hoop and Grapes
47 Aldgate High Street EC3.
Tel: 020 7265 5171.
Pub open 11.00–22.00 Mon–Wed, 11.00–23.00 Thur and Fri. Closed Sat and Sun.
Underground: Aldgate (Metropolitan and Circle Lines).

BIBLIOGRAPHY

A good deal of the information in this book came from personal observation, correspondence and conversations, and from ephemeral sources such as cuttings, leaflets and brochures. Periodicals I found most useful were *London's Industrial Archaeology* and *Country Life*, which has a special London number every November. *The Times London History Atlas*, the *History of the King's Works*, the *Victoria County History for Middlesex*, the *Survey of London*, *Who's Who* and the one-volume *London Encyclopedia* all proved indispensable reference works. On individual subjects I made use of the following:

Barton, N., *The Lost Rivers of London*, 1992
Bell, W. G., *Unknown London*, 1966
Beresford, P., *The Sunday Times Book of the Rich*, 1991
Borg, A., *War Memorials*, 1991
Boyne, H., *The Houses of Parliament*, 1981
Campbell, D., *War Plan UK*, 1982
Connor, J. E. and Halford, B. L., *The Forgotten Stations of Greater London*, 1991
Cormack, P., *Westminster Palace and Parliament*, 1981
Fitter, R. S. R., *London's Natural History*, 1945
Freeman, J., *London Revealed*, 1989
Friedman, J., *Inside London*, 1988
Georgano, G. N., *A History of the London Taxicab*, 1972
Gill, C., ed., *The Duchy of Cornwall*, 1987
GLC, *Historic Buildings in London*, 1975
Green, S., *Who Owns London?*, 1986
Imray, J., *The Charity of Richard Whittington*, 1968
Kelly, A., *Mrs Coade's Stone*, 1990
Laune, P., *Beneath City Streets*, 1979
Lejeune, A., *The Gentlemen's Clubs of London*, 1979
Ormsby, H., *London on the Thames*, 1924
Tanner, L., *History and Treasures of Westminster Abbey*, 1953
Tanner, L., *Westminster School*, 1951
Trench, R., and Hillman, E., *London Under London*, 1985
Tyburn, Nuns of, *Tyburn Hill of Glory*, 1953
Wooldridge, S. W. and Hutchings, G., *London's Countryside*, 1957

INDEX

Abbey Mills pumping
station 53, 163
Abchurch Lane 139
Adam, Robert 108, 128,
153
Addle Hill 12
Adelphi Terrace 12
Admiralty 45, 108–110
citadel 45
First Lord's house
109–10
Admiralty Arch 110
Adoration of the Sacred
Heart of Jesus of
Montmartre 152
Air Pilots and Air Navi-
gators, Guild of 132
Albert Gate 26
Albion pub 19, 20
Aldgate 158
Aldwych 54
Alexander, General Sir
James 81
Alexander estate 56, 70
Alexandra Road 23
Alfred Dunhill Museum
120, 165
All Hallows Church (City)
140
All Hallows London Wall
Church 22
Alleyn, Edward 61
Amwell Street 19, 20
Angel Court 124, 142
Anne of Cleves 122–3
Annigoni, Pietro 135
Anstruther, Ian Fife
Campbell 70
Apothecaries' Company
132
Argyll, Duke of 70, 155
Arlington Club 114
Armstrong, Captain
George 77
Army and Navy Club
112, 115
Ashburnham House 96,
98–9
Ashentree Court 149
Ashworth, Mr and Mrs 85
Athenaeum 112, 114, 115,
116
Aubrey House 16

Austin Friars 141
Austin Friars Passage 141
Avery Row 31, 65
Aybrook Street 30
Aye Brook *see* Tyburn river
Ayres, Alice 144

Babmaes Street 125–6
Back Hill 40
Bacon, Sir Francis 67
Bacon, Sir Nicholas 67
Bacon estate 56, 67, 148
Bagnigge Wells 39–40
Baker Street 29 30
Bank of England 50, 60,
127, 128, 138, 142
Museum 166
banks, private 154–6, 169
Banqueting House 107,
165
Barbican 55
Barham, Lord 109
Barker's Stores 151
Barkstone Gardens 71
Barnard Park 20
Barnard's Inn 147
Barnsbury Road 20
Barnsbury Street 19, 20
Battersea Park 29
Battersea Power Station
18, 28–9
Bayard's Watering 24
Bayswater Road 24–5,
61–2, 152
Bazalgette, Sir Joseph 52
Beaufort, Duke of 117
Beaufort Street 69
Beck, Henry 83
Bedford estate 56, 66–7
Bedford Row 61, 67
Bedford School 61
Belgravia 17, 65, 66, 77
Belgravia estate 27
Belsize Park tube station
46–7
Belsize Road 23, 68
Bengal Court 140
Bennet's Hill 12
Berkeley Square 31, 71,
153
Berry Bros. & Rudd
123–4
Bethnal Green Road 46

Beverley Brook 43
Bevis Marks 141
Big Ben *see* Westminster,
Palace of
Billingsgate Bath–house
127, 165
Billingsgate fish market 58,
127, 129, 132, 134
Billiter Street 158
Bishopsgate 60, 141
Blackfriars 38, 42
Blackfriars Bridge 46, 49,
50, 59
Blackfriars Monastery 149
Blackfriar's Playhouse 149
Blake, William 58
Blanchard family 154
Blitz 47, 55, 78, 143, 146,
156
Blue Ball Yard 120
blue plaques 73, 84–5
Boltons, The 71
Boodle Hatfield 118
Boodle's Club 117, 118
Borough High Street 59
Borough Station 49
Botolph Alley 140
Botolph Lane 140
Bourne, Widow 124
Bouverie family 67–8
Bouverie Street 67, 148
Bow Church 138
Bow Lane 138
Brangwyn, Frank 133
Branson, Richard 80, 151
Brick Street 33–4
Bridewell Place 42
Bridewell Prison 42, 53
Bridge House Estates 59
Bridgewater House 121
British Museum 66, 69
Research Laboratory 78
Britton Court 149
Broderers' Company 143
Brompton Road 48, 54
Brompton Road tube
station 48
Brook Mews North 23,
24
Brook's Mews 31
Brooks's Club 112, 115,
117, 118, 120
Brook Street 31, 58

Bruton Lane 31
Bruton Place 31, 65
Bruton Street 32
BT Tower 16, 19, 20, 73,
79, 80
Buckingham Palace 18,
35, 45, 80, 155, 162
Budge Row 22
Burbage, Richard 149
Burton, Decimus 114
Bushy Park 63
Byrd, William 122
Byron, Lord 108

cabbies' shelters 77
Cabinet Office 45, 105,
107; *see also*
Whitehall Palace
Cabinet War Rooms
44–5, 46, 47, 163
Cable and Wireless
Communications 50,
51
Cabmen's Shelter Fund
Cadogan, Earl 69
Cadogan estate 56, 69
Cadogan Lane 28
Caledonian market
clocktower 11, 18
Caledonian Park 18,
Calthorpe Street 40
Camden Lock 53
Camden Passage antiques
market 19
Camden Town
Catacombs 53
Camden Town tube
station 46–7
Campbell, John 155
Campden Hill 13, 16, 71
Campden Hill Road 16,
17
Cannon Street 12, 22, 139
Cannon Street Station 22,
133
Canonbury estate 68
Canonbury Square 68
Carlisle Place 35
Carlton Club 115, 116
Carlton Gardens 110
Carlton House 63
Carlton House Terrace 63,
114, 153

Carlyle, Thomas 125
Carpenters' Company 59,
142
Hall 59, 129, 142
Carrington Street 33
Carteret Street 61
Carter Lane 143, 149
Cartwright Gardens 60
Cash estate 58–9
Cathcart Hill 18
Cecil Court 67
Cecil estate 67
Cecil Lane 67
Central Criminal Courts
146, 166
Century House 110
Chadwell Street 19
Chalcot estate 60
Chamberlain, Robert 158
Chancery, Inns of 147
Chancery Lane 67
shelter 46
Chancery Lane tube
station 46
Change Alley 139–40
Chapel Royal *see* St
James's Palace
Charing Cross loop 49
Charing Cross Road 50, 67
Charlbert Bridge 29
Charles I 58
Charles II 40, 96, 104, 106
Charles, Prince 64
Charterhouse 152, 156, 167
Charterhouse School 156
Charterhouse Street 146
Cheapside 138, 140, 143
Chelsea 11, 69, 135, 148
Chelsea, Viscount 69
Chelsea Bridge Road 28,
29, 65
Chelsea Embankment
28
Chelsea Hospital 28–9,
162
Chelsea Waterworks
Company 29
Chesterfield, Lord 68
Chester Wharf 36
Child, Francis 154
Child & Co 154, 167
Christie's 11, 120, 125,
165
Christ's Hospital estate 57,
61
Church Commissioners
61

Church Court 140
Church Entry 149–50
Church estates 57, 61–2
Churchill, Winston 44,
47
Church of England 61
City 11, 12, 18, 22, 47, 50,
55–60, 61, 65,
127–49, 150
markets 128–9
walks 136–50
City and South London
Railway 47, 49
City Corporation 55, 58,
59, 136, 148
Planning Estate 55
City Information Office
133, 135, 166
City of London School
122
Clapham Common 12
Clapham Common tube
station 46, 47
Clapham North tube sta-
tion 46, 47
Clapham South tube sta-
tion 46, 47
Claremont Square 19
Clarence House 121
Clements Lane 140
Cleopatra's Needle 73,
81–2
Clerkenwell 40–41, 49
Clerkenwell Green 37, 41
Clerkenwell House of
Detention 53, 163
Clerkenwell Parish
Church 40, 53
Clerks' Well 40–41, 163
Cloak Lane 22
Clothworkers' Company
142
Cloudesley Square 22
clubs *see* gentlemen's clubs
Coade, Eleanor 77–9
Coade stone 77–9
Coade Stone Lion 77–8
Cobb's Court 149
Coke, Lady Mary 16
Colfe's School 132
College Hill 12, 85–6
College Street 133
Colombo House 45
Colonial Office 101
Colville estate 67
Commons, House of *see*
Westminster, Palace of

Commonwealth Institute
17, 162
Conduit Mead 58–9, 65
Conduit Mews 24
Conduit Place 24
Conduit Street 58
Connaught Street 62
Constitution Arch 80
Constitution Hill 12, 34,
Contemporary Arts,
Institute of 45
Cornhill 22, 60
Cornwall, Dukes of 64
Corporation of London
estate 57
Cosmati family 94
Cottage Place 48
Counter's Creek 13, 16,
17, 38
Court, Inns of 147
Coutts, Thomas 155
Coutts & Co. 139, 155,
167
Covent Garden 51, 60, 67,
70
Cranborne, Viscount 67
Crawford Street 66
Creechurch Lane 141
Creed Lane 149
Croker, John Wilson 114
Cromwell, Oliver 103,
104
Crossness pumping station
53, 163
Crown Estate 55, 57,
62–4, 74, 163
Crown Estate
Commissioners 63,
153
Crown Passage 119, 124–5
Crown Reach Riverside
Walk 36
Cubitt Street 40
Culture, Media and Sport
Department of 165
Cumberland Gardens 20
Cumberland Gate 80–1
Cunard Place 141
Curzon Street 32, 45
Cutlers' Company 144

Dartmouth Park Road 18
Davies Mews 31
Davies Street 31, 66
Day, Benjamin 70
Day, Simon 70
Day estate 56, 70

Defence, Ministry of 45,
106–7
Derby Gate 88
Derry & Toms 63, 151
Derry Street 151
Devonshire, Duke of 117
Devonshire Club 116
Devonshire House 32
Dickens, Charles 146, 153
Directors, Institute of
114
Disraeli, Benjamin 142
Dixon, John 81–2
Docklands 50, 58, 132
Dr Johnson's House 148,
166
Dodemead, Walter 70
Doggett, Thomas 135
Doggett's Coat and Badge
Race 135
Dollis Hill 45
Dombey Street 61
Dorset Buildings 12
Dorset Rise 12
Dove Court 142
Dover House *see* Scottish
Office
Dowgate Hill 12, 133
Dowgate ward 23
Downing, George 103–4
Downing Street 103–5
No. 10 104, 106
No. 11 104
No. 12 104–105
Down Street tube station
33, 47
D'Oyley, Ann 71
D'Oyley Street 28
Drapers' Company 20–2,
59–60, 129, 142
Drapers Gardens 60
Drayton Gardens 70
Dresdner Kleinwort
Benson 140
drinking fountains 73, 75
Drummonds 154, 167
Duchess of Bedford's Walk
17
Duchy of Cornwall estate
56, 62, 64
Duchy of Lancaster estate
56, 62, 64
Duke of York's Memorial
114
Duke of York's Steps 45
Duke of York Street 126
Duke's Hotel 120–1

Duke Street St James's 12, 52, 120, 125
Dulwich 43, 61
Dulwich College 61
Dulwich Picture Gallery 61, 163
Dunhills *see* Alfred Dunhill Museum

Ealing 60
Ealing tube station 48
Earl's Court 38, 51, 71
Earl's Sluice 43
Eastcheap 12, 140
East End 46, 61, 150
East India Company 77, 102, 116
East India, Devonshire Sports and Public Schools Club 115
East Smithfield 63
Eaton Square 65
Ebury Bridge Road 65
Edgware Road 61, 66, 151
Edith Grove 71
Edward the Confessor 89, 94, 95
Edward III 64, 90, 156
Edward VI 61
Effra river 36, 43
Eisenhower, Dwight D. 46
Eleanor of Castile 64
Elizabeth I 67, 147
Elizabeth II 121, 135
Ellesmere, Lord 121
Elms Mews 24
Elsworthy Rise 18
Ely, Bishops of 40, 41, 146
Ely Court 147
Ely Place 144, 146
Embankment 50
Emerald Street 61
Epping Forest 59
Eros, Statue of 74–5
Essex Street 12
Eton College 60, 61
Eton College estate 57, 60
Eton Villas 60
Euston Station 18, 53
Evelyn Gardens 69
Eyre estate 56, 68
Eyre Street Hill 40

Falcon Brook 43
Fan Makers' Company 132
Farmers' Company 132

Farrell, Terry 110
Farriers' Company 132
Farringdon Road 40, 41
Farringdon Station 38, 41
Farringdon Street 41, 146
Fenchurch Buildings 141
Fenchurch Street 58, 128, 141
Fetter Lane 148
ffrench-Beytagh, Canon Gonville 143
Finch, Lady Isabella 153
Finch Lane 60
Finchley Road 17
Fishmeters 132
Fishmongers' Company 129, 132, 133, 134, 135
Fish Street Hill 12
Fitzjohn's Avenue 17, 29
Fleet Market 41
Fleet river 10, 11, 13, 18, 23
 outflow 42–3
 valley 12, 20, 37, 38, 40, 41, 68
 walk 37–43
Fleet Road 37
Fleet Sewer 54
Fleet Street 12, 42, 67, 143, 148, 149, 154–5
Fleming, Sir John 70
Folkestone, Viscount 68
Foreign and Commonwealth Office 101–3, 150, 164
Forest Hill 12
Foster Lane 143
Founders' Company Hall 129, 138
Fox, Charles James 71, 117
Fraser, House of 151
Frederick's Place 142–3
French Ordinary Court 140–1
Freshfields 148
Fulham Road 69
Furnival Street 46

Galway, Lord 71
Garlick Hill 12
Garrick Street 51
General Post Office 139
gentlemen's clubs 112–18
 see also individual club names

George, Bernard 151
George II 104
George III 71, 106, 108
George IV (Prince Regent) 63, 80
George Yard 140
Gielgud Theatre 61
Gilbert, Sir Arthur 74–5
Gilbert Street 31
Giltspur Street 128
Glasshouse Street 73
Gloucester Mews West 23
Gloucester Road 70, 77
Gloucester Terrace 24
Goldsmiths' Company 60, 132
 Fair 135
 Hall 129, 133, 135, 166
 Passing Out Exhibition 135
Goldsmith Street 143
Goodge Street tube station 46, 47
Goodrich, Bishop 147
Gosling's Bank 154, 167
Government Art Collection 110–11, 165
Gower Street 110
Gowing, Lawrence 111
Gracechurch Street 127, 140
Grafton Street 58
Grant, Duncan 111
Great Eastern Hotel 128, 129
Great Fire (1666) 22, 86, 138, 156
Great George Street 44
Great Ormond Street Hospital 60
Great Percy Street 20
Great Portland Street 66
Great St Thomas Apostle Street 134
Greek Street 153–4
Green Park 12, 34–5, 54, 63, 64, 121
Green Park tube station 47
Greenwich 11, 12
Greenwich Observatory 53
Greenwich Park 53, 64
Gresham, Sir Thomas 147, 148
Gresham College 147–8, 166

Greville Street 41
Greyfriars' Monastery 85
Grocers' Company 60, 142
Grocers' Hall Gardens 60
Grosvenor Canal 29
Grosvenor estate 26, 56, 65, 118, 163
Grosvenor family 29
Grosvenor Gardens 77
Grosvenor Place 65
Grosvenor Road 29, 36
Grosvenor Square 52, 65
Grosvenor Street 31, 153
Guildhall 86, 138
Guildhall amphitheatre 127, 129
Gunmakers' Company 132
Gunter, Robert 71
Gunter, Sir Ronald 71
Gunter estate 56, 71
Gunter Grove 71
Gurney, Samuel 76
Gutter Lane 143
Gwynne, Nell 40
Gwynne Place 40

Haberdashers' Hall 129, 133
Hammersmith 11, 50
Hampden, John 104
Hampstead 12, 17, 18, 23, 29, 37, 83
Hampstead Heath 10, 37, 42, 48, 59
Hampstead Tube Company 48
Hampstead Way 48
Hampton Court 105, 106, 143
Hampton Court Park 63
Handel, George Frederick 122
Harley family 66
Harley Street 66
Harmsworth House 67
Harper estate 61
Harrington, 3rd Earl of 70
Harrington estate 56, 70
Harrington Gardens 70
Harrods 54, 69
Harrow Road 69
Harrow School 62
Hart Street 140
Hatfield House 67
Hatton Garden 147

Haverstock Hill 29
Hay Hill 32
Haymarket 63
Hay's Wharf 59
Heneage Lane 141
Henry III 94,
Henry IV 97
Henry V 122
Henry VI 60
Henry VII 96
Henry VIII 62, 66, 91, 99, 101, 105, 107, 122–3
Herbal Hill 40
Hereford Square 70
Herland, Hugh 100
Hertford Street 33
Highgate 11, 12,18, 37, 86
Highgate Hill 86
Highgate Wood 59
High Holborn 46
Hippodrome 14
Hoare's Bank 155, 167
Hockney, David 111
Holbein, Hans 122–3
Holborn 41, 46, 50, 54, 147
Holborn Viaduct 41, 50, 63
Holland, 1st Lord 71
Holland, 3rd Lord 16
Holland House estate 71
Holland Park 13, 16–17,
Holland Street 17
Holland Walk 16, 17
Home House 153
Home Office 101
Hoop and Grapes pub, 160, 167
Homers' Company 132
Hornton Street 17
Horseferry Road 44
Horse Guards 105, 107, 108, 109
Horseguards Avenue 107
Horse Guards building 101
Horse Guards Parade 104, 105, 108, 109–110
Horse Guards Road 44, 45
Horsham 61
Houghton, John 152
Howard, Catherine 123
Howard de Walden, 9th Baron 66

Howard de Walden estate 56, 66
Huggin Hill 12, 129, 167
Hughes family 134, 158
Hungerford Bridge 49
Hyde Park 17, 23, 24, 25, 54, 63–4, 68, 80, 150
Hyde Park Corner 47, 80
Hyde Park Comer tube station 47
Hyde Park estate 61, 62

Ice House gallery (Holland Park) 14, 162
Ilchester, Earls of 71
India Office 101–103
Information Technologists' Company 132
International Financial Centre 141
Ireland, William 149
Ireland Yard 149
Ironmonger Lane 127
Islington 13, 19, 61, 68
Islington estate 68

James I 157
James II 106
James Street 31
Jason Court 31
Jermyn Street 118, 120, 126
John, Augustus 111
Johnson, Samuel 148
Johnson's Court 148
Joint Grand Gresham Committee 148
Jones Street 31
Judd, Sir Andrew 60
Judd Street 60
Junior Carlton Club 115

Kempster, William 128
Kennington 64
Kensal Rise 23
Kensington 14, 55, 71, 77
Kensington and Chelsea, London Borough of 69–72
Kensington estate 63
Kensington Gardens 17, 64
Kensington High Street 13, 17, 63, 71, 150
Kensington Palace 25

Kensington Palace Gardens 63
Kensington Park Road 77
Kensington Road 77
Kensington Roof Gardens 150–1, 167
Kent, William 106
Kentish Town Road 37
Kenwood 37
Kew 63
Kilburn High Road 23
Kilburn Wells 23
King Charles Street 101
King Edward Street 49, 128
King Henry's Road 18, 60
Kings Arms Tavern (City) 139–40
King's Cross Bridge 37–8
King's Cross Road 38–9
King's Cross Station 18, 37, 54
King's Road, Chelsea 62, 69
King's Scholars 36
King's Scholars' Passage 35–6
King's Scholars' Pond Sewer 36
King Street (EC2) 143
King Street (SW1) 124, 125
King's Troop, Royal Horse Artillery 68
Kingsway telephone exchange 46
Kingsway tram tunnel 54
King William Street 47, 139
King William Street tube station 47, 49
Kinnerton Street 24, 26–7, 66
Knightsbridge 26, 62, 65, 69
Knightsbridge cavalry barracks 25
Kyoto water garden (Holland Park) 17

Ladbroke estate 13, 14
Ladbroke Grove 14–16
Ladbroke Road 14
Ladbroke Square 14
Lamb, Lady Caroline 108
Lambeth 11, 62, 110, 139
Lambeth Bridge 110

Lambeth Hill 12
Lamb's Conduit Street 60–61, 162
Lancaster, Edmund, Earl of 64
Lancaster Gate 62
Lancaster Place 64
Lansdowne Crescent 14–16
Lansdowne House 32
Lansdowne Row 32
Latsis, Captain John 121
Laurence Pountney Hill 12
Leadenhall Market 22, 58, 127
Leadenhall Street 63, 102, 141
Lea river 13, 23
Leathersellers' Company 60, 132, 141
Hall 60,129, 141
Legard family 72
Leicester Square 52, 54, 67
Liberty's 63
Lichfield, Earl of 104
Lichfield House 104
Limehouse 51
Lincoln's Inn Fields 54
Linley Sambourne Museum 164
Lion brewery 78
Little St James's Street 121
Liverpool Road 22
Liverpool Street Station 49, 128
livery companies 129–35
estates 57 59–60
halls 129, 132–5, 151
schools 132
see also individual Company names
Lloyd Baker family 20
Lloyd's 128,129, 139
Lloyd's building 141
Lloyd's Coffee House 139
Lloyd Square 20
Lobb's 124
Lock's (hatters) 124
Lombard Court 140
Lombard Lane 148
Lombard Street 139, 140
London Bridge 46, 49, 50, 59, 134, 135
London Bridge Sewer 22
see also Walbrook river

London College of
Printing 84
London Electricity plc 52
London Hydraulic Power
Company 50, 51
London International
Financial Futures and
Options Exchange
128
London Library 125–6
London Metal Exchange
128–9, 166
London Stone 139
London Tunnel Ring
Main 51–2, 54
London Underground
47–50, 83–4
Group 83
map 83–4
London Wall 60, 129, 141
Long Water 17, 25
Lonsdale Square 20–22
Lord, Thomas 68
Lords, House of *see*
Westminster, Palace of
Lord's cricket ground 68
Lothbury 142
Lovat Lane 140
Lower Marsh 11
Lower Regent Street 63,
73
Lower Sloane Street 29
Lower Thames Street 127
Lowndes Street 28
Ludgate Broadway 149
Ludgate Hill 22, 42, 51,
149
Ludgate Square 149

Madame Tussaud's Rock
Circus 74, 164
Maddox Street 58
Magpie Alley 149
Maida Vale 23, 62
Mail Rail 49, 128, 163
Mall 45, 80, 110
Mall House 110
Manchester Square 66
Manny, Sir Edward 156
Mansion House 128, 129,
138, 166
Mappin & Webb 63
Marble Arch 17, 25, 80–1,
151
Marine Society 139–40
Mark Lane 140
Marlborough Gate 25

Marlborough Road 122
Marsden, William 109
Marsham Street 44, 45
Martyn, W. 159, 167
Mary II 106
Marylebone 30–31, 35
Marylebone High Street
30, 66
Marylebone Lane 30–31,
37
Marylebone Road 30, 66
Mason's Yard 125
May, Baptist 126
Mayfair 29, 30, 31–2, 45,
51, 58, 65–6, 71, 110,
118
Melbourne, Lord 108
Mercers' Company 60, 85,
86, 132, 147, 148
estate 57
Hall 129, 143
Mercers' School 86, 147
Mercer Street 60
Merchant Taylors'
Company 60, 134
Metropolitan Board of
Works 52
Metropolitan Drinking
Fountain and Cattle
Trough Association
75–7, 146
MI5 45, 110
MI6 36, 110
Milford Lane 12
Millbank 63, 110
Mithras, Temple of 22, 138
Mitre Court 143
Monck Street 45
Montague Street 67
Monument to the Great
Fire 136, 140, 166
Moore, Albert 83
Moorgate tube station 47,
173
Moravians 148
Moreton Street 36
Morrison, Hon. Charlotte
71
Morrison estate 56, 71
Motcomb Street 27–8
Mount Pleasant 40
Mount Pleasant Sorting
Office 40, 49, 163
Moxon Street 30
Museum of London 127
Muswell Hill Broadway
159

Myddelton, Sir Hugh 20
Myddelton Square 19, 20

Nash, John 63, 68, 80, 81,
156
National Heritage,
Department of 111
National Trust 61, 154
Natural History Museum
45
Naval and Military Club
113, 116, 126
Neckinger river 43
Nelson, Lord 96, 109
New Bond Street 58
New Bridge Street 42, 149
New Broad Street 58
New Change 138
New Court 138
New Cross 49
New Fetter Lane 148
Newgate Prison 86, 146,
151, 152
Newgate Street 41, 76,
144
New River Company 20
Nine Elms Lane 36
Norfolk Road 68
Northampton, 7th
Marquess of 68
Northampton estate 56,
68
Northcliffe House West
68
North End Road 48
North End (Bull and
Bush) tube station
48–9
Northern Heights 12, 13,
17, 25, 37
Northern line 46–7 49
Northumberland Avenue
45
Notting Barns 72
Notting Dale 14
Notting Hill 13, 14–16,
69
Notting Hill carnival 14
Notting Hill Gate 13, 14

Octavia Hill housing
estates 62
Old Bailey 58, 128, 129,
146
Old Broad Street 141
Old Brompton Road 70

Old Deer Park 63
Olde Mitre pub 144,
147
Old Fish Street Hill 12
Old Fleet Lane 42
Old Jewry 60, 142
Old Queen Street 61
Old St Pancras Church 37
Old Seacoal Lane 42
Ormiston, Thomas 142
Orr, Brigadier James 44
Oval cricket ground 64
Over-Seas House 120
Owen, Robert 153
Oxford, Earls of 66
Oxford and Cambridge
Club 116
Oxford Court 139
Oxford Street 18, 31, 51,
65, 66, 80, 152
Oxo Tower 82–3

Paddington 46
Paddington Station 45
Pakenham Street 40
Palace Green 63
Palace Street 35
Pall Mall 114, 115, 116,
117–18, 123, 124,
125
Pancras Lane 138
Pankhurst, Emily 91–2
Pantechnicon 27–8
Panyer Alley Steps 22
Parish Clerks, Company
of 40
Park Lane 51, 65
Park Place 117, 120
Parliament, Houses of *see*
Westminster, Palace
of
Parliament Hill 10, 11, 17
Parliament Street 88, 92,
101
Paul's Walk 42
Payne & Gunter 71
Peasants' Revolt 135
Peel Street 16
Pelham Street 69
Pemberton Row 148
Pembridge Road 14
Penton Street 20
Pentonville Road 19, 20,
37
Pepys, Samuel 140
Perryn, John 60
Petersham, Viscount 70

Peters Hill 12
Phillimore, 5th Baron 72
Phillimore, Joseph 71
Phillimore estate 56, 71–2
Phoenix Place 40
Piccadilly 12, 18, 31, 32,
   33, 34, 47, 114, 118,
   120, 126
Piccadilly Arcade 120
Piccadilly Circus 50, 63,
   73–5, 112, 118, 126
Pickering, William 124
Pickering Place 124
Pilgrim Street 149
Pimlico 17, 52, 65
Pimlico Road 28
Piper, John 111
Plantation House 128
Playhouse Yard 149
Pleydell-Bouverie estate
   56, 67–8
Pleydell Court 148
Plumstead 52
Plunket, Blessed Oliver
   152
Poets' Coener *see*
   Westminster Abbey
Pont Street 28, 77
Portland, Dukes of 66
Portland Place, 63
Portman, Edward, 9th
   Viscount 66
Portman, Lord Chief
   Justice 66
Portman estate 56, 66
Portman Square 66, 153
Portobello Road 14
Postman's Park 144
Post Office 45, 49, 82
   cable tunnels 45–6,
   49, 50
Chief Post Office 128,
   129, 144
Research Station 45
Tower *see* BT Tower *see
   also* Mail Rail
Post Office Court 139
Pratt, William 117
Pratt's Club 117, 120
Pratt Street 37
Priest's Court 136, 143
Primrose Hill 13, 17–18,
   53, 60, 63, 149
Primrose Hill Park 64
Primrose Hill Road 18
Prince's Arcade 120
Princes Place 125

Prince's Street 60
Provost Road 60
Prudent Passage 143
Public Record Office 148
Purcell, Henry 122

Queen Anne's Gate 61
Queen's Gallery 35, 163
Queen's Park 59
Queen Square 54
Queen's Scholars 122
Queen's Theatre 61
Queen Street 138
Queen's Walk 121
Queen Victoria Street 22,
   127, 138

RAC Club 115
Radnor, 8th Earl of 68
Radnor estate 67–8,
   148
Railton, David 93
Ranelagh Gardens 28
Ranelagh Sewer 25, 28
Ravensbourne river 43
Ray Street Bridge 40
Red Lion pub (Crown
   Passage) 119, 125
Red Lion pub (Parliament
   Street) 92
Reform Act (1832) 115,
   116, 149
Reformation 61, 156
Reform Club 115
Regent's Canal 18, 20, 23,
   29, 37
Regent's Park 29, 55, 62,
   63, 64, 68
Regent's Park lake 29
Regent's Park Road 18
Regent Street 50, 63, 73
Richmond 12, 63
Richmond Avenue 22
Richmond Park 63
Rio Cottage 36
River Street 19, 20
Rogers, Richard 128
Rolls Passage 67
Roman era/remains 11,
   22, 127, 138, 146
   bath-houses 127, 129,
   165
Rosary Gardens 70
Rothschild, Lord 55, 121
Rothschild's Bank 51, 138
Rotten Row 25
Rotunda citadel 44–S

Royal Arsenal 54
Royal Artillery 54
Royal Automobile Club
   see RAC Club
Royal Exchange 138, 139
Royal Festival Hall 78
Royal Horseguards Hotel
   92
Royal Institution of Great
   Britain 157–8, 167
Royal Mint 63
Royal Over-Seas League
   120
Rugby School estate 57, 60
Rugby Street 60
Russell, Lord William 67
Russell Court 121
Russell Square 54, 67
Russia Row 143
Rutland House 120

Saddlers' Company 132
   Hall 129, 143
Saffron Hill 41
St Andrew's Hill 12
St Ann Blackfriars 149
St Anselm's Place 31
St Barnabas-in-Soho,
   House of 153–4, 167
St Bartholomew, Priory of
   68
St Bartholomew's
   Hospital 86, 157
St Benet Sherehog 138
St Botolph Aldgate 141
St Bride Institute 149
St Bride Printing Library
   144, 149, 166
St Bride's Church 149
St Bride's Passage 149
St Chad's Place 38
St Chad's spa 38
St Clement's Church 140
St Dunstan's Hill 12
St Etheldreda's Church
   144, 147
St Helen's Church 141
St Helen's Place 60, 141
St James's 12, 55, 63,
   112–26
   clubs 112–18; *see also
   individual club names*
   walk 118–26
St James's, Court of 123
St James's Church 120
St James's Palace 112, 118,
   121–3, 124

Chapel Royal 118, 120,
   122, 165
Queen's Chapel 122
St James's Park 18, 34, 54,
   63, 64, 101, 105, 106
St James's Place 116, 120
St James's Square 115,
   116, 125, 126, 153
St James's Street 12, 116,
   117, 118, 120, 123,
   124
St John's Church (Notting
   Hill) 14, 16
St John Street 19
St John's Wood 68
St John the Baptist upon
   Walbrook Church 22
St Katharine Coleman
   140
St Katherine's Row 140
St Margaret Lothbury 22,
   142
St Margaret's Close 142
St Mark's Church (EC1)
   19
St Martin's Lane 67
St Martin's le Grand 144
St Mary Abbots 17, 151
St Mary Abchurch 139
St Mary-at-Hill 12, 133,
   140
St Mary Axe 60, 141
St Mary-le-Bow 138
St Mary Woolnoth 138
St Michael Paternoster
   Church 85
St Olave Jewry 143
St Olave's Church 140
St Olave's Court 143
St Pancras 60
St Pancras Church 138
St Pancras Station 18, 20,
   37, 49, 60
St Pancras Way 37
St Paul's Cathedral 12, 22,
   49, 51, 128, 129, 132,
   133, 136, 148, 149,
   162
St Paul's Churchyard 12
St Paul's School 132
St Paul's tube station 22
St Quintin Avenue 72
St Quintin estate 56 72
St Saviour's Dock 43
St Sepulchre's Church 76,
   146
St Stephens, College of 91

St Stephen Walbrook 138
St Swithin's Lane 60, 138, 139
St Swithin's London Stone 139
St Thomas's Hospital 85
St Vedast Foster Lane 143
Salisbury, Marquesses of 67
Salisbury estate 56
Salisbury Square 12, 149
Salters' Company 132, 139
Salters Hall Court 139
Sambourne, Edward Linley 72
Savoy Chapel 64
Savoy Hotel 64
Savoy Palace 64
Savoy Street 64
Scattergood, Thomas 159
Sclater Street 46
Scott, Sir George Gilbert 101
Scottish Office 107–108
Serpentine 17, 24, 25
sewers 52–3
Shaftesbury, Earl of 74–5
Shaftesbury Avenue 50, 61, 73
Shakespeare, William 149
Shepherd Market 30, 32–3
Shepherd's Bush 14, 46, 48
Shepherd's Bush tube station 48
Shepherd's Walk 29
Sherborne Lane 139
Shooters Hill 54
Shoreditch 46
Sickert, Walter 111
Skinners Arms pub 60
Skinners' Company 60, 132, 134
Hall 86,129, 133–4
Sloane, Sir Hans 69
Sloane Square 28, 29, 69
Sloane Square tube station 28
Sloane Street 65, 69
Sloane Terrace 28
Smallbrook Mews 24
Smith, Alderman Henry 69
Smith, Captain John 138
Smithfield 49, 68, 139, 157

Smithfield Market 19, 41, 58, 146, 156
Smith's Charity estate 56, 69, 70, 164
Smith Street 69
Snow Hill 146
Snow Hill Court 146
Snow Hill railway tunnel 51
Soho 61, 150, 153–4
Soho Square 153–4
Southampton Buildings 67
South Audley Street 153
South Bank Lion see Coade Stone Lion
South Kensington 45
South Molton Lane 31, 65
South Molton Street 58
South Street 65
Southwark 11
Southwark Bridge 59, 138
Spanish and Portuguese Synagogue 141,166
Spencer, Earl 55
Spencer, Elizabeth 68
Spencer, John 68
Spencer House 55, 120, 121, 165
Spencer Rise 18
Spitalfields market 58
Stafford Hotel 120, 121
Stafford Place 35
Stamford Brook 13, 17
Stanhope Gardens 711
Stock Exchange 128, 129, 142
Stockwell tube station 46, 47
Stoke Newington 20, 62
Storey's Gate 44
Strand 12, 154–6
Streatham 86
Surrey County Cricket Club 64
Sussex Gardens 61
Sutherland, Graham 111
Sutton, Thomas 156
Swan Inn 25
Swiss Cottage 29
synagogues 141, 166

Tachbrook Street 36
Talbot Court 136, 140
Tavistock, Henry Russell, Marquess of 67

Tawyers' Hall 134
Taylors of Loughborough 158
Telegraph Street 142
Temple Lane 148
Thames Barrier 11, 54
Visitor Centre 162
Thames House 110
Thameslink line 38
Thameslink tunnel 54
Thamesmead 49, 54
Thames river *passim, et* 10–22, 23, 28, 32, 35–6, 42–3, 59, 80–82, 86,134
bridges 59; *see also individual bridge names*
estuary 29
flood plain 11, 18, 26, 34–5
tides 24, 30, 37
tunnels under 44, 47, 49
Thames valley 10–22, 79
spurs 13–22, 25
terraces 11–13, 17, 20
Thames Water plc 51
Theatre Royal 63
Theobald's Road 54
Thornhill Road 20
Threadneedle Street 60, 141
Throgmorton Avenue 60, 142
Throgmorton Street 60, 142
Thurloe, John 70
Thurloe Place 77
Thurloe Square 70
Tokenhouse Yard 142
Tomb of the Unknown Soldier *see* Westminster Abbey
Tonbridge School 60, 132
Tonbridge School estate 57, 60
Tonbridge Street 60
Tooley Street 50
Tower Bridge 50, 59
Tower Hill 50
Tower of London 50, 140
Tower Subway 50, 51
Trafalgar Square 11, 45–6, 50, 63, 80, 101, 108, 154
Travellers Club 113–15, 116, 165
Treasury 45, 111

Treasury Green 105
Treasury Passage 105, 106
Trocadero 74
Trollope, Anthony 114
Trump Street 143
tube *see* London Underground; Underground railways
Tudor Street 12
Tufnell Park tube Station 18
Turf Club 114
Turnagain Lane 42
Turners' Company 132
Turnmill Street 41
Tutbury Ceramics 85
Tyburn Brook 25
Tyburn convent 151–3, 167
Tyburn House 36
Tyburn martyrs 152
Tyburn river (Aye Brook) 13, 18, 23, 25, 37, 58, 65, 80
outflow 35–6 42
walk 29–36, 110
Tyburn Walk 152–3
Tyburn Tree 151
Tyler, Wat 135

Underground railways 47–50; *see also* London
Undershaft 141
United Oxford and Cambridge University Club 116
Unknown Soldier, Tomb of *see* Westminster Abbey
Upbrook Mews 23, 24
Upper Tachbrook Street 36
utility subways 50–53

Vauxhall Cross 110
Vernon House 120
Victoria & Albert Museum 70, 77, 83
Victoria Embankment 82
Victoria Gardens 14
Victoria Station 17, 65, 93
Victoria Street 35, 62, 63
Vine Hill 40
Vine Lane 50
Vintners' Company 132

Waithman, Robert 149
Walbrook river (London
    Bridge Sewer) 13,
    22–3,134,138
Walpole, Sir Robert 104,
    106
Walton Street 69
Walworth, Sir William 135
Wandle river 43
Warwick, Earls of 146
Warwick Lane 144
Warwick Passage 146
Warwick Square 146
Warwick Way 36
Watergate 42
Waterloo Bridge 12, 54
Waterloo Place 73, 114
Waterloo Station 11, 45
Watermen and
    Lightermen's
    Company 133, 135
Watts, G.F. 144
Wellcome Trust 69, 164
Westbourne river 13, 17,
    65
  outflows 25, 29, 42
  walk 23–9
Westminster 11, 25, 51,
    61, 69, 87–100, 101
Westminster, Dukes of 26,
    65
Westminster, Palace of
    (Houses of
    Parliament) 25, 50,
    77, 87–92, 97, 164
  Big Ben 88, 89, 91–2,
    158
  Central Lobby 89
  Commons, House of
    88, 89, 90, 115
  Commons division bell
    92
  Jewel Tower 91
  Lord Chancellor's
    Department 89
  Lord Chancellor's house
    88

Lords, House of 88, 89,
    90
Lords' Bar 89
Press Gallery 91
Princes Gallery 87
Prison Cell 91
Record Office 89
Robing Room 87
Royal Gallery 87
St Stephen's Chapel
    90–1
St Stephen's Cloisters
    90–91
Speaker 88
Speaker's Chair 89
Speaker's House 88
Strangers 88–9
Victoria Tower 89
Westminster Hall 90, 91,
    100
Woolsack 89
Westminster Abbey 87,
    92–7, 158, 164
  Abbot's house 97,100
  Abbot's Pew 93
  Chapter House 95, 164
  College Garden 93, 96,
    100, 164
  Cosmati pavement
    93–4
  Dark Passage 96
  Dean's Yard 97, 98, 100
  East Cloister 95, 96,
    97
  Edward the Confessor's
    tomb 94
  farm 98, 100
  garden *see* College
    Garden
  Henry III's tomb 94
  High Altar 94
  Infirmary (Little)
    Cloister 96
  Jericho Parlour 97
  Jerusalem Chamber 97
  Library 93, 95, 96, 99,
    164

Little (Infirmary)
    Cloister 96
  Museum 95–6, 164
  North Cloister 97
  Poets' Corner 94
  Pyx Chamber 95–6,
    164
  Quire 94
  St Faith's Chapel 95
  St Katharine's Chapel
    96
  Song School 97
  South Transept 95
  Tomb of the Unknown
    Soldier 93
  West Cloister 97
Westminster Hall *see*
    Westminster, Palace
    of
Westminster Hospital 45
Westminster School 36,
    87, 92, 95, 96, 97,
    98–100, 164
  Dr Busby's Library
    99
  Greaze 99
  Little Dean's Yard 98
  'School' 99
Wetherby Place 70
White, Francis 118
Whitechapel 49
Whitechapel Bell Foundry
    134, 146, 153–9,
    167
Whitechapel Road 158
White City tube station 48
Whitefriars 58, 149
  Crypt 166
Whitefriars Street 149
Whitehall 11, 44–5, 63,
    101–111, 151
Whitehall Court 92
Whitehall Palace 90, 101,
    104–106 107
  Cockpit 105, 106
  Cockpit Gallery
    105–106

Great Close Tennis
    Court 105
  Kent's Treasury 105,
    106, 108
  Little Close Tennis
    Court 105
  Treasury Board Room
    106
White Lion Hill 12
White's Club 117, 118
Whittington, Dick 73,
    85–6
Whittington, Sir William
    85
Whittington College 86
Whittington Stone 86
Wigmore Street 31, 66
Wilkes, John 148
William the Conqueror
    65, 92
William III 106
Wilson, Erasmus 81
Wilton Place 26
Wise, Henry 36
Woburn Abbey 67
Woburn Square 54
Wolsey, Cardinal 107
Woodington, W. F. 78
Wood Lane tube station
    48
Wood Street Compter
    143
Woolwich Arsenal 54
Woolwich Reach 50
World's End 148
Wren, Sir Christopher
    139
Wyatt, Matthew Digby
    101

Yarmouth Place 33
York, Duke of 108
York Place 107
York Road curve 54
York Way 37, 54

Zafferano's Restaurant 27